MznLnx

Missing Links Exam Preps

Exam Prep for

International Financial Management

Eun & Resnick, 4th Edition

The MznLnx Exam Prep is your link from the texbook and lecture to your exams.
The MznLnx Exam Preps are unauthorized and comprehensive reviews of your textbooks.

All material provided by MznLnx and Rico Publications (c) 2010
Textbook publishers and textbook authors do not particpate in or contribute to these reviews.

MznLnx

Rico Publications

Exam Prep for International Financial Management
4th Edition
Eun & Resnick

Publisher: Raymond Houge	*Product Manager:* Dave Mason
Assistant Editor: Michael Rouger	*Editorial Assitant:* Rachel Guzmanji
Text and Cover Designer: Lisa Buckner	*Pedagogy:* Debra Long
Marketing Manager: Sara Swagger	*Cover Image:* Jim Reed/Getty Images
Project Manager, Editorial Production: Jerry Emerson	*Text and Cover Printer:* City Printing, Inc.
Art Director: Vernon Lowerui	*Compositor:* Media Mix, Inc.

(c) 2010 Rico Publications

ALL RIGHTS RESERVED. No part of this work covered by the copyright may be reproduced or used in any form or by an means--graphic, electronic, or mechanical, including photocopying, recording, taping, Web distribution, information storage, and retrieval systems, or in any other manner--without the written permission of the publisher.

Printed in the United States
ISBN:

For more information about our products, contact us at:
Dave.Mason@RicoPublications.com

For permission to use material from this text or product, submit a request online to:
Dave.Mason@RicoPublications.com

Contents

CHAPTER 1
Globalization and the Multinational Firm,   1

CHAPTER 2
International Monetary System,   13

CHAPTER 3
Balance of Payments,   23

CHAPTER 4
Corporate Governance around the World,   32

CHAPTER 5
The Market for Foreign Exchange,   41

CHAPTER 6
International Parity Relationships and Forecasting Foreign Exchange Rates,   50

CHAPTER 7
Futures and Options on Foreign Exchange,   59

CHAPTER 8
Management of Transaction Exposure,   68

CHAPTER 9
Management of Economic Exposure,   79

CHAPTER 10
Management of Translation Exposure,   89

CHAPTER 11
International Banking and Money Market,   96

CHAPTER 12
International Bond Market,   107

CHAPTER 13
International Equity Markets,   117

CHAPTER 14
Interest Rate and Currency Swaps,   126

CHAPTER 15
International Portfolio Investment,   134

CHAPTER 16
Foreign Direct Investment and Cross-Border Acquisitions,   147

CHAPTER 17
International Capital Structure and the Cost of Capital,   156

CHAPTER 18
International Capital Budgeting,   169

CHAPTER 19
Multinational Cash Management,   180

CHAPTER 20
International Trade Finance,   189

Contents (Cont.)

CHAPTER 21
  International Tax Environment,   195
ANSWER KEY   203

TO THE STUDENT

COMPREHENSIVE

The *MznLnx* Exam Prep series is designed to help you pass your exams. Editors at MznLnx review your textbooks and then prepare these practice exams to help you master the textbook material. Unlike study guides, workbooks, and practice tests provided by the texbook publisher and textbook authors, *MznLnx* gives you **all** of the material in each chapter in exam form, not just samples, so you can be sure to nail your exam.

MECHANICAL

The MznLnx Exam Prep series creates exams that will help you learn the subject matter as well as test you on your understanding. Each question is designed to help you master the concept. Just working through the exams, you gain an understanding of the subject--its a simple mechanical process that produces success.

INTEGRATED STUDY GUIDE AND REVIEW

MznLnx is not just a set of exams designed to test you, its also a comprehensive review of the subject content. Each exam question is also a review of the concept, making sure that you will get the answer correct without having to go to other sources of material. You learn as you go! Its the easiest way to pass an exam.

HUMOR

Studying can be tedious and dry. MznLnx's instructional design includes moderate humor within the exam questions on occassion, to break the tedium and revitalize the brain

Chapter 1. Globalization and the Multinational Firm, 1

1. The _____ is a private, not-for-profit organization whose primary purpose is to develop generally accepted accounting principles (GAAP) within the United States in the public's interest. The Securities and Exchange Commission (SEC) designated the _____ as the organization responsible for setting accounting standards for public companies in the U.S. It was created in 1973, replacing the Accounting Principles Board and the Committee on Accounting Procedure of the American Institute of Certified Public Accountants. The _____'s mission is 'to establish and improve standards of financial accounting and reporting for the guidance and education of the public, including issuers, auditors, and users of financial information.'

The _____ is not a governmental body.

  a. Credit karma   b. MRU Holdings
  c. PlaNet Finance   d. FASB

2. _____ is the branch of economics that studies the dynamics of exchange rates, foreign investment, and how these affect international trade. It also studies international projects, international investments and capital flows, and trade deficits. It includes the study of futures, options and currency swaps.

  a. ABN Amro   b. A Random Walk Down Wall Street
  c. AAB   d. International finance

3. A _____ is a professionally managed type of collective investment scheme that pools money from many investors and invests it in stocks, bonds, short-term money market instruments, and/or other securities. The _____ will have a fund manager that trades the pooled money on a regular basis. Currently, the worldwide value of all _____s totals more than $26 trillion.

Since 1940, there have been three basic types of investment companies in the United States: open-end funds, also known in the US as _____s; unit investment trusts (UITs); and closed-end funds.

  a. Financial intermediary   b. Trust company
  c. Net asset value   d. Mutual fund

4. The institution most often referenced by the word '_____' is a public or publicly traded _____, the shares of which are traded on a public stock exchange (e.g., the New York Stock Exchange or Nasdaq in the United States) where shares of stock of _____s are bought and sold by and to the general public. Most of the largest businesses in the world are publicly traded _____s. However, the majority of _____s are said to be closely held, privately held or close _____s, meaning that no ready market exists for the trading of shares.

  a. Depository Trust Company   b. Federal Home Loan Mortgage Corporation
  c. Corporation   d. Protect

5. _____ is the removal or simplification of government rules and regulations that constrain the operation of market forces. _____ does not mean elimination of laws against fraud, but eliminating or reducing government control of how business is done, thereby moving toward a more free market.

The stated rationale for '_____' is often that fewer and simpler regulations will lead to a raised level of competitiveness, therefore higher productivity, more efficiency and lower prices overall.

a. Demand shock
b. Value added
c. Supply shock
d. Deregulation

6. When companies conduct business across borders, they must deal in foreign currencies. Companies must exchange foreign currencies for home currencies when dealing with receivables, and vice versa for payables. This is done at the current exchange rate between the two countries. _____ is the risk that the exchange rate will change unfavorably before the currency is exchanged.

a. Lower of cost or market rule
b. 4-4-5 Calendar
c. 529 plan
d. Foreign exchange risk

7. The _____ or Plaza Agreement was an agreement between the governments of France, West Germany, Japan, the United States and the United Kingdom, agreeing to depreciate the US dollar in relation to the Japanese yen and German Deutsche Mark by intervening in currency markets. The five governments signed the accord on September 22, 1985 at the Plaza Hotel in New York City.

The exchange rate value of the dollar versus the yen declined by 51% from 1985 to 1987.

a. 4-4-5 Calendar
b. 529 plan
c. 7-Eleven
d. Plaza Accord

8. _____ is a type of risk faced by investors, corporations, and governments. It is a risk that can be understood and managed with proper aforethought and investment.

Broadly, _____ refers to the complications businesses and governments may face as a result of what are commonly referred to as political decisions--or 'any political change that alters the expected outcome and value of a given economic action by changing the probability of achieving business objectives.' .

a. Mid price
b. Single-index model
c. Political risk
d. Capital asset

9. The _____ was a December 1971 agreement that ended the fixed exchange rates established at the Bretton Woods Conference of 1944.

The Bretton Woods Conference of 1944 established an international fixed exchange rate regime in which currencies were pegged to the United States dollar, which was based on the gold standard.

By 1970, however, it was clear that the exchange rate regime was under threat, as the United States dollar was greatly overvalued because of heavy American spending on Lyndon B. Johnson's Great Society and the Vietnam War.

a. 4-4-5 Calendar
b. Smithsonian Agreement
c. 7-Eleven
d. 529 plan

10. A _____ is a private or public market for the trading of company stock and derivatives of company stock at an agreed price; these are securities listed on a stock exchange as well as those only traded privately.

Chapter 1. Globalization and the Multinational Firm,

The size of the world _____ is estimated at about $36.6 trillion US at the beginning of October 2008. The world derivatives market has been estimated at about $480 trillion face or nominal value, 12 times the size of the entire world economy.

a. Stock market
b. Andrew Tobias
c. Anton Gelonkin
d. Adolph Coors

11. In finance, the _____ between two currencies specifies how much one currency is worth in terms of the other. For example an _____ of 102 Japanese yen to the United States dollar means that JPY 102 is worth the same as USD 1. The foreign exchange market is one of the largest markets in the world.

a. ABN Amro
b. Exchange rate
c. A Random Walk Down Wall Street
d. AAB

12. _____ is a form of risk that arises from the change in price of one currency against another. Whenever investors or companies have assets or business operations across national borders, they face _____ if their positions are not hedged.

- Transaction risk is the risk that exchange rates will change unfavourably over time. It can be hedged against using forward currency contracts;
- Translation risk is an accounting risk, proportional to the amount of assets held in foreign currencies. Changes in the exchange rate over time will render a report inaccurate, and so assets are usually balanced by borrowings in that currency.

The exchange risk associated with a foreign denominated instrument is a key element in foreign investment. This risk flows from differential monetary policy and growth in real productivity, which results in differential inflation rates.

a. Credit risk
b. Tracking error
c. Market risk
d. Currency risk

13. In economics, a _____ is a mechanism that allows people to easily buy and sell (trade) financial securities (such as stocks and bonds), commodities (such as precious metals or agricultural goods), and other fungible items of value at low transaction costs and at prices that reflect the efficient-market hypothesis.

_____s have evolved significantly over several hundred years and are undergoing constant innovation to improve liquidity.

Both general markets (where many commodities are traded) and specialized markets (where only one commodity is traded) exist.

a. Cost of carry
b. Secondary market
c. Financial market
d. Delta hedging

14. In business and finance, a _____ (also referred to as equity _____) of stock means a _____ of ownership in a corporation (company.) In the plural, stocks is often used as a synonym for _____s especially in the United States, but it is less commonly used that way outside of North America.

In the United Kingdom, South Africa, and Australia, stock can also refer to completely different financial instruments such as government bonds or, less commonly, to all kinds of marketable securities.

    a. Bucket shop
    b. Share
    c. Margin
    d. Procter ' Gamble

15. _____ most frequently refers to the standard deviation of the continuously compounded returns of a financial instrument with a specific time horizon. It is often used to quantify the risk of the instrument over that time period. _____ is typically expressed in annualized terms, and it may either be an absolute number ($5) or a fraction of the mean (5%).

    a. Portfolio insurance
    b. Seasoned equity offering
    c. Currency swap
    d. Volatility

16. The _____ was a period of financial crisis that gripped much of Asia beginning in July 1997, and raised fears of a worldwide economic meltdown (financial contagion).

The crisis started in Thailand with the financial collapse of the Thai baht caused by the decision of the Thai government to float the baht, cutting its peg to the USD, after exhaustive efforts to support it in the face of a severe financial overextension that was in part real estate driven. At the time, Thailand had acquired a burden of foreign debt that made the country effectively bankrupt even before the collapse of its currency.

    a. Asian Financial Crisis
    b. Internal control
    c. OTC Bulletin Board
    d. International trade

17. A _____ is an exchange of promises between two or more parties to do an act which is enforceable in a court of law. It is where an unqualified offer meets a qualified acceptance and the parties reach Consensus ad Idem. The parties must have the necessary capacity to _____ and the _____ must not be either trifling, indeterminate, impossible or illegal.

    a. 529 plan
    b. 4-4-5 Calendar
    c. 7-Eleven
    d. Contract

18. _____ refers to the various forms of financial support and financial transactions used in international trade. _____ uses a range of instruments to provide finance to exporters and importers, including documentary credits such as letters of credit.

While a seller (the exporter) can require the purchaser (an importer) to prepay for goods shipped, the purchaser (importer) may wish to reduce risk by requiring the seller to document that the goods have been shipped.

    a. Forfaiting
    b. Trade finance
    c. Free cash flow
    d. Debtor-in-possession financing

Chapter 1. Globalization and the Multinational Firm,

19. In economics, _____ refers to the ability of a party to produce a good or service using fewer real resources than another entity producing the same good or service. A party has an _____ when using the same input as another party, it can produce a greater output. Since _____ is determined by a simple comparison of labor productivities, it is possible for a a party to have no _____ in anything. It can be contrasted with the concept of comparative advantage which refers to the ability to produce a particular good at a lower opportunity cost.
   a. A Random Walk Down Wall Street
   b. AAB
   c. Economic depreciation
   d. Absolute advantage

20. A _____ is a document that indicates that the bearer of the document has title to property, such as shares or bonds. They differ from normal registered instruments, in that no records are kept of who owns the underlying property, or of the transactions involving transfer of ownership. Whoever physically holds the bearer bond papers owns the property.
   a. Book entry
   b. Marketable
   c. Securities lending
   d. Bearer instrument

21. _____ is a form of corporation equity ownership represented in the securities. It is dangerous in comparison to preferred shares and some other investment options, in that in the event of bankruptcy, _____ investors receive their funds after preferred stockholders, bondholders, creditors, etc. On the other hand, common shares on average perform better than preferred shares or bonds over time.
   a. Stock market bubble
   b. Common stock
   c. Stop-limit order
   d. Stock split

22. In economics and finance, _____ represents passive holdings of securities such as foreign stocks, bonds, or other financial assets, none of which entails active management or control of the securities' issuer by the investor; where such control exists, it is known as foreign direct investment. Generally, this means the investor holds less than 10% of the total shares or less than the amount needed to hold the majority vote.

Some examples of _____ are:

- purchase of shares in a foreign company.
- purchase of bonds issued by a foreign government.
- acquisition of assets in a foreign country.

Factors affecting international _____:

- tax rates on interest or dividends (investors will normally prefer countries where the tax rates are relatively low)
- interest rates (money tends to flow to countries with high interest rates)
- exchange rates (foreign investors may be attracted if the local currency is expected to strengthen)

_____ is part of the capital account on the balance of payments statistics.

   a. Tactical asset allocation
   b. Portfolio investment
   c. Divestment
   d. Portable alpha

23. In economics, the _____, measures the payments that flow between any individual country and all other countries. It is used to summarize all international economic transactions for that country during a specific time period, usually a year. The _____ is determined by the country's exports and imports of goods, services, and financial capital, as well as financial transfers.

   a. Balance of payments
   b. Gross national product
   c. Purchasing power parity
   d. 4-4-5 Calendar

24. _____ in its classic form is defined as a company from one country making a physical investment into building a factory in another country. It is the establishment of an enterprise by a foreigner. Its definition can be extended to include investments made to acquire lasting interest in enterprises operating outside of the economy of the investor.

   a. Public company
   b. Dow Jones ' Company
   c. MicroPlace
   d. Foreign direct investment

25. _____ is a business valuation method. _____ is the net present value of a project if financed solely by ownership equity plus the present value of all the benefits of financing. Usually, the main benefit is a tax shield resulted from tax deductibility of interest payments. Another one can be a subsidized borrowing.

   a. A Random Walk Down Wall Street
   b. AAB
   c. ABN Amro
   d. Adjusted present value

26. A _____ is an international bond that is denominated in a currency not native to the country where it is issued. It can be categorised according to the currency in which it is issued. London is one of the centers of the _____ market, but _____s may be traded throughout the world - for example in Singapore or Tokyo.

   a. Eurobond
   b. Interest rate option
   c. Economic entity
   d. Education production function

27. In finance, a _____ is a derivative in which two counterparties agree to exchange one stream of cash flows against another stream. These streams are called the legs of the _____.

The cash flows are calculated over a notional principal amount, which is usually not exchanged between counterparties.

   a. Volatility arbitrage
   b. Swap
   c. Volatility swap
   d. Local volatility

28. A _____ is a set of companies with interlocking business relationships and shareholdings. It is a type of business group.

The prototypical _____ are those which appeared in Japan during the 'economic miracle' following World War II.

   a. Relative strength Index
   b. Stock split
   c. Zero-coupon bond
   d. Keiretsu

29. A _____, reserve bank, or monetary authority is the entity responsible for the monetary policy of a country or of a group of member states. It is a bank that can lend money to other banks in times of need. Its primary responsibility is to maintain the stability of the national currency and money supply, but more active duties include controlling subsidized-loan interest rates, and acting as a lender of last resort to the banking sector during times of financial crisis (private banks often being integral to the national financial system.)
   a. 529 plan
   b. 7-Eleven
   c. 4-4-5 Calendar
   d. Central Bank

30. _____ is the set of processes, customs, policies, laws and institutions affecting the way a corporation is directed, administered or controlled. _____ also includes the relationships among the many stakeholders involved and the goals for which the corporation is governed. The principal stakeholders are the shareholders, management and the board of directors.
   a. Due diligence
   b. Foreign Corrupt Practices Act
   c. Patent
   d. Corporate governance

31. In business, _____ is the total assets minus total outside liabilities of an individual or a company. For a company, this is called shareholders' equity and may be referred to as book value. _____ is stated as at a particular point in time.
   a. Certified International Investment Analyst
   b. Moneylender
   c. Restructuring
   d. Net worth

32. The _____ is the market for securities, where companies and governments can raise longterm funds. The _____ includes the stock market and the bond market. Financial regulators, such as the U.S. Securities and Exchange Commission, oversee the _____s in their designated countries to ensure that investors are protected against fraud.
   a. Spot rate
   b. Capital market
   c. Forward market
   d. Delta neutral

33.

A _____ is a type of financial intermediary and a type of bank. Commercial banking is also known as business banking. It is a bank that provides checking accounts, savings accounts, and money market accounts and that accepts time deposits.

   a. 529 plan
   b. 4-4-5 Calendar
   c. Commercial bank
   d. 7-Eleven

34. The _____ of 1933 established the Federal Deposit Insurance Corporation (FDIC) in the United States and included banking reforms, some of which were designed to control speculation. Some provisions such as Regulation Q, which allowed the Federal Reserve to regulate interest rates in savings accounts, were repealed by the Depository Institutions Deregulation and Monetary Control Act of 1980. Provisions that prohibit a bank holding company from owning other financial companies were repealed on November 12, 1999, by the Gramm-Leach-Bliley Act.
   a. 4-4-5 Calendar
   b. 529 plan
   c. Glass-Steagall Act
   d. 7-Eleven

35. _____ is the incidence or process of transferring ownership of a business, enterprise, agency or public service from the public sector (government) to the private sector (business.) In a broader sense, _____ refers to transfer of any government function to the private sector including governmental functions like revenue collection and law enforcement.

The term '_____' also has been used to describe two unrelated transactions. The first is a buyout, by the majority owner, of all shares of a public corporation or holding company's stock, privatizing a publicly traded stock. The second is a demutualization of a mutual organization or cooperative to form a joint stock company.

a. 529 plan
b. Privatization
c. 7-Eleven
d. 4-4-5 Calendar

36. A _____, securities exchange or (in Europe) bourse is a corporation or mutual organization which provides 'trading' facilities for stock brokers and traders, to trade stocks and other securities. _____s also provide facilities for the issue and redemption of securities as well as other financial instruments and capital events including the payment of income and dividends. The securities traded on a _____ include: shares issued by companies, unit trusts and other pooled investment products and bonds.

a. 7-Eleven
b. 529 plan
c. 4-4-5 Calendar
d. Stock Exchange

37. The phrase _____ refers to the aspect of corporate strategy, corporate finance and management dealing with the buying, selling and combining of different companies that can aid, finance, or help a growing company in a given industry grow rapidly without having to create another business entity.

An acquisition, also known as a takeover, is the buying of one company (the 'target') by another. An acquisition may be friendly or hostile.

a. 7-Eleven
b. 529 plan
c. 4-4-5 Calendar
d. Mergers and acquisitions

38. _____ is the process by which the government, or monetary authority of a country controls (i) the supply of money central bank (ii) availability of money, and (iii) cost of money or rate of interest, in order to attain a set of objectives oriented towards the growth and stability of the economy. Monetary theory provides insight into how to craft optimal _____.

_____ is referred to as either being an expansionary policy where an expansionary policy increases the total supply of money in the economy, and a contractionary policy decreases the total money supply.

a. Federal Open Market Committee
b. Tax exemption
c. Natural resources consumption tax
d. Monetary policy

39. In financial accounting, the term _____ is most commonly used to describe any part of shareholders' equity, except for basic share capital. Sometimes, the term is used instead of the term provision; such a use, however, is inconsistent with the terminology suggested by International Accounting Standards Board. For more information about provisions, see provision (accounting.)

a. Closing entries
b. Reserve
c. Treasury stock
d. FIFO and LIFO accounting

Chapter 1. Globalization and the Multinational Firm, 9

40. In economics and finance, _____ is the practice of taking advantage of a price differential between two or more markets: striking a combination of matching deals that capitalize upon the imbalance, the profit being the difference between the market prices. When used by academics, an _____ is a transaction that involves no negative cash flow at any probabilistic or temporal state and a positive cash flow in at least one state; in simple terms, a risk-free profit.
   a. Efficient-market hypothesis
   b. Arbitrage
   c. Initial margin
   d. Issuer

41. In finance, a _____ is a debt security, in which the authorized issuer owes the holders a debt and, depending on the terms of the _____, is obliged to pay interest (the coupon) and/or to repay the principal at a later date, termed maturity.

Thus a _____ is a loan: the issuer is the borrower, the _____ holder is the lender, and the coupon is the interest. _____ s provide the borrower with external funds to finance long-term investments, or, in the case of government _____ s, to finance current expenditure.

   a. Catastrophe bonds
   b. Convertible bond
   c. Puttable bond
   d. Bond

42. The _____ is where currency trading takes place. It is where banks and other official institutions facilitate the buying and selling of foreign currencies. FX transactions typically involve one party purchasing a quantity of one currency in exchange for paying a quantity of another.
   a. Foreign exchange market
   b. Foreign exchange option
   c. Spot market
   d. Floating exchange rate

43. The _____ is one of the measures of national income and input for a given country's economy. _____ is defined as the total cost of all finished goods and services produced within the country in a stipulated period of time (usually a 365-day year.) It is sometimes regarded as the sum of profits added at every level of production (the intermediate stages) of all final goods and services produced within a country in a stipulated timeframe, and it is rarely given a monetary value.
   a. Recession
   b. Behavioral finance
   c. Macroeconomics
   d. Gross domestic product

44. In economics, _____ refers to the ability of a person or a country to produce a particular good at a lower marginal cost and opportunity cost than another person or country. It is the ability to produce a product most efficiently given all the other products that could be produced. It can be contrasted with absolute advantage which refers to the ability of a person or a country to produce a particular good at a lower absolute cost than another.
   a. Case-Shiller Home Price Indices
   b. Comparative advantage
   c. Reputational risk
   d. Loans and interest, in Judaism

45. In economics, business, and accounting, a _____ is the value of money that has been used up to produce something, and hence is not available for use anymore. In business, the _____ may be one of acquisition, in which case the amount of money expended to acquire it is counted as _____. In this case, money is the input that is gone in order to acquire the thing.
   a. Cost
   b. Sliding scale fees
   c. Fixed costs
   d. Marginal cost

46. In economics and related disciplines, a _____ is a cost incurred in making an economic exchange. For example, most people, when buying or selling a stock, must pay a commission to their broker; that commission is a _____ of doing the stock deal. Or consider buying a banana from a store; to purchase the banana, your costs will be not only the price of the banana itself, but also the energy and effort it requires to find out which of the various banana products you prefer, where to get them and at what price, the cost of traveling from your house to the store and back, the time waiting in line, and the effort of the paying itself; the costs above and beyond the cost of the banana are the _____s.
   a. Variable costs
   b. Transaction cost
   c. Marginal cost
   d. Fixed costs

47. The _____ was the outcome of the failure of negotiating governments to create the International Trade Organization (ITO). _____ was formed in 1947 and lasted until 1994, when it was replaced by the World Trade Organization. The Bretton Woods Conference had introduced the idea for an organization to regulate trade as part of a larger plan for economic recovery after World War II.
   a. 7-Eleven
   b. 529 plan
   c. 4-4-5 Calendar
   d. General Agreement on Tariffs and Trade

48. The _____ is an important selective, mainly private, international organization designed by its founders to supervise and liberalize international trade. The organization officially commenced on 1 January 1995, under the Marrakesh Agreement, succeeding the 1947 General Agreement on Tariffs and Trade (GATT.)

The _____ deals with regulation of trade between participating countries; it provides a framework for negotiating and formalising trade agreements, and a dispute resolution process aimed at enforcing participants' adherence to _____ agreements which are signed by representatives of member governments and ratified by their parliaments.

   a. World Trade Organization
   b. Financial Crimes Enforcement Network
   c. Public Company Accounting Oversight Board
   d. Gamelan Council

49. _____ is subcontracting a process, such as product design or manufacturing, to a third-party company. The decision to outsource is often made in the interest of lowering cost or making better use of time and energy costs, redirecting or conserving energy directed at the competencies of a particular business, or to make more efficient use of land, labor, capital, (information) technology and resources. _____ became part of the business lexicon during the 1980s.
   a. OTC Bulletin Board
   b. Exchange Rate Mechanism
   c. AT'T Inc.
   d. Outsourcing

50. A _____ is a fungible, negotiable instrument representing financial value. They are broadly categorized into debt securities (such as banknotes, bonds and debentures), and equity securities; e.g., common stocks. The company or other entity issuing the _____ is called the issuer.
   a. Securities lending
   b. Book entry
   c. Security
   d. Tracking stock

51. _____ is a type of trade policy that allows traders to act and transact without interference from government. Thus, the policy permits trading partners mutual gains from trade, with goods and services produced according to the theory of comparative advantage.

Under a _____ policy, prices are a reflection of true supply and demand, and are the sole determinant of resource allocation.

- a. Monte Carlo methods
- b. Yield spread
- c. Seasoned equity offering
- d. Free Trade

52. The _____ is a trilateral trade bloc in North America created by the governments of the United States, Canada, and Mexico. The agreement creating the trade bloc came into force on January 1, 1994. It superseded the Canada-United States Free Trade Agreement between the U.S. and Canada.
- a. 529 plan
- b. 7-Eleven
- c. 4-4-5 Calendar
- d. North American Free Trade Agreement

53. _____ is that which is owed; usually referencing assets owed, but the term can cover other obligations. In the case of assets, _____ is a means of using future purchasing power in the present before a summation has been earned. Some companies and corporations use _____ as a part of their overall corporate finance strategy.
- a. Cross-collateralization
- b. Credit cycle
- c. Debt
- d. Partial Payment

54. _____, in microeconomics, are the cost advantages that a business obtains due to expansion. _____ may be utilized by any size firm expanding its scale of operation.
- a. Articles of incorporation
- b. Economies of scale
- c. Uniform Commercial Code
- d. Employee Retirement Income Security Act

55. _____ stands for Singapore Interbank Offered Rate and is a daily reference rate based on the interest rates at which banks offer to lend unsecured funds to other banks in the Singapore wholesale money market (or interbank market.) It is similar to the widely used LIBOR (London Interbank Offered Rate), and Euribor (Euro Interbank Offered Rate.) Using _____ is more common in the Asian region and set by the Association of Banks in Singapore (ABS.)
- a. Repo rate
- b. SONIA
- c. Fixed interest
- d. SIBOR

56. _____ refers to the pricing of contributions (assets, tangible and intangible, services, and funds) transferred within an organization. For example, goods from the production division may be sold to the marketing division, or goods from a parent company may be sold to a foreign subsidiary. Since the prices are set within an organization (i.e. controlled), the typical market mechanisms that establish prices for such transactions between third parties may not apply.
- a. Transfer pricing
- b. Price discrimination
- c. Discounts and allowances
- d. Price index

57. _____ proposes how rational investors will use diversification to optimize their portfolios, and how a risky asset should be priced. The basic concepts of the theory are Markowitz diversification, the efficient frontier, capital asset pricing model, the alpha and beta coefficients, the Capital Market Line and the Securities Market Line.

_____ models an asset's return as a random variable, and models a portfolio as a weighted combination of assets so that the return of a portfolio is the weighted combination of the assets' returns.

a. Payback period
b. Modern portfolio theory
c. Market value
d. Consumer basket

58. The _____ is an American financial and commodity derivative exchange based in Chicago. The _____ was founded in 1898 as the Chicago Butter and Egg Board. Originally, the exchange was a non-profit organization.
   a. Financial Crimes Enforcement Network
   b. Chicago Mercantile Exchange
   c. Public Company Accounting Oversight Board
   d. Gamelan Council

59. _____ or economic opportunity loss is the value of the next best alternative foregone as the result of making a decision. _____ analysis is an important part of a company's decision-making processes but is not treated as an actual cost in any financial statement. The next best thing that a person can engage in is referred to as the _____ of doing the best thing and ignoring the next best thing to be done.
   a. AAB
   b. A Random Walk Down Wall Street
   c. ABN Amro
   d. Opportunity cost

Chapter 2. International Monetary System, 13

1. The _____ of monetary management established the rules for commercial and financial relations among the world's major industrial states in the mid 20th Century. The _____ was the first example of a fully negotiated monetary order intended to govern monetary relations among independent nation-states.

Preparing to rebuild the international economic system as World War II was still raging, 730 delegates from all 44 Allied nations gathered at the Mount Washington Hotel in Bretton Woods, New Hampshire, United States, for the United Nations Monetary and Financial Conference.

   a. Fixed Asset Register
   b. Cash budget
   c. The Hong Kong Securities Institute
   d. Bretton Woods System

2. _____ is a business valuation method. _____ is the net present value of a project if financed solely by ownership equity plus the present value of all the benefits of financing. Usually, the main benefit is a tax shield resulted from tax deductibility of interest payments. Another one can be a subsidized borrowing.
   a. ABN Amro
   b. AAB
   c. A Random Walk Down Wall Street
   d. Adjusted present value

3. The _____ was a period of financial crisis that gripped much of Asia beginning in July 1997, and raised fears of a worldwide economic meltdown (financial contagion).

The crisis started in Thailand with the financial collapse of the Thai baht caused by the decision of the Thai government to float the baht, cutting its peg to the USD, after exhaustive efforts to support it in the face of a severe financial overextension that was in part real estate driven. At the time, Thailand had acquired a burden of foreign debt that made the country effectively bankrupt even before the collapse of its currency.

   a. Internal control
   b. OTC Bulletin Board
   c. International trade
   d. Asian Financial Crisis

4. In economics, _____ is a monetary standard in which the value of the monetary unit is defined as equivalent either to a certain quantity of gold or to a certain quantity of silver. Such a system effectively establishes a fixed rate of exchange for the two metals. The merits of the system were the subject of debate in the late 19th century.
   a. 4-4-5 Calendar
   b. 7-Eleven
   c. 529 plan
   d. Bimetallism

5. In finance, the _____ between two currencies specifies how much one currency is worth in terms of the other. For example an _____ of 102 Japanese yen to the United States dollar means that JPY 102 is worth the same as USD 1. The foreign exchange market is one of the largest markets in the world.
   a. ABN Amro
   b. A Random Walk Down Wall Street
   c. AAB
   d. Exchange rate

6. The _____ is where currency trading takes place. It is where banks and other official institutions facilitate the buying and selling of foreign currencies. FX transactions typically involve one party purchasing a quantity of one currency in exchange for paying a quantity of another.
   a. Spot market
   b. Foreign exchange option
   c. Floating exchange rate
   d. Foreign exchange market

Chapter 2. International Monetary System,

7. A _____ secures the proper functioning of money by regulating economic agents, transaction types, and money supply.

They are traditionally formed by the policy decisions of individual governments and administrated as a domestic economic issue.

The current trend, however, is to use international trade and investment to alter the policy and legislation of individual governments.

- a. Bond credit rating
- b. Monetary system
- c. Pattern day trader
- d. Payback period

8. The _____ is a monetary system in which the standard economic unit of account is a fixed weight of silver. The _____ was widespread until the 19th century, when it was replaced in most countries by the gold standard.

The first metal used as a currency was silver more than 4,000 years ago, when silver ingots were used in trade.

- a. 4-4-5 Calendar
- b. 529 plan
- c. 7-Eleven
- d. Silver standard

9. The _____ is a monetary system in which a region's common medium of exchange are paper notes that are normally freely convertible into pre-set, fixed quantities of gold. The _____ is not currently used by any government, having been replaced completely by fiat currency.
- a. Gold standard
- b. 529 plan
- c. 7-Eleven
- d. 4-4-5 Calendar

10. In economics, the _____, measures the payments that flow between any individual country and all other countries. It is used to summarize all international economic transactions for that country during a specific time period, usually a year. The _____ is determined by the country's exports and imports of goods, services, and financial capital, as well as financial transfers.
- a. Balance of payments
- b. Purchasing power parity
- c. 4-4-5 Calendar
- d. Gross national product

11. An _____ represents the ownership in the shares of a foreign company trading on US financial markets. The stock of many non-US companies trades on US exchanges through the use of _____s. _____s enable US investors to buy shares in foreign companies without undertaking cross-border transactions.
- a. American depository receipt
- b. AAB
- c. ABN Amro
- d. A Random Walk Down Wall Street

12. _____ is a term used in accounting, economics and finance to spread the cost of an asset over the span of several years.

In simple words we can say that _____ is the reduction in the value of an asset due to usage, passage of time, wear and tear, technological outdating or obsolescence, depletion or other such factors.

In accounting, _____ is a term used to describe any method of attributing the historical or purchase cost of an asset across its useful life, roughly corresponding to normal wear and tear.

a. Matching principle
b. Deferred financing costs
c. Depreciation
d. Bottom line

13. A _____ is a certificate issued by a depository bank, which purchases shares of foreign companies and deposits it on the account. _____s represent ownership of an underlying number of shares.

They facilitate trade of shares, and are commonly used to invest in companies from developing or emerging markets.

a. Global depository receipt
b. Short positions
c. Special journals
d. The Security Industry Association

14. In economics, _____ is inflation that is very high or 'out of control', a condition in which prices increase rapidly as a currency loses its value. Definitions used by the media vary from a cumulative inflation rate over three years approaching 100% to 'inflation exceeding 50% a month.' In informal usage the term is often applied to much lower rates. As a rule of thumb, normal inflation is reported per year, but _____ is often reported for much shorter intervals, often per month.

a. 529 plan
b. 4-4-5 Calendar
c. 7-Eleven
d. Hyperinflation

15. The _____ was a worldwide economic downturn starting in most places in 1929 and ending at different times in the 1930s or early 1940s for different countries. It was the largest and most important economic depression in the 20th century, and is used in the 21st century as an example of how far the world's economy can fall. The _____ originated in the United States; historians most often use as a starting date the stock market crash on October 29, 1929, known as Black Tuesday.

a. Great Depression
b. 7-Eleven
c. 4-4-5 Calendar
d. 529 plan

16. The _____ is a bank that provides financial and technical assistance to developing countries for development programs (e.g. bridges, roads, schools, etc.) with the stated goal of reducing poverty.

The _____ differs from the _____ Group, in that the _____ comprises only two institutions:

- International Bank for Reconstruction and Development (IBRD)
- International Development Association (IDA)

Whereas the latter incorporates these two in addition to three more:

- International Finance Corporation (IFC)
- Multilateral Investment Guarantee Agency (MIGA)
- International Centre for Settlement of Investment Disputes (ICSID)

Chapter 2. International Monetary System,

John Maynard Keynes (right) represented the UK at the conference, and Harry Dexter White represented the US.

The _____ was created following the ratification of the United Nations Monetary and Financial Conference | Bretton Woods agreement. The concept was originally conceived in July 1944 at the United Nations Monetary and Financial Conference.

- a. 7-Eleven
- b. 529 plan
- c. World Bank
- d. 4-4-5 Calendar

17. _____, in finance and accounting, means stated value or face value. From this comes the expressions at par (at the _____), over par (over _____) and under par (under _____.)

The term '_____' has several meanings depending on context and geography.

- a. Par value
- b. Global Squeeze
- c. FIDC
- d. Sinking fund

18. In financial accounting, the term _____ is most commonly used to describe any part of shareholders' equity, except for basic share capital. Sometimes, the term is used instead of the term provision; such a use, however, is inconsistent with the terminology suggested by International Accounting Standards Board. For more information about provisions, see provision (accounting.)

- a. Reserve
- b. Closing entries
- c. Treasury stock
- d. FIFO and LIFO accounting

19. A _____ is a currency which is held in significant quantities by many governments and institutions as part of their foreign exchange reserves. It also tends to be the international pricing currency for products traded on a global market, such as oil, gold, etc.

This permits the issuing country to purchase the commodities at a marginally cheaper rate than other nations, which must exchange their currency with each purchase and pay a transaction cost.

- a. Hard currency
- b. Devaluation
- c. Reserve currency
- d. Functional currency

20. _____ is the provision of resources (such as granting a loan) by one party to another party where that second party does not reimburse the first party immediately, thereby generating a debt, and instead arranges either to repay or return those resources (or material(s) of equal value) at a later date. The first party is called a creditor, also known as a lender, while the second party is called a debtor, also known as a borrower.

Movements of financial capital are normally dependent on either _____ or equity transfers.

Chapter 2. International Monetary System, 17

    a. Clearing house
    b. Warrant
    c. Comparable
    d. Credit

21. _____ is a fee paid on borrowed assets. It is the price paid for the use of borrowed money, or, money earned by deposited funds. Assets that are sometimes lent with _____ include money, shares, consumer goods through hire purchase, major assets such as aircraft, and even entire factories in finance lease arrangements.
    a. AAB
    b. Interest
    c. Insolvency
    d. A Random Walk Down Wall Street

22. _____ was a domestic tax measure implemented by U.S. President John F. Kennedy in July 1963. It was meant to make it less profitable for U.S. investors to invest abroad by taxing the interest on foreign securities. It was seen by some as retaliation against Canadian attempts to repatriate their economy one month earlier under the direction of Finance Minister Walter Gordon.
    a. Interest Equalization Tax
    b. ABN Amro
    c. A Random Walk Down Wall Street
    d. AAB

23. The _____ of 2002 (Pub.L. 107-204, 116 Stat. 745, enacted July 30, 2002), also known as the Public Company Accounting Reform and Investor Protection Act of 2002 and commonly called Sarbanes-Oxley, Sarbox or SOX, is a United States federal law enacted on July 30, 2002 in response to a number of major corporate and accounting scandals including those affecting Enron, Tyco International, Adelphia, Peregrine Systems and WorldCom.
    a. Sarbanes-Oxley Act
    b. Blue sky law
    c. Foreign Corrupt Practices Act
    d. Duty of loyalty

24. The _____, is the fundamental problem of the United States dollar's role as reserve currency in the Bretton Woods system, or more generally of a national currency as reserve currency.

Briefly, the use of a national currency as global reserve currency leads to a tension between national monetary policy and global monetary policy.

This is reflected in fundamental imbalances in the balance of payments, specifically the current account: to maintain all desired goals, dollars must both overall flow out of the United States, but must also flow in to the United States, which cannot both happen at once.

    a. 529 plan
    b. 7-Eleven
    c. 4-4-5 Calendar
    d. Triffin dilemma

25. A _____ or a flexible exchange rate is a type of exchange rate regime wherein a currency's value is allowed to fluctuate according to the foreign exchange market. A currency that uses a _____ is known as a floating currency. The opposite of a _____ is a fixed exchange rate.
    a. Foreign exchange market
    b. Spot market
    c. Currency pair
    d. Floating exchange rate

26. The _____ was a December 1971 agreement that ended the fixed exchange rates established at the Bretton Woods Conference of 1944.

Chapter 2. International Monetary System,

The Bretton Woods Conference of 1944 established an international fixed exchange rate regime in which currencies were pegged to the United States dollar, which was based on the gold standard.

By 1970, however, it was clear that the exchange rate regime was under threat, as the United States dollar was greatly overvalued because of heavy American spending on Lyndon B. Johnson's Great Society and the Vietnam War.

a. 7-Eleven
b. 529 plan
c. 4-4-5 Calendar
d. Smithsonian Agreement

27. The _____ or Plaza Agreement was an agreement between the governments of France, West Germany, Japan, the United States and the United Kingdom, agreeing to depreciate the US dollar in relation to the Japanese yen and German Deutsche Mark by intervening in currency markets. The five governments signed the accord on September 22, 1985 at the Plaza Hotel in New York City.

The exchange rate value of the dollar versus the yen declined by 51% from 1985 to 1987.

a. 529 plan
b. 7-Eleven
c. 4-4-5 Calendar
d. Plaza Accord

28. A _____ is a monetary authority which is required to maintain a fixed exchange rate with a foreign currency. This policy objective requires the conventional objectives of a central bank to be subordinated to the exchange rate target.

a. Devaluation
b. Hard currency
c. Functional currency
d. Currency board

29. The _____ was signed by the then G6 on February 22, 1987 in Paris, France. Italy had been an invited member, but declined to finalize the agreement. The goal of the _____ was to stabilize the international currency markets and halt the continued decline of the US Dollar caused by the Plaza Accord.

a. 529 plan
b. 4-4-5 Calendar
c. 7-Eleven
d. Louvre Accord

30. _____ was an arrangement established in 1979 under the Jenkins European Commission where most nations of the European Economic Community (EEC) linked their currencies to prevent large fluctuations relative to one another.

After the collapse of the Bretton Woods system in 1971, most of the EEC countries agreed in 1972 to maintain stable exchange rates by preventing exchange fluctuations of more than 2.25% (the European 'currency snake'.) In March 1979, this system was replaced by the _____, and the European Currency Unit (ECU) was defined.

a. Exchange Rate Mechanism
b. Euro Interbank Offered Rate
c. A Random Walk Down Wall Street
d. European Monetary System

Chapter 2. International Monetary System,

31. _____ is the process by which the government, or monetary authority of a country controls (i) the supply of money central bank (ii) availability of money, and (iii) cost of money or rate of interest, in order to attain a set of objectives oriented towards the growth and stability of the economy. Monetary theory provides insight into how to craft optimal _____.

_____ is referred to as either being an expansionary policy where an expansionary policy increases the total supply of money in the economy, and a contractionary policy decreases the total money supply.

   a. Tax exemption
   b. Federal Open Market Committee
   c. Monetary policy
   d. Natural resources consumption tax

32. A _____, reserve bank, or monetary authority is the entity responsible for the monetary policy of a country or of a group of member states. It is a bank that can lend money to other banks in times of need. Its primary responsibility is to maintain the stability of the national currency and money supply, but more active duties include controlling subsidized-loan interest rates, and acting as a lender of last resort to the banking sector during times of financial crisis (private banks often being integral to the national financial system.)
   a. 7-Eleven
   b. 4-4-5 Calendar
   c. 529 plan
   d. Central Bank

33. The _____ was a basket of the currencies of the European Community member states, used as the unit of account of the European Community before being replaced by the euro on January 1, 1999, at parity. The _____ itself replaced the European Unit of Account, also at parity, on March 13, 1979. The European Exchange Rate Mechanism attempted to minimize fluctuations between member state currencies and the _____.
   a. OTC Bulletin Board
   b. Outsourcing
   c. Electronic communication network
   d. European Currency Unit

34. The European _____, was a system introduced by the European Community in March 1979, as part of the European Monetary System (EMS), to reduce exchange rate variability and achieve monetary stability in Europe, in preparation for Economic and Monetary Union and the introduction of a single currency, the euro, which took place on 1 January 1999. Subsequent exchange rate agreements made with countries wishing to join the Eurozone are known as _____ II.

The _____ is based on the concept of fixed currency exchange rate margins, but with exchange rates variable within those margins.

   a. A Random Walk Down Wall Street
   b. Exchange Rate Mechanism
   c. Euro Interbank Offered Rate
   d. European Monetary System

35. In finance, a _____ is a debt security, in which the authorized issuer owes the holders a debt and, depending on the terms of the _____, is obliged to pay interest (the coupon) and/or to repay the principal at a later date, termed maturity.

Thus a _____ is a loan: the issuer is the borrower, the _____ holder is the lender, and the coupon is the interest. _____s provide the borrower with external funds to finance long-term investments, or, in the case of government _____s, to finance current expenditure.

a. Convertible bond
c. Puttable bond
b. Bond
d. Catastrophe bonds

36. The _____ is one of the measures of national income and input for a given country's economy. _____ is defined as the total cost of all finished goods and services produced within the country in a stipulated period of time (usually a 365-day year.) It is sometimes regarded as the sum of profits added at every level of production (the intermediate stages) of all final goods and services produced within a country in a stipulated timeframe, and it is rarely given a monetary value.
   a. Gross domestic product
   b. Macroeconomics
   c. Behavioral finance
   d. Recession

37. In economics and related disciplines, a _____ is a cost incurred in making an economic exchange. For example, most people, when buying or selling a stock, must pay a commission to their broker; that commission is a _____ of doing the stock deal. Or consider buying a banana from a store; to purchase the banana, your costs will be not only the price of the banana itself, but also the energy and effort it requires to find out which of the various banana products you prefer, where to get them and at what price, the cost of traveling from your house to the store and back, the time waiting in line, and the effort of the paying itself; the costs above and beyond the cost of the banana are the _____s.
   a. Fixed costs
   b. Marginal cost
   c. Variable costs
   d. Transaction cost

38. In economics, business, and accounting, a _____ is the value of money that has been used up to produce something, and hence is not available for use anymore. In business, the _____ may be one of acquisition, in which case the amount of money expended to acquire it is counted as _____. In this case, money is the input that is gone in order to acquire the thing.
   a. Cost
   b. Marginal cost
   c. Sliding scale fees
   d. Fixed costs

39. In economics, an _____ is a geographical region in which it would maximize economic efficiency to have the entire region share a single currency. It describes the optimal characteristics for the merger of currencies or the creation of a new currency. The theory is used often to argue whether or not a certain region is ready to become a monetary union, one of the final stages in economic integration.
   a. ABN Amro
   b. A Random Walk Down Wall Street
   c. Optimum currency area
   d. AAB

40. In economics, a _____ is a general slowdown in economic activity in a country over a sustained period of time, or a business cycle contraction. During _____s, many macroeconomic indicators vary in a similar way. Production as measured by Gross Domestic Product (GDP), employment, investment spending, capacity utilization, household incomes and business profits all fall during _____s.
   a. Recession
   b. Mercantilism
   c. Fixed exchange rate
   d. Behavioral finance

41. The term _____ is used to describe a nation's social, or business activity in the process of rapid industrialization. _____ are generally less-wealthy than the developed world, and are wealthier (or the wealthiest of) the developing world. According to The Economist many people find the term dated, but a new term has yet to gain much traction.
   a. ABN Amro
   b. Emerging markets
   c. A Random Walk Down Wall Street
   d. AAB

Chapter 2. International Monetary System,

42. _____ is the branch of economics that studies the dynamics of exchange rates, foreign investment, and how these affect international trade. It also studies international projects, international investments and capital flows, and trade deficits. It includes the study of futures, options and currency swaps.
a. ABN Amro
b. AAB
c. A Random Walk Down Wall Street
d. International finance

43. _____ is the removal or simplification of government rules and regulations that constrain the operation of market forces. _____ does not mean elimination of laws against fraud, but eliminating or reducing government control of how business is done, thereby moving toward a more free market.

The stated rationale for '_____' is often that fewer and simpler regulations will lead to a raised level of competitiveness, therefore higher productivity, more efficiency and lower prices overall.

a. Value added
b. Supply shock
c. Demand shock
d. Deregulation

44. A _____ is the suggested tax on all trade of currency across borders. The tax is intended to put a penalty on short-term speculation in currencies. The original tax rate he proposed was 1%, which was subsequently lowered to between 0.1% and 0.25%.
a. 7-Eleven
b. Tobin tax
c. 4-4-5 Calendar
d. 529 plan

45. In economics, the _____ is a term used in discussing the problems associated with creating a stable international financial system. It refers to the trade-offs among the following three goals: a fixed exchange rate, national independence in monetary policy, and capital mobility. According to the Mundell-Fleming model, a small, open economy cannot achieve all three of these policy goals at the same time: in pursuing any two of these goals, a nation must forgo the third.
a. 4-4-5 Calendar
b. 7-Eleven
c. 529 plan
d. Trilemma

46. _____ is the quality of paper money substitutes which entitles the holder to redeem them on demand into money proper.

Historically, the banknote has followed a common or very similar pattern in the western nations. Originally decentralized and issued from various independent banks, it was gradually brought under state control and became a monopoly privilege of the central banks.

a. Devaluation
b. Convertibility
c. Petrodollar recycling
d. Functional currency

47. The _____ is a private, not-for-profit organization whose primary purpose is to develop generally accepted accounting principles (GAAP) within the United States in the public's interest. The Securities and Exchange Commission (SEC) designated the _____ as the organization responsible for setting accounting standards for public companies in the U.S. It was created in 1973, replacing the Accounting Principles Board and the Committee on Accounting Procedure of the American Institute of Certified Public Accountants. The _____'s mission is 'to establish and improve standards of financial accounting and reporting for the guidance and education of the public, including issuers, auditors, and users of financial information.'

The _____ is not a governmental body.

- a. Credit karma
- c. MRU Holdings
- b. PlaNet Finance
- d. FASB

48. A _____, sometimes called a pegged exchange rate, is a type of exchange rate regime wherein a currency's value is matched to the value of another single currency or to a basket of other currencies, or to another measure of value such as gold.

A _____ is usually used to stabilize the value of a currency, vis-a-vis the currency it is pegged to. This facilitates trade and investments between the two countries, and is especially useful for small economies where external trade forms a large part of their GDP.

- a. Deflation
- c. Market structure
- b. Human capital
- d. Fixed exchange rate

Chapter 3. Balance of Payments,

1. _____ is the recording of the value of assets, liabilities, income, and expenses in the daybooks and in ledgers which debit and credit entries are chronologically posted to record changes in value. _____ is often confused with accounting which is the system of recording, verifying, and reporting such information. Practitioners of accounting are called accountants.
   - a. Resources, Events, Agents
   - b. Bookkeeping
   - c. Debit and credit
   - d. Standard accounting practices

2. The institution most often referenced by the word '_____' is a public or publicly traded _____, the shares of which are traded on a public stock exchange (e.g., the New York Stock Exchange or Nasdaq in the United States) where shares of stock of _____s are bought and sold by and to the general public. Most of the largest businesses in the world are publicly traded _____s. However, the majority of _____s are said to be closely held, privately held or close _____s, meaning that no ready market exists for the trading of shares.
   - a. Protect
   - b. Federal Home Loan Mortgage Corporation
   - c. Corporation
   - d. Depository Trust Company

3. _____ is a system that ensures the integrity of the financial values recorded in a financial accounting system. It does this by ensuring that each individual transaction is recorded in at least two different (sections) nominal ledgers of the financial accounting system and so implementing a double checking system for every transaction. It does this by first identifying values as either a Debit or a Credit value.
   - a. Resources, Events, Agents
   - b. Momentum Accounting and Triple-Entry Bookkeeping
   - c. Single-entry bookkeeping system
   - d. Double-entry bookkeeping

4. _____ is exchange of capital, goods, and services across international borders or territories. In most countries, it represents a significant share of gross domestic product (GDP.) While _____ has been present throughout much of history, its economic, social, and political importance has been on the rise in recent centuries.
   - a. Index number
   - b. OTC Bulletin Board
   - c. United States Treasury security
   - d. International trade

5. In economics, the _____, measures the payments that flow between any individual country and all other countries. It is used to summarize all international economic transactions for that country during a specific time period, usually a year. The _____ is determined by the country's exports and imports of goods, services, and financial capital, as well as financial transfers.
   - a. 4-4-5 Calendar
   - b. Gross national product
   - c. Purchasing power parity
   - d. Balance of payments

6. In financial accounting, the _____ is one of the accounts in shareholders' equity. Sole proprietorships have a single _____ in the owner's equity. Partnerships maintain a _____ for each of the partners.
   - a. Bed Bath ' Beyond Inc.
   - b. Duty of loyalty
   - c. Market maker
   - d. Capital account

7. In economics, the _____ is one of the two primary components of the balance of payments, the other being the capital account. It is the sum of the balance of trade (exports minus imports of goods and services), net factor income (such as interest and dividends) and net transfer payments (such as foreign aid.)

The _____ balance is one of two major metrics of the nature of a country's foreign trade (the other being the net capital outflow).

- a. Cash budget
- b. Consols
- c. Rights issue
- d. Current account

8. In financial accounting, the term _____ is most commonly used to describe any part of shareholders' equity, except for basic share capital. Sometimes, the term is used instead of the term provision; such a use, however, is inconsistent with the terminology suggested by International Accounting Standards Board. For more information about provisions, see provision (accounting.)

- a. Treasury stock
- b. FIFO and LIFO accounting
- c. Closing entries
- d. Reserve

9. _____, in bookkeeping, refers to assets, liabilities, income, and expenses recorded on individual pages of the so called book of final entry or ledger. Changes in _____ value are made by chronologically posting debit (DR) and credit (CR) entries to its page. Examples of _____ s are cash, _____ s receivable, mortgages, loans, land and buildings, common stock, sales, services provided, wages, and payroll overhead.

- a. Alpha
- b. Option
- c. Account
- d. Accretion

10. The _____ or balance of trade on services is that part of the balance of trade that refers to services and other products that do not result in the transfer of physical objects. Examples include consulting services, tourism, and patent license revenues. This figure is usually generated by tertiary industry.

- a. AAB
- b. ABN Amro
- c. A Random Walk Down Wall Street
- d. Invisible balance

11. The _____ of 2002 (Pub.L. 107-204, 116 Stat. 745, enacted July 30, 2002), also known as the Public Company Accounting Reform and Investor Protection Act of 2002 and commonly called Sarbanes-Oxley, Sarbox or SOX, is a United States federal law enacted on July 30, 2002 in response to a number of major corporate and accounting scandals including those affecting Enron, Tyco International, Adelphia, Peregrine Systems and WorldCom.

- a. Sarbanes-Oxley Act
- b. Foreign Corrupt Practices Act
- c. Duty of loyalty
- d. Blue sky law

12. _____ refers to the various forms of financial support and financial transactions used in international trade. _____ uses a range of instruments to provide finance to exporters and importers, including documentary credits such as letters of credit.

While a seller (the exporter) can require the purchaser (an importer) to prepay for goods shipped, the purchaser (importer) may wish to reduce risk by requiring the seller to document that the goods have been shipped.

- a. Debtor-in-possession financing
- b. Forfaiting
- c. Free cash flow
- d. Trade finance

13. In economics, _____ refers to the ability of a party to produce a good or service using fewer real resources than another entity producing the same good or service. A party has an _____ when using the same input as another party, it can produce a greater output. Since _____ is determined by a simple comparison of labor productivities, it is possible for a a party to have no _____ in anything. It can be contrasted with the concept of comparative advantage which refers to the ability to produce a particular good at a lower opportunity cost.
   a. Absolute advantage
   c. AAB
   b. Economic depreciation
   d. A Random Walk Down Wall Street

14. The _____ is the difference between a nation's exports of goods and services and its imports of goods and services, if all financial transfers and investments and the like are ignored. A nation is said to have a trade deficit if it is importing more than it exports.

In economics, the current account is one of the two primary components of the balance of payments, the other being the capital account.

   a. Value added
   c. Demand shock
   b. Supply shock
   d. Balance of Trade

15. In finance, the _____ between two currencies specifies how much one currency is worth in terms of the other. For example an _____ of 102 Japanese yen to the United States dollar means that JPY 102 is worth the same as USD 1. The foreign exchange market is one of the largest markets in the world.
   a. A Random Walk Down Wall Street
   c. ABN Amro
   b. AAB
   d. Exchange rate

16. _____ is the returns received on factors of production: rent is return on land, wages on labor, interest on capital, and profit on entrepreneurship. It is also known as Net Factor Payments (NFP.)

Part of current account with balance of trade (exports minus imports of goods and services) and net transfer payments (such as foreign aid).

   a. 7-Eleven
   c. Factor income
   b. 4-4-5 Calendar
   d. 529 plan

17. The _____ is where currency trading takes place. It is where banks and other official institutions facilitate the buying and selling of foreign currencies. FX transactions typically involve one party purchasing a quantity of one currency in exchange for paying a quantity of another.
   a. Foreign exchange market
   c. Spot market
   b. Foreign exchange option
   d. Floating exchange rate

18. _____ is an accounting term used to reflect the portion of the book value of a business entity not directly attributable to its assets and liabilities; it normally arises only in case of an acquisition. It reflects the ability of the entity to make a higher profit than would be derived from selling the tangible assets. _____ is also known as an intangible asset.
   a. Consolidation
   c. Net profit
   b. Cost of goods sold
   d. Goodwill

19. _____ is a term used in accounting, economics and finance to spread the cost of an asset over the span of several years.

In simple words we can say that _____ is the reduction in the value of an asset due to usage, passage of time, wear and tear, technological outdating or obsolescence, depletion or other such factors.

In accounting, _____ is a term used to describe any method of attributing the historical or purchase cost of an asset across its useful life, roughly corresponding to normal wear and tear.

- a. Matching principle
- b. Bottom line
- c. Deferred financing costs
- d. Depreciation

20. _____, refers to consumption opportunity gained by an entity within a specified time frame, which is generally expressed in monetary terms. However, for households and individuals, '_____ is the sum of all the wages, salaries, profits, interests payments, rents and other forms of earnings received... in a given period of time.' For firms, _____ generally refers to net-profit: what remains of revenue after expenses have been subtracted.

- a. OIBDA
- b. Accrual
- c. Annual report
- d. Income

21. _____ is a business valuation method. _____ is the net present value of a project if financed solely by ownership equity plus the present value of all the benefits of financing. Usually, the main benefit is a tax shield resulted from tax deductibility of interest payments. Another one can be a subsidized borrowing.

- a. ABN Amro
- b. A Random Walk Down Wall Street
- c. AAB
- d. Adjusted present value

22. _____ in its classic form is defined as a company from one country making a physical investment into building a factory in another country. It is the establishment of an enterprise by a foreigner. Its definition can be extended to include investments made to acquire lasting interest in enterprises operating outside of the economy of the investor.

- a. Foreign direct investment
- b. Dow Jones ' Company
- c. Public company
- d. MicroPlace

23. In economics and finance, _____ represents passive holdings of securities such as foreign stocks, bonds, or other financial assets, none of which entails active management or control of the securities' issuer by the investor; where such control exists, it is known as foreign direct investment. Generally, this means the investor holds less than 10% of the total shares or less than the amount needed to hold the majority vote.

Some examples of _____ are:

- purchase of shares in a foreign company.
- purchase of bonds issued by a foreign government.
- acquisition of assets in a foreign country.

Chapter 3. Balance of Payments, 27

Factors affecting international _____:

- tax rates on interest or dividends (investors will normally prefer countries where the tax rates are relatively low)
- interest rates (money tends to flow to countries with high interest rates)
- exchange rates (foreign investors may be attracted if the local currency is expected to strengthen)

_____ is part of the capital account on the balance of payments statistics.

a. Divestment
c. Tactical asset allocation
b. Portable alpha
d. Portfolio investment

24. In finance, a _____ is a debt security, in which the authorized issuer owes the holders a debt and, depending on the terms of the _____, is obliged to pay interest (the coupon) and/or to repay the principal at a later date, termed maturity.

Thus a _____ is a loan: the issuer is the borrower, the _____ holder is the lender, and the coupon is the interest. _____s provide the borrower with external funds to finance long-term investments, or, in the case of government _____s, to finance current expenditure.

a. Catastrophe bonds
c. Puttable bond
b. Bond
d. Convertible bond

25. _____ is an economic term describing capital flowing out of (or leaving) a particular economy. _____ can be caused by any number of economic or political reasons but can often originate from instability in either sphere.

Regardless of cause, _____ is generally perceived as always undesirable and many countries create laws to restrict the movement of capital out of the nations' borders (called capital controls).

a. Break-even point
c. Defined contribution plan
b. Fixed asset turnover
d. Capital outflow

26. _____ is an accounting term which frequently appears as a balance sheet item as a component of shareholders' equity. _____ is used to account for any funds the issuing firm has received over and above the par value of the common stock. It may also be used to account for any gains the firm may derive from selling treasury stock, although this is less commonly seen.

a. Commercial finance
c. Stock market index option
b. Capital surplus
d. Flight-to-quality

27. A _____ is a bond issued by a corporation. The term is usually applied to longer-term debt instruments, generally with a maturity date falling at least a year after their issue date. (The term 'commercial paper' is sometimes used for instruments with a shorter maturity.)

Chapter 3. Balance of Payments,

a. Brady bonds
b. Government bond
c. Serial bond
d. Corporate bond

28. _____ is a fee paid on borrowed assets. It is the price paid for the use of borrowed money, or, money earned by deposited funds. Assets that are sometimes lent with _____ include money, shares, consumer goods through hire purchase, major assets such as aircraft, and even entire factories in finance lease arrangements.

a. A Random Walk Down Wall Street
b. Insolvency
c. AAB
d. Interest

29. An _____ is the price a borrower pays for the use of money they do not own, and the return a lender receives for deferring the use of funds, by lending it to the borrower. _____s are normally expressed as a percentage rate over the period of one year.

_____s targets are also a vital tool of monetary policy and are used to control variables like investment, inflation, and unemployment.

a. ABN Amro
b. Interest rate
c. A Random Walk Down Wall Street
d. AAB

30. _____ is that which is owed; usually referencing assets owed, but the term can cover other obligations. In the case of assets, _____ is a means of using future purchasing power in the present before a summation has been earned. Some companies and corporations use _____ as a part of their overall corporate finance strategy.

a. Cross-collateralization
b. Partial Payment
c. Credit cycle
d. Debt

31. In economics and finance, _____ is the practice of taking advantage of a price differential between two or more markets: striking a combination of matching deals that capitalize upon the imbalance, the profit being the difference between the market prices. When used by academics, an _____ is a transaction that involves no negative cash flow at any probabilistic or temporal state and a positive cash flow in at least one state; in simple terms, a risk-free profit.

a. Efficient-market hypothesis
b. Initial margin
c. Issuer
d. Arbitrage

32. _____ is an event or condition under the contract between a buyer and a seller to exchange an asset for payment. In accounting, it is recognized by an entry in the books of account. It involves a change in the status of the finances of two or more businesses or individuals.

a. Tax shield
b. Financial transaction
c. Negative gearing
d. Nominal value

33. A _____ is a fungible, negotiable instrument representing financial value. They are broadly categorized into debt securities (such as banknotes, bonds and debentures), and equity securities; e.g., common stocks. The company or other entity issuing the _____ is called the issuer.

a. Securities lending
b. Security
c. Book entry
d. Tracking stock

Chapter 3. Balance of Payments,

34. In business and accounting, _____s are everything of value that is owned by a person or company. The balance sheet of a firm records the monetary value of the _____s owned by the firm. The two major _____ classes are tangible _____s and intangible _____s.
   a. Accounts payable
   b. EBITDA
   c. Income
   d. Asset

35. _____ in a strict sense are only the foreign currency deposits and bonds held by central banks and monetary authorities. However, the term in popular usage commonly includes foreign exchange and gold, SDRs and IMF reserve positions. This broader figure is more readily available, but it is more accurately termed official international reserves or international reserves.
   a. Floating exchange rate
   b. Foreign exchange reserves
   c. Currency swap
   d. Spot market

36. The _____ is a monetary system in which a region's common medium of exchange are paper notes that are normally freely convertible into pre-set, fixed quantities of gold. The _____ is not currently used by any government, having been replaced completely by fiat currency.
   a. 4-4-5 Calendar
   b. Gold standard
   c. 529 plan
   d. 7-Eleven

37. A _____ secures the proper functioning of money by regulating economic agents, transaction types, and money supply.

They are traditionally formed by the policy decisions of individual governments and administrated as a domestic economic issue.

The current trend, however, is to use international trade and investment to alter the policy and legislation of individual governments.

   a. Bond credit rating
   b. Pattern day trader
   c. Payback period
   d. Monetary system

38. The _____ was a period of financial crisis that gripped much of Asia beginning in July 1997, and raised fears of a worldwide economic meltdown (financial contagion).

The crisis started in Thailand with the financial collapse of the Thai baht caused by the decision of the Thai government to float the baht, cutting its peg to the USD, after exhaustive efforts to support it in the face of a severe financial overextension that was in part real estate driven. At the time, Thailand had acquired a burden of foreign debt that made the country effectively bankrupt even before the collapse of its currency.

   a. Internal control
   b. OTC Bulletin Board
   c. International trade
   d. Asian Financial Crisis

39. The _____ was a basket of the currencies of the European Community member states, used as the unit of account of the European Community before being replaced by the euro on January 1, 1999, at parity. The _____ itself replaced the European Unit of Account, also at parity, on March 13, 1979. The European Exchange Rate Mechanism attempted to minimize fluctuations between member state currencies and the _____.

a. European Currency Unit
b. Outsourcing
c. OTC Bulletin Board
d. Electronic communication network

40. A _____, reserve bank, or monetary authority is the entity responsible for the monetary policy of a country or of a group of member states. It is a bank that can lend money to other banks in times of need. Its primary responsibility is to maintain the stability of the national currency and money supply, but more active duties include controlling subsidized-loan interest rates, and acting as a lender of last resort to the banking sector during times of financial crisis (private banks often being integral to the national financial system.)

a. 4-4-5 Calendar
b. 7-Eleven
c. Central bank
d. 529 plan

41. _____ in finance is a risk management technique, related to hedging, that mixes a wide variety of investments within a portfolio. Because the fluctuations of a single security have less impact on a diverse portfolio, _____ minimizes the risk from any one investment.

A simple example of _____ is the following: On a particular island the entire economy consists of two companies: one that sells umbrellas and another that sells sunscreen.

a. 529 plan
b. 4-4-5 Calendar
c. 7-Eleven
d. Diversification

42. A _____ or a flexible exchange rate is a type of exchange rate regime wherein a currency's value is allowed to fluctuate according to the foreign exchange market. A currency that uses a _____ is known as a floating currency. The opposite of a _____ is a fixed exchange rate.

a. Spot market
b. Currency pair
c. Floating exchange rate
d. Foreign exchange market

43. The _____ or Plaza Agreement was an agreement between the governments of France, West Germany, Japan, the United States and the United Kingdom, agreeing to depreciate the US dollar in relation to the Japanese yen and German Deutsche Mark by intervening in currency markets. The five governments signed the accord on September 22, 1985 at the Plaza Hotel in New York City.

The exchange rate value of the dollar versus the yen declined by 51% from 1985 to 1987.

a. 4-4-5 Calendar
b. 7-Eleven
c. 529 plan
d. Plaza Accord

44. _____ is an economic theory that holds that the prosperity of a nation is dependent upon its supply of capital, and that the global volume of international trade is 'unchangeable.' Economic assets or capital, are represented by bullion (gold, silver, and trade value) held by the state, which is best increased through a positive balance of trade with other nations (exports minus imports). _____ suggests that the ruling government should advance these goals by playing a protectionist role in the economy; by encouraging exports and discouraging imports, notably through the use of tariffs and subsidies.

_____ was the dominant school of thought throughout the early modern period (from the 16th to the 18th century).

a. Macroeconomics
b. Business cycle
c. Fixed exchange rate
d. Mercantilism

45. A _____ is a party (e.g. person, organization, company, or government) that has a claim to the services of a second party. The first party, in general, has provided some property or service to the second party under the assumption (usually enforced by contract) that the second party will return an equivalent property or service. The second party is frequently called a debtor or borrower.
   a. False billing
   b. NOPLAT
   c. Redemption value
   d. Creditor

46. Gross domestic product (GDP) is defined as the 'value of all final goods and services produced in a country in one year'. On the other hand, _____ is defined as the 'value of all (final) goods and services produced in a country in one year, plus income earned by its citizens abroad, minus income earned by foreigners in the country'. The key difference between the two is that GDP is the total output of a region, eg.
   a. 4-4-5 Calendar
   b. TED spread
   c. Purchasing power parity
   d. Gross national product

1. _____ is the set of processes, customs, policies, laws and institutions affecting the way a corporation is directed, administered or controlled. _____ also includes the relationships among the many stakeholders involved and the goals for which the corporation is governed. The principal stakeholders are the shareholders, management and the board of directors.
   a. Corporate governance
   b. Foreign Corrupt Practices Act
   c. Patent
   d. Due diligence

2. The institution most often referenced by the word '_____' is a public or publicly traded _____, the shares of which are traded on a public stock exchange (e.g., the New York Stock Exchange or Nasdaq in the United States) where shares of stock of _____s are bought and sold by and to the general public. Most of the largest businesses in the world are publicly traded _____s. However, the majority of _____s are said to be closely held, privately held or close _____s, meaning that no ready market exists for the trading of shares.
   a. Depository Trust Company
   b. Protect
   c. Federal Home Loan Mortgage Corporation
   d. Corporation

3. _____ is a term used in corporate law to describe a fiduciaries' 'conflicts of interest and requires fiduciaries to put the corporation's interests ahead of their own.' 'Corporate fiduciaries breach their _____ when they divert corporate assets, opportunities, or information for personal gain.'

It is generally acceptable if a director makes a decision for the corporation that profits both him and the corporation. The _____ is breached when the director puts their interest in front of that of the corporation.

- Flagrant Diversion: corporate official stealing tangible corporate assets - 'a plain breach of the fiduciary's _____ since the diversion was unauthorized and the corporation received no benefit in the transaction.'
- Self-Dealing: A key player and the corporation are on opposite sides of the transaction or the key player has helped influence the corporation's decisions to enter the transaction. 'When a fiduciary enters into a transaction with the corporation on unfair terms, the effect is the same as if he had appropriated the difference between the transaction's fair value and the transaction's price.'
- Executive Compensation
- Usurping Corporate Opportunity
- Disclosure to Shareholders
- Trading on Inside Information
- Selling out
- Entrenchment
- The key player's personal financial interest are at least potentially in conflict with the financial interests of the corporation.

- By showing approval by a majority of disinterested directors
- Showing ratification by shareholders (MBCA 8.63)
- Showing transaction was inherently fair (MBCA 8.61)

Section 8.60 of the Model Business Corporation Act states there is a conflict of interest when the director knows that at the time of a commitment that he or a related person is 1) a party to the transaction or 2) has a beneficial financial interest in the transaction that the interest and exercises his influence to the detriment of the corporation.

Chapter 4. Corporate Governance around the World, 33

   a. Corporate governance
   c. Duty of loyalty
   b. Fraud deterrence
   d. Law of one price

4. A _____ is a private or public market for the trading of company stock and derivatives of company stock at an agreed price; these are securities listed on a stock exchange as well as those only traded privately.

The size of the world _____ is estimated at about $36.6 trillion US at the beginning of October 2008 . The world derivatives market has been estimated at about $480 trillion face or nominal value, 12 times the size of the entire world economy.

   a. Andrew Tobias
   c. Adolph Coors
   b. Anton Gelonkin
   d. Stock market

5. In economics, collective bargaining, psychology and political science, 'free riders' are those who consume more than their fair share of a resource, or shoulder less than a fair share of the costs of its production. Free riding is usually considered to be an economic 'problem' only when it leads to the non-production or under-production of a public good (and thus to Pareto inefficiency), or when it leads to the excessive use of a common property resource. The _____ is the question of how to prevent free riding from taking place (or at least limit its negative effects) in these situations.
   a. 529 plan
   c. Free rider problem
   b. 7-Eleven
   d. 4-4-5 Calendar

6. In business, _____ is the total assets minus total outside liabilities of an individual or a company. For a company, this is called shareholders' equity and may be referred to as book value. _____ is stated as at a particular point in time.
   a. Restructuring
   c. Certified International Investment Analyst
   b. Moneylender
   d. Net worth

7. The phrase _____ refers to the aspect of corporate strategy, corporate finance and management dealing with the buying, selling and combining of different companies that can aid, finance, or help a growing company in a given industry grow rapidly without having to create another business entity.

An acquisition, also known as a takeover, is the buying of one company (the 'target') by another. An acquisition may be friendly or hostile.

   a. 7-Eleven
   c. 4-4-5 Calendar
   b. 529 plan
   d. Mergers and acquisitions

8. The term _____ usually refers to a company that is permitted to offer its registered securities for sale to the general public, typically through a stock exchange, or occasionally a company whose stock is traded over the counter via market makers who use non-exchange quotation services.

The term '_____' may also refer to a company owned by the government.

   a. First Prudential Markets
   c. Public company
   b. Corporation
   d. General partnership

Chapter 4. Corporate Governance around the World,

9. An _____ is an economic concept that relates to the cost incurred by an entity (such as organizations) associated with problems such as divergent management-shareholder objectives and information asymmetry. The costs consist of two main sources:

   1. The costs inherently associated with using an agent (e.g., the risk that agents will use organizational resource for their own benefit) and
   2. The costs of techniques used to mitigate the problems associated with using an agent (e.g., the costs of producing financial statements or the use of stock options to align executive interests to shareholder interests.)

Though effects of _____ are present in any agency relationship, the term is most used in business contexts.

The information asymmetry that exists between shareholders and the Chief Executive Officer is generally considered to be a classic example of a principal-agent problem. The agent (the manager) is working on behalf of the principal (the shareholders), who does not observe the actions of the agent.

  a. AAB
  b. ABN Amro
  c. A Random Walk Down Wall Street
  d. Agency Cost

10. In political science and economics, the _____ or agency dilemma treats the difficulties that arise under conditions of incomplete and asymmetric information when a principal hires an agent. Various mechanisms may be used to try to align the interests of the agent with those of the principal, such as piece rates/commissions, profit sharing, efficiency wages, performance measurement (including financial statements), the agent posting a bond, or fear of firing. The _____ is found in most employer/employee relationships, for example, when stockholders hire top executives of corporations.
  a. 7-Eleven
  b. 529 plan
  c. 4-4-5 Calendar
  d. Principal-agent problem

11. In economics, business, and accounting, a _____ is the value of money that has been used up to produce something, and hence is not available for use anymore. In business, the _____ may be one of acquisition, in which case the amount of money expended to acquire it is counted as _____. In this case, money is the input that is gone in order to acquire the thing.
  a. Sliding scale fees
  b. Marginal cost
  c. Cost
  d. Fixed costs

12. _____ is the balance of the amounts of cash being received and paid by a business during a defined period of time, sometimes tied to a specific project. Measurement of _____ can be used

   - to evaluate the state or performance of a business or project.
   - to determine problems with liquidity. Being profitable does not necessarily mean being liquid. A company can fail because of a shortage of cash, even while profitable.
   - to generate project rate of returns. The time of _____s into and out of projects are used as inputs to financial models such as internal rate of return, and net present value.
   - to examine income or growth of a business when it is believed that accrual accounting concepts do not represent economic realities. Alternately, _____ can be used to 'validate' the net income generated by accrual accounting.

Chapter 4. Corporate Governance around the World, 35

_____ as a generic term may be used differently depending on context, and certain _____ definitions may be adapted by analysts and users for their own uses. Common terms include operating _____ and free _____.

_____s can be classified into:

1. Operational _____s: Cash received or expended as a result of the company's core business activities.
2. Investment _____s: Cash received or expended through capital expenditure, investments or acquisitions.
3. Financing _____s: Cash received or expended as a result of financial activities, such as interests and dividends.

All three together - the net _____ - are necessary to reconcile the beginning cash balance to the ending cash balance. Loan draw downs or equity injections, that is just shifting of capital but no expenditure as such, are not considered in the net _____.

a. Corporate finance
b. Shareholder value
c. Cash flow
d. Real option

13. A _____ is an exchange of promises between two or more parties to do an act which is enforceable in a court of law. It is where an unqualified offer meets a qualified acceptance and the parties reach Consensus ad Idem. The parties must have the necessary capacity to _____ and the _____ must not be either trifling, indeterminate, impossible or illegal.
a. 4-4-5 Calendar
b. Contract
c. 7-Eleven
d. 529 plan

14. A _____ is a payment made by a corporation to its shareholder members. When a corporation earns a profit or surplus, that money can be put to two uses: it can either be re-invested in the business (called retained earnings), or it can be paid to the shareholders as a _____. Many corporations retain a portion of their earnings and pay the remainder as a _____.

a. Special dividend
b. Dividend puzzle
c. Dividend
d. Dividend yield

15. The _____ duty is a legal relationship of confidence or trust between two or more parties, most commonly a _____ or trustee and a principal or beneficiary. One party, for example a corporate trust company or the trust department of a bank, holds a _____ relation or acts in a _____ capacity to another, such as one whose funds are entrusted to it for investment. In a _____ relation one person justifiably reposes confidence, good faith, reliance and trust in another whose aid, advice or protection is sought in some matter.
a. Financial Institutions Reform Recovery and Enforcement Act
b. Legal tender
c. General obligation
d. Fiduciary

16. In corporate finance, _____ is a cash flow available for distribution among all the security holders of a company. They include equity holders, debt holders, preferred stock holders, convertible security holders, and so on.

Note that the first three lines above are calculated for you on the standard Statement of Cash Flows.

a. Free cash flow
b. Funding
c. Safety stock
d. Forfaiting

17. _____ refers to the pricing of contributions (assets, tangible and intangible, services, and funds) transferred within an organization. For example, goods from the production division may be sold to the marketing division, or goods from a parent company may be sold to a foreign subsidiary. Since the prices are set within an organization (i.e. controlled), the typical market mechanisms that establish prices for such transactions between third parties may not apply.

a. Price discrimination
b. Transfer pricing
c. Discounts and allowances
d. Price index

18. _____ is a business valuation method. _____ is the net present value of a project if financed solely by ownership equity plus the present value of all the benefits of financing. Usually, the main benefit is a tax shield resulted from tax deductibility of interest payments. Another one can be a subsidized borrowing.

a. ABN Amro
b. AAB
c. A Random Walk Down Wall Street
d. Adjusted present value

19. _____ is the value on a given date of a future payment or series of future payments, discounted to reflect the time value of money and other factors such as investment risk. _____ calculations are widely used in business and economics to provide a means to compare cash flows at different times on a meaningful 'like to like' basis.

The most commonly applied model of the time value of money is compound interest.

a. Present value of benefits
b. Negative gearing
c. Net present value
d. Present value

20. In economics, the _____, measures the payments that flow between any individual country and all other countries. It is used to summarize all international economic transactions for that country during a specific time period, usually a year. The _____ is determined by the country's exports and imports of goods, services, and financial capital, as well as financial transfers.

a. Gross national product
b. Balance of payments
c. Purchasing power parity
d. 4-4-5 Calendar

21. An _____ is a contract written by a seller that conveys to the buyer the right -- but not the obligation -- to buy (in the case of a call _____) or to sell (in the case of a put _____) a particular asset, such as a piece of property such as, among others, a futures contract. In return for granting the _____, the seller collects a payment (the premium) from the buyer.

For example, buying a call _____ provides the right to buy a specified quantity of a security at a set strike price at some time on or before expiration, while buying a put _____ provides the right to sell.

a. AT'T Mobility LLC
b. Option
c. Amortization
d. Annuity

22. _____ LLP, based in Chicago, was once one of the 'Big Five' accounting firms among PricewaterhouseCoopers, Deloitte Touche Tohmatsu, Ernst ' Young and KPMG, providing auditing, tax, and consulting services to large corporations. In 2002, the firm voluntarily surrendered its licenses to practice as Certified Public Accountants in the United States after being found guilty of criminal charges relating to the firm's handling of the auditing of Enron, the energy corporation, resulting in the loss of 85,000 jobs. Although the verdict was subsequently overturned by the Supreme Court of the United States, it has not returned as a viable business.

a. Institute of Financial Accountants
b. Information Systems Audit and Control Association
c. Accion USA
d. Arthur Andersen

23. The _____ was a period of financial crisis that gripped much of Asia beginning in July 1997, and raised fears of a worldwide economic meltdown (financial contagion).

The crisis started in Thailand with the financial collapse of the Thai baht caused by the decision of the Thai government to float the baht, cutting its peg to the USD, after exhaustive efforts to support it in the face of a severe financial overextension that was in part real estate driven. At the time, Thailand had acquired a burden of foreign debt that made the country effectively bankrupt even before the collapse of its currency.

a. OTC Bulletin Board
b. International trade
c. Internal control
d. Asian Financial Crisis

24. In accounting terms, after all liabilities are paid, _____ is the remaining interest in assets. If valuations placed on assets do not exceed liabilities, negative equity exists.

Shareholders' equity (or stockholders' equity, shareholders' funds, shareholders' capital employed) is this interest in remaining assets, spread among individual shareholders of common or preferred stock.

a. Asset-backed commercial paper
b. Amortising swap
c. Intelligent investor
d. Ownership Equity

25. In economics, _____ is a monetary standard in which the value of the monetary unit is defined as equivalent either to a certain quantity of gold or to a certain quantity of silver. Such a system effectively establishes a fixed rate of exchange for the two metals. The merits of the system were the subject of debate in the late 19th century.

a. 4-4-5 Calendar
b. 7-Eleven
c. 529 plan
d. Bimetallism

26. A _____ is a set of companies with interlocking business relationships and shareholdings. It is a type of business group.

The prototypical _____ are those which appeared in Japan during the 'economic miracle' following World War II.

a. Zero-coupon bond
b. Keiretsu
c. Relative strength Index
d. Stock split

Chapter 4. Corporate Governance around the World,

27. In finance, a _____ is a debt security, in which the authorized issuer owes the holders a debt and, depending on the terms of the _____, is obliged to pay interest (the coupon) and/or to repay the principal at a later date, termed maturity.

Thus a _____ is a loan: the issuer is the borrower, the _____ holder is the lender, and the coupon is the interest. _____s provide the borrower with external funds to finance long-term investments, or, in the case of government _____s, to finance current expenditure.

 a. Catastrophe bonds
 b. Bond
 c. Puttable bond
 d. Convertible bond

28. The _____ is a financial market where participants buy and sell debt securities, usually in the form of bonds. As of 2006, the size of the international _____ is an estimated $45 trillion, of which the size of the outstanding U.S. _____ debt was $25.2 trillion.

Nearly all of the $923 billion average daily trading volume in the U.S. _____ takes place between broker-dealers and large institutions in a decentralized, over-the-counter market.

 a. Bond market
 b. Fixed income
 c. 4-4-5 Calendar
 d. 529 plan

29. The _____ of 2002 (Pub.L. 107-204, 116 Stat. 745, enacted July 30, 2002), also known as the Public Company Accounting Reform and Investor Protection Act of 2002 and commonly called Sarbanes-Oxley, Sarbox or SOX, is a United States federal law enacted on July 30, 2002 in response to a number of major corporate and accounting scandals including those affecting Enron, Tyco International, Adelphia, Peregrine Systems and WorldCom.
 a. Blue sky law
 b. Duty of loyalty
 c. Foreign Corrupt Practices Act
 d. Sarbanes-Oxley Act

30. _____ is that which is owed; usually referencing assets owed, but the term can cover other obligations. In the case of assets, _____ is a means of using future purchasing power in the present before a summation has been earned. Some companies and corporations use _____ as a part of their overall corporate finance strategy.
 a. Partial Payment
 b. Credit cycle
 c. Debt
 d. Cross-collateralization

31. The _____ is a description of the role of equity markets in facilitating corporate takeovers first put forward by Alan Manne.
 a. Gross profit margin
 b. Preferred stock
 c. Market for corporate control
 d. Trade-off theory

32. A _____ is a fungible, negotiable instrument representing financial value. They are broadly categorized into debt securities (such as banknotes, bonds and debentures), and equity securities; e.g., common stocks. The company or other entity issuing the _____ is called the issuer.
 a. Tracking stock
 b. Securities lending
 c. Book entry
 d. Security

Chapter 4. Corporate Governance around the World,

33. The _____ of 1934 is a law governing the secondary trading of securities (stocks, bonds, and debentures) in the United States of America. The Act, 48 Stat. 881 (enacted June 6, 1934), codified at 15 U.S.C. § 78a et seq., was a sweeping piece of legislation. The Act and related statutes form the basis of regulation of the financial markets and their participants in the United States.
   a. 7-Eleven
   b. 529 plan
   c. 4-4-5 Calendar
   d. Securities Exchange Act

34. In business, a _____ is the purchase of one company (the target) by another (the acquirer or bidder). In the UK the term refers to the acquisition of a public company whose shares are listed on a stock exchange, in contrast to the acquisition of a private company.

Before a bidder makes an offer for another company, it usually first informs that company's board of directors.

   a. Takeover
   b. 529 plan
   c. Stock swap
   d. 4-4-5 Calendar

35. The _____ is the market for securities, where companies and governments can raise longterm funds. The _____ includes the stock market and the bond market. Financial regulators, such as the U.S. Securities and Exchange Commission, oversee the _____s in their designated countries to ensure that investors are protected against fraud.
   a. Capital market
   b. Spot rate
   c. Forward market
   d. Delta neutral

36. In finance, the _____ between two currencies specifies how much one currency is worth in terms of the other. For example an _____ of 102 Japanese yen to the United States dollar means that JPY 102 is worth the same as USD 1. The foreign exchange market is one of the largest markets in the world.
   a. A Random Walk Down Wall Street
   b. Exchange rate
   c. ABN Amro
   d. AAB

37. _____ is the premiums paid in block transactions, which is indeed how much the new Large minority shareholder would pay more per share, than the stock price two days after the transaction.

Block Premuim per share is derived as

   a. Market order
   b. Wash sale
   c. Stock split
   d. Block premium

38. In finance, _____ is the process of estimating the potential market value of a financial asset or liability. they can be done on assets (for example, investments in marketable securities such as stocks, options, business enterprises, or intangible assets such as patents and trademarks) or on liabilities (e.g., Bonds issued by a company.) _____s are required in many contexts including investment analysis, capital budgeting, merger and acquisition transactions, financial reporting, taxable events to determine the proper tax liability, and in litigation.

a. Valuation
b. Share
c. Procter ' Gamble
d. Margin

39. A _____, securities exchange or (in Europe) bourse is a corporation or mutual organization which provides 'trading' facilities for stock brokers and traders, to trade stocks and other securities. _____s also provide facilities for the issue and redemption of securities as well as other financial instruments and capital events including the payment of income and dividends. The securities traded on a _____ include: shares issued by companies, unit trusts and other pooled investment products and bonds.

a. 4-4-5 Calendar
b. 7-Eleven
c. 529 plan
d. Stock Exchange

40. _____ (also branded as Deloitte) is one of the largest professional services firms in the world and one of the Big Four auditors, along with PricewaterhouseCoopers, Ernst ' Young, and KPMG.

According to the firm's website as of 2008, Deloitte has approximately 165,000 professionals at work in 140 countries, delivering audit, tax, consulting, and financial advisory services. _____ is a Swiss Verein, a membership organization under the Swiss Civil Code whereby each member firm is a separate and independent legal entity.

a. Gold exchange-traded fund
b. Deloitte Touche Tohmatsu
c. World Congress of Accountants
d. Chio Lim Stone Forest

Chapter 5. The Market for Foreign Exchange,

1. In finance, the _____ between two currencies specifies how much one currency is worth in terms of the other. For example an _____ of 102 Japanese yen to the United States dollar means that JPY 102 is worth the same as USD 1. The foreign exchange market is one of the largest markets in the world.

   a. ABN Amro
   b. AAB
   c. A Random Walk Down Wall Street
   d. Exchange rate

2. The _____ is where currency trading takes place. It is where banks and other official institutions facilitate the buying and selling of foreign currencies. FX transactions typically involve one party purchasing a quantity of one currency in exchange for paying a quantity of another.

   a. Floating exchange rate
   b. Foreign exchange option
   c. Spot market
   d. Foreign exchange market

3. A _____ secures the proper functioning of money by regulating economic agents, transaction types, and money supply.

   They are traditionally formed by the policy decisions of individual governments and administrated as a domestic economic issue.

   The current trend, however, is to use international trade and investment to alter the policy and legislation of individual governments.

   a. Payback period
   b. Bond credit rating
   c. Monetary system
   d. Pattern day trader

4. _____ refers to a business or organization attempting to acquire goods or services to accomplish the goals of the enterprise. Though there are several organizations that attempt to set standards in the _____ process, processes can vary greatly between organizations. Typically the word '_____' is not used interchangeably with the word 'procurement', since procurement typically includes Expediting, Supplier Quality, and Traffic and Logistics (T'L) in addition to _____.

   a. Purchasing
   b. 7-Eleven
   c. 529 plan
   d. 4-4-5 Calendar

5. _____ is the value of goods/services compared to the amount paid with a currency. Currency can be either a commodity money, like gold or silver, or fiat currency like US dollars which are the world reserve currency. As Adam Smith noted, having money gives one the ability to 'command' others' labor, so _____ to some extent is power over other people, to the extent that they are willing to trade their labor or goods for money or currency.

   a. 4-4-5 Calendar
   b. 529 plan
   c. 7-Eleven
   d. Purchasing power

6. The _____ is the top-level foreign exchange market where banks exchange different currencies. The banks can either deal with one another directly, or through electronic brokering platforms. The Electronic Brokering Services (EBS) and Reuters Dealing 3000 Matching are the two competitors in the electronic brokering platform business and together connect over 1000 banks.

   a. AAB
   b. ABN Amro
   c. A Random Walk Down Wall Street
   d. Interbank market

7. _____ refers to the various forms of financial support and financial transactions used in international trade. _____ uses a range of instruments to provide finance to exporters and importers, including documentary credits such as letters of credit.

While a seller (the exporter) can require the purchaser (an importer) to prepay for goods shipped, the purchaser (importer) may wish to reduce risk by requiring the seller to document that the goods have been shipped.

   a. Debtor-in-possession financing
   b. Trade finance
   c. Free cash flow
   d. Forfaiting

8. In economics, _____ refers to the ability of a party to produce a good or service using fewer real resources than another entity producing the same good or service. A party has an _____ when using the same input as another party, it can produce a greater output. Since _____ is determined by a simple comparison of labor productivities, it is possible for a a party to have no _____ in anything. It can be contrasted with the concept of comparative advantage which refers to the ability to produce a particular good at a lower opportunity cost.
   a. Absolute advantage
   b. A Random Walk Down Wall Street
   c. Economic depreciation
   d. AAB

9. _____s are deposits denominated in United States dollars at banks outside the United States, and thus are not under the jurisdiction of the Federal Reserve. Consequently, such deposits are subject to much less regulation than similar deposits within the United States, allowing for higher margins. There is nothing 'European' about _____ deposits; a US dollar-denominated deposit in Tokyo or Caracas would likewise be deemed _____ deposits.
   a. Eurodollar
   b. A Random Walk Down Wall Street
   c. AAB
   d. ABN Amro

10. _____ consists of the sale of goods or merchandise from a fixed location, such as a department store, boutique or kiosk in small or individual lots for direct consumption by the purchaser. _____ may include subordinated services, such as delivery. Purchasers may be individuals or businesses.
   a. 7-Eleven
   b. 4-4-5 Calendar
   c. Retailing
   d. 529 plan

11. A _____ is an exchange of promises between two or more parties to do an act which is enforceable in a court of law. It is where an unqualified offer meets a qualified acceptance and the parties reach Consensus ad Idem. The parties must have the necessary capacity to _____ and the _____ must not be either trifling, indeterminate, impossible or illegal.
   a. 7-Eleven
   b. 4-4-5 Calendar
   c. Contract
   d. 529 plan

12. _____ is a business valuation method. _____ is the net present value of a project if financed solely by ownership equity plus the present value of all the benefits of financing. Usually, the main benefit is a tax shield resulted from tax deductibility of interest payments. Another one can be a subsidized borrowing.
   a. A Random Walk Down Wall Street
   b. Adjusted present value
   c. AAB
   d. ABN Amro

13. In economics and finance, _____ is the practice of taking advantage of a price differential between two or more markets: striking a combination of matching deals that capitalize upon the imbalance, the profit being the difference between the market prices. When used by academics, an _____ is a transaction that involves no negative cash flow at any probabilistic or temporal state and a positive cash flow in at least one state; in simple terms, a risk-free profit.
   a. Initial margin
   b. Issuer
   c. Arbitrage
   d. Efficient-market hypothesis

14. A _____, reserve bank, or monetary authority is the entity responsible for the monetary policy of a country or of a group of member states. It is a bank that can lend money to other banks in times of need. Its primary responsibility is to maintain the stability of the national currency and money supply, but more active duties include controlling subsidized-loan interest rates, and acting as a lender of last resort to the banking sector during times of financial crisis (private banks often being integral to the national financial system.)
   a. Central bank
   b. 7-Eleven
   c. 4-4-5 Calendar
   d. 529 plan

15. A _____ is an international bond that is denominated in a currency not native to the country where it is issued. It can be categorised according to the currency in which it is issued. London is one of the centers of the _____ market, but _____s may be traded throughout the world - for example in Singapore or Tokyo.
   a. Interest rate option
   b. Eurobond
   c. Education production function
   d. Economic entity

16. In financial accounting, the term _____ is most commonly used to describe any part of shareholders' equity, except for basic share capital. Sometimes, the term is used instead of the term provision; such a use, however, is inconsistent with the terminology suggested by International Accounting Standards Board. For more information about provisions, see provision (accounting.)
   a. FIFO and LIFO accounting
   b. Closing entries
   c. Treasury stock
   d. Reserve

17. A _____, also FX future or foreign exchange future, is a futures contract to exchange one currency for another at a specified date in the future at a price (exchange rate) that is fixed on the purchase date. Typically, one of the currencies is the US dollar. The price of a future is then in terms of US dollars per unit of other currency.
   a. Non-deliverable forward
   b. Currency swap
   c. Foreign exchange controls
   d. Currency future

18. In finance, a _____ is a standardized contract, to buy or sell a specified commodity of standardized quality at a certain date in the future, at a market determined price (the futures price.)

The price is determined by the instantaneous equilibrium between the forces of supply and demand among competing buy and sell orders on the exchange at the time of the purchase or sale of the contract.

In many cases, the items may be such non-traditional 'commodities' as foreign currencies, commercial or government paper [e.g., bonds], or 'baskets' of corporate equity ['stock indices'] or other financial instruments.

   a. Financial future
   b. Futures contract
   c. Heston model
   d. Repurchase agreement

19. In banking and finance, _____ denotes all activities from the time a commitment is made for a transaction until it is settled. _____ is necessary because the speed of trades is much faster than the cycle time for completing the underlying transaction.

In its widest sense _____ involves the management of post-trading, pre-settlement credit exposures, to ensure that trades are settled in accordance with market rules, even if a buyer or seller should become insolvent prior to settlement.

a. Procter ' Gamble
b. Share
c. Clearing
d. Clearing house

20. A _____ is a financial services company that provides clearing and settlement services for financial transactions, usually on a futures exchange, and often acts as central counterparty (the payor actually pays the _____, which then pays the payee). A _____ may also offer novation, the substitution of a new contract or debt for an old, or other credit enhancement services to its members.

The term is also used for banks like Suffolk Bank that acted as a restraint on the over-issuance of private bank notes.

a. Warrant
b. Bucket shop
c. Valuation
d. Clearing House

21. The _____ is the main privately held clearing house for large-value transactions in the United States, settling well over US$1 trillion a day in around 250,000 interbank payments. Together with the Fedwire Funds Service (which is operated by the Federal Reserve Banks), _____ forms the primary U.S. network for large-value domestic and international USD payments (where it has a market share of around 96%).

a. 7-Eleven
b. 4-4-5 Calendar
c. 529 plan
d. Clearing House Interbank Payments System

22. In finance, the _____ is the global financial market for short-term borrowing and lending. It provides short-term liquidity funding for the global financial system. The _____ is where short-term obligations such as Treasury bills, commercial paper and bankers' acceptances are bought and sold.

a. Cramdown
b. Consumer debt
c. Debt-for-equity swap
d. Money market

23. The _____ or cash market is a commodities or securities market in which goods are sold for cash and delivered immediately. Contracts bought and sold on these markets are immediately effective. _____s can operate wherever the infrastructure exists to conduct the transaction.

a. Currency swap
b. Foreign exchange controls
c. Spot market
d. Non-deliverable forward

24. The institution most often referenced by the word '_____' is a public or publicly traded _____, the shares of which are traded on a public stock exchange (e.g., the New York Stock Exchange or Nasdaq in the United States) where shares of stock of _____s are bought and sold by and to the general public. Most of the largest businesses in the world are publicly traded _____s. However, the majority of _____s are said to be closely held, privately held or close _____s, meaning that no ready market exists for the trading of shares.

a. Depository Trust Company
c. Federal Home Loan Mortgage Corporation
b. Protect
d. Corporation

25. _____ is the value on a given date of a future payment or series of future payments, discounted to reflect the time value of money and other factors such as investment risk. _____ calculations are widely used in business and economics to provide a means to compare cash flows at different times on a meaningful 'like to like' basis.

The most commonly applied model of the time value of money is compound interest.

a. Negative gearing
c. Present value of benefits
b. Net present value
d. Present value

26. The _____ was a period of financial crisis that gripped much of Asia beginning in July 1997, and raised fears of a worldwide economic meltdown (financial contagion).

The crisis started in Thailand with the financial collapse of the Thai baht caused by the decision of the Thai government to float the baht, cutting its peg to the USD, after exhaustive efforts to support it in the face of a severe financial overextension that was in part real estate driven. At the time, Thailand had acquired a burden of foreign debt that made the country effectively bankrupt even before the collapse of its currency.

a. Asian Financial Crisis
c. OTC Bulletin Board
b. Internal control
d. International trade

27. _____ is a mathematical science pertaining to the collection, analysis, interpretation or explanation, and presentation of data. It also provides tools for prediction and forecasting based on data. It is applicable to a wide variety of academic disciplines, from the natural and social sciences to the humanities, government and business.

a. Sample size
c. Covariance
b. Mean
d. Statistics

28. The _____ or Plaza Agreement was an agreement between the governments of France, West Germany, Japan, the United States and the United Kingdom, agreeing to depreciate the US dollar in relation to the Japanese yen and German Deutsche Mark by intervening in currency markets. The five governments signed the accord on September 22, 1985 at the Plaza Hotel in New York City.

The exchange rate value of the dollar versus the yen declined by 51% from 1985 to 1987.

a. Plaza Accord
c. 4-4-5 Calendar
b. 7-Eleven
d. 529 plan

29. _____ offer, asking price is a price a seller of a good is willing to accept for that particular good.

In bid and ask, the term _____ is used in contrast to the term bid price. The difference between the _____ and the bid price is called the spread.

a. AAB
b. Ask price
c. A Random Walk Down Wall Street
d. Interest rate parity

30. A _____ or market-based mechanism is any of a wide variety of ways to match up buyers and sellers.

An example of a _____ uses announced bid and ask prices. Generally speaking, when two parties wish to engage in a trade, the purchaser will announce a price he is willing to pay (the bid price) and seller will announce a price he is willing to accept (the ask price).

a. Price mechanism
b. 7-Eleven
c. 4-4-5 Calendar
d. 529 plan

31. The _____ for securities is the difference between the price quoted by a market maker for an immediate sale and an immediate purchase The size of the bid-offer spread in a given commodity is a measure of the liquidity of the market.

The trader initiating the transaction is said to demand liquidity, and the other party to the transaction supplies liquidity.

a. Capital outflow
b. Defined contribution plan
c. Bid/offer spread
d. Trade-off

32. In economics, _____ refers to the ability of a person or a country to produce a particular good at a lower marginal cost and opportunity cost than another person or country. It is the ability to produce a product most efficiently given all the other products that could be produced. It can be contrasted with absolute advantage which refers to the ability of a person or a country to produce a particular good at a lower absolute cost than another.

a. Case-Shiller Home Price Indices
b. Comparative advantage
c. Reputational risk
d. Loans and interest, in Judaism

33. _____ is a branch of finance concerned with the details of how exchange occurs in markets. While the theory of _____ applies to the exchange of real or financial assets, more evidence is available on the microstructure of financial markets due to the availability of transactions data from financial markets. The major thrust of _____ research examines the ways in which the working processes of a market affects determinants of transaction costs, prices, quotes, volume, and trading behavior.

a. Break-even point
b. Fixed asset turnover
c. Trade-off
d. Market microstructure

34. _____ refers to taking advantage of a state of imbalance between three foreign exchange markets: a combination of matching deals are struck that exploit the imbalance, the profit being the difference between the market prices.

_____ offers a risk-free profit (in theory), so opportunities for _____ usually disappear quickly, as many people are looking for them, or simply never occur as everybody knows the pricing relation.

Consider the three foreign exchange rates among the Canadian dollar, the U.S. dollar, and the Australian dollar.

Chapter 5. The Market for Foreign Exchange, 47

  a. Currency future
  b. Floating exchange rate
  c. Currency pair
  d. Triangular arbitrage

35. The concept was first developed in game theory and consequently zero-sum situations are often called _____s though this does not imply that the concept applies only to what are commonly referred to as games.

For 2-player finite _____s, the different game theoretic Solution concepts of Nash equilibrium, minimax, and maximin all give the same solution. In the solution, players play a mixed strategy.

  a. 4-4-5 Calendar
  b. 529 plan
  c. 7-Eleven
  d. Zero-sum game

36. An _____ represents the ownership in the shares of a foreign company trading on US financial markets. The stock of many non-US companies trades on US exchanges through the use of _____s. _____s enable US investors to buy shares in foreign companies without undertaking cross-border transactions.
  a. American depository receipt
  b. ABN Amro
  c. A Random Walk Down Wall Street
  d. AAB

37. _____ is a term used in accounting, economics and finance to spread the cost of an asset over the span of several years.

In simple words we can say that _____ is the reduction in the value of an asset due to usage, passage of time, wear and tear, technological outdating or obsolescence, depletion or other such factors.

In accounting, _____ is a term used to describe any method of attributing the historical or purchase cost of an asset across its useful life, roughly corresponding to normal wear and tear.

  a. Depreciation
  b. Matching principle
  c. Bottom line
  d. Deferred financing costs

38. The _____ is the over-the-counter financial market in contracts for future delivery, so called forward contracts. Forward contracts are personalized between parties. The _____ is a general term used to describe the informal market by which these contracts are entered into.
  a. Limits to arbitrage
  b. Delta hedging
  c. Spot rate
  d. Forward market

39. The _____ or forward rate is the agreed upon price of an asset in a forward contract. Using the rational pricing assumption, we can express the _____ in terms of the spot price and any dividends etc., so that there is no possibility for arbitrage.

The _____ is given by:

where

F is the _____ to be paid at time T
e^x is the exponential function
r is the risk-free interest rate
q is the cost-of-carry
S_0 is the spot price of the asset (i.e. what it would sell for at time 0)
D_i is a dividend which is guaranteed to be paid at time t_i where $0 < t_i < T$.

The two questions here are what price the short position (the seller of the asset) should offer to maximize his gain, and what price the long position (the buyer of the asset) should accept to maximize his gain?

At the very least we know that both do not want to lose any money in the deal.

a. Biweekly Mortgage
b. Security interest
c. Financial Gerontology
d. Forward price

40. A _____ is a certificate issued by a depository bank, which purchases shares of foreign companies and deposits it on the account. _____s represent ownership of an underlying number of shares.

They facilitate trade of shares, and are commonly used to invest in companies from developing or emerging markets.

a. The Security Industry Association
b. Special journals
c. Short positions
d. Global depository receipt

41. The term _____, as used in currency trading, refers to the premium (or discount) resulting from a forward contract to be executed in the future at a forward rate. The premium is calculated as follows:

((forwardrate >− spotrate) / spotrate) * (12 / numberofmonthsforward) * 100

The resulting value is a percentage and termed a premium if it is positive. If the resulting percentage is negative, it is a forward discount.

a. 529 plan
b. Forward Premium
c. 4-4-5 Calendar
d. 7-Eleven

42. _____ is a term used in accounting relating to the increase in value of an asset. In this sense it is the reverse of depreciation, which measures the fall in value of assets over their normal life-time.

_____ is a rise of a currency in a floating exchange rate.

a. A Random Walk Down Wall Street
b. Operating cash flow
c. Other Comprehensive Basis of Accounting
d. Appreciation

43. In finance, a _____ in a security, such as a stock or a bond means the holder of the position owns the security and will profit if the price of the security goes up.

Similarly, a _____ in a futures contract or similar derivative, means the holder of the position will profit if the price of the underlying security goes up. Going long is the more conventional practice of investing and is contrasted with going short

- Short (finance)

a. Delta hedging
b. Forward market
c. Central Securities Depository
d. Long position

44. Days to Cover (DTC) is a numerical term that describes the relationship between the amount of shares in a given equity that have been short sold and the number of days of typical trading that it would require to 'cover' all _____ outstanding. For example, if there are ten million shares of XYZ Inc. that are currently short sold and the average daily volume of XYZ shares traded each day is one million, it would require ten days of trading for all _____ to be covered (10 million / 1 million.)

a. Guaranteed investment contracts
b. Stock or scrip dividends
c. Short positions
d. Cash budget

45. In finance, a _____ is a derivative in which two counterparties agree to exchange one stream of cash flows against another stream. These streams are called the legs of the _____.

The cash flows are calculated over a notional principal amount, which is usually not exchanged between counterparties.

a. Volatility arbitrage
b. Local volatility
c. Volatility swap
d. Swap

46. A _____ is an agreement between two parties to buy or sell an asset at a specified point of time in the future. The price of the underlying instrument, in whatever form, is paid before control of the instrument changes. This is one of the many forms of buy/sell orders where the time of trade is not the time where the securities themselves are exchanged.

a. Constant maturity credit default swap
b. Derivatives markets
c. Loan Credit Default Swap Index
d. Forward contract

47. A '_____' is a 'Charge' that is paid to obtain the right to delay a payment. Essentially, the payer purchases the right to make a given payment in the future instead of in the Present. The '_____', or 'Charge' that must be paid to delay the payment, is simply the difference between what the payment amount would be if it were paid in the present and what the payment amount would be paid if it were paid in the future.

a. Risk aversion
b. Risk modeling
c. Value at risk
d. Discount

Chapter 6. International Parity Relationships and Forecasting Foreign Exchange Rates,

1. _____ is a business valuation method. _____ is the net present value of a project if financed solely by ownership equity plus the present value of all the benefits of financing. Usually, the main benefit is a tax shield resulted from tax deductibility of interest payments. Another one can be a subsidized borrowing.
    a. A Random Walk Down Wall Street
    b. ABN Amro
    c. AAB
    d. Adjusted present value

2. In economics and finance, _____ is the practice of taking advantage of a price differential between two or more markets: striking a combination of matching deals that capitalize upon the imbalance, the profit being the difference between the market prices. When used by academics, an _____ is a transaction that involves no negative cash flow at any probabilistic or temporal state and a positive cash flow in at least one state; in simple terms, a risk-free profit.
    a. Initial margin
    b. Efficient-market hypothesis
    c. Issuer
    d. Arbitrage

3. _____ is a fee paid on borrowed assets. It is the price paid for the use of borrowed money, or, money earned by deposited funds. Assets that are sometimes lent with _____ include money, shares, consumer goods through hire purchase, major assets such as aircraft, and even entire factories in finance lease arrangements.
    a. A Random Walk Down Wall Street
    b. AAB
    c. Interest
    d. Insolvency

4. An _____ is the price a borrower pays for the use of money they do not own, and the return a lender receives for deferring the use of funds, by lending it to the borrower. _____s are normally expressed as a percentage rate over the period of one year.

    _____s targets are also a vital tool of monetary policy and are used to control variables like investment, inflation, and unemployment.

    a. AAB
    b. A Random Walk Down Wall Street
    c. Interest rate
    d. ABN Amro

5. _____ is an economic concept, expressed as a basic algebraic identity that relates interest rates and exchange rates. The identity is theoretical, and usually follows from assumptions imposed in economics models. There is evidence to support as well as to refute the concept.
    a. A Random Walk Down Wall Street
    b. AAB
    c. Unit price
    d. Interest rate parity

6. The _____ is a private, not-for-profit organization whose primary purpose is to develop generally accepted accounting principles (GAAP) within the United States in the public's interest. The Securities and Exchange Commission (SEC) designated the _____ as the organization responsible for setting accounting standards for public companies in the U.S. It was created in 1973, replacing the Accounting Principles Board and the Committee on Accounting Procedure of the American Institute of Certified Public Accountants. The _____'s mission is 'to establish and improve standards of financial accounting and reporting for the guidance and education of the public, including issuers, auditors, and users of financial information.'

    The _____ is not a governmental body.

Chapter 6. International Parity Relationships and Forecasting Foreign Exchange Rates, 51

a. MRU Holdings
b. Credit karma
c. FASB
d. PlaNet Finance

7. The _____ is an economic law stated as: 'In an efficient market all identical goods must have only one price.'

The intuition for this law is that all sellers will flock to the highest prevailing price, and all buyers to the lowest current market price. In an efficient market the convergence on one price is instant.

Commodities can be traded on financial markets, where there will be a single offer price, and bid price.

a. Liability
b. Letter of credit
c. Law of one price
d. Personal property

8. _____ is the value on a given date of a future payment or series of future payments, discounted to reflect the time value of money and other factors such as investment risk. _____ calculations are widely used in business and economics to provide a means to compare cash flows at different times on a meaningful 'like to like' basis.

The most commonly applied model of the time value of money is compound interest.

a. Negative gearing
b. Net present value
c. Present value of benefits
d. Present value

9. _____ is the investment strategy where an investor buys a financial instrument denominated in a foreign currency, and hedges his foreign exchange risk by selling a forward contract in the amount of the proceeds of the investment back into his base currency. The proceeds of the investment are only known exactly if the financial instrument is risk-free and only pays interest once, on the date of the forward sale of foreign currency. Otherwise, some foreign exchange risk remains.

a. Floating exchange rate
b. Covered interest arbitrage
c. Triangular arbitrage
d. Currency future

10. _____ is the term used to describe deposits residing in banks that are located outside the borders of the country that issues the currency the deposit is denominated in. For example a deposit denominated in US dollars residing in a Japanese bank is a _____ deposit, or more specifically a Eurodollar deposit.

Key points are the location of the bank and the denomination of the currency, not the nationality of the bank or the owner of the deposit/loan.

a. A Random Walk Down Wall Street
b. AAB
c. Eurocurrency
d. ABN Amro

11. In finance, the _____ between two currencies specifies how much one currency is worth in terms of the other. For example an _____ of 102 Japanese yen to the United States dollar means that JPY 102 is worth the same as USD 1. The foreign exchange market is one of the largest markets in the world.

a. AAB
b. A Random Walk Down Wall Street
c. Exchange rate
d. ABN Amro

52 *Chapter 6. International Parity Relationships and Forecasting Foreign Exchange Rates,*

12. The _____ is where currency trading takes place. It is where banks and other official institutions facilitate the buying and selling of foreign currencies. FX transactions typically involve one party purchasing a quantity of one currency in exchange for paying a quantity of another.

a. Floating exchange rate
b. Foreign exchange option
c. Foreign exchange market
d. Spot market

13. The _____ or forward rate is the agreed upon price of an asset in a forward contract. Using the rational pricing assumption, we can express the _____ in terms of the spot price and any dividends etc., so that there is no possibility for arbitrage.

The _____ is given by:

$$F >$$

where

F is the _____ to be paid at time T
e^x is the exponential function
r is the risk-free interest rate
q is the cost-of-carry
S_0 is the spot price of the asset (i.e. what it would sell for at time 0)
D_i is a dividend which is guaranteed to be paid at time t_i where $0 < t_i < T$.

The two questions here are what price the short position (the seller of the asset) should offer to maximize his gain, and what price the long position (the buyer of the asset) should accept to maximize his gain?

At the very least we know that both do not want to lose any money in the deal.

a. Financial Gerontology
b. Security interest
c. Biweekly Mortgage
d. Forward price

14. The _____ was a December 1971 agreement that ended the fixed exchange rates established at the Bretton Woods Conference of 1944.

The Bretton Woods Conference of 1944 established an international fixed exchange rate regime in which currencies were pegged to the United States dollar, which was based on the gold standard.

By 1970, however, it was clear that the exchange rate regime was under threat, as the United States dollar was greatly overvalued because of heavy American spending on Lyndon B. Johnson's Great Society and the Vietnam War.

a. Smithsonian Agreement
b. 7-Eleven
c. 4-4-5 Calendar
d. 529 plan

Chapter 6. International Parity Relationships and Forecasting Foreign Exchange Rates,

15. In economics, the _____, measures the payments that flow between any individual country and all other countries. It is used to summarize all international economic transactions for that country during a specific time period, usually a year. The _____ is determined by the country's exports and imports of goods, services, and financial capital, as well as financial transfers.
   a. 4-4-5 Calendar
   b. Balance of payments
   c. Purchasing power parity
   d. Gross national product

16. In finance, a _____ is a debt security, in which the authorized issuer owes the holders a debt and, depending on the terms of the _____, is obliged to pay interest (the coupon) and/or to repay the principal at a later date, termed maturity.

   Thus a _____ is a loan: the issuer is the borrower, the _____ holder is the lender, and the coupon is the interest. _____s provide the borrower with external funds to finance long-term investments, or, in the case of government _____s, to finance current expenditure.

   a. Convertible bond
   b. Catastrophe bonds
   c. Puttable bond
   d. Bond

17. In economics, _____ is the monetary policy device that a country's government (i.e., sovereign power) uses to regulate the flows into and out of a country's capital account, i.e., the flows of investment-oriented money into and out of a country or currency. _____ has become more prominent in the years since the Clinton administration blessed the efforts of the world community to create the World Trade Organization (WTO), primarily because globalization has increased the acceleration of currency domain strength, in other words, giving some currencies utility far beyond their physical geographic boundaries.
   a. Tail risk
   b. Capital control
   c. Monte Carlo methods
   d. Debtor-in-possession financing

18. A _____ is something for which there is demand, but which is supplied without qualitative differentiation across a market. It is a product that is the same no matter who produces it, such as petroleum, notebook paper, or milk. In other words, copper is copper.
   a. 7-Eleven
   b. 4-4-5 Calendar
   c. 529 plan
   d. Commodity

19. In economics, _____ is inflation that is very high or 'out of control', a condition in which prices increase rapidly as a currency loses its value. Definitions used by the media vary from a cumulative inflation rate over three years approaching 100% to 'inflation exceeding 50% a month.' In informal usage the term is often applied to much lower rates. As a rule of thumb, normal inflation is reported per year, but _____ is often reported for much shorter intervals, often per month.
   a. 7-Eleven
   b. 4-4-5 Calendar
   c. 529 plan
   d. Hyperinflation

20. _____ refers to a business or organization attempting to acquire goods or services to accomplish the goals of the enterprise. Though there are several organizations that attempt to set standards in the _____ process, processes can vary greatly between organizations. Typically the word '_____' is not used interchangeably with the word 'procurement', since procurement typically includes Expediting, Supplier Quality, and Traffic and Logistics (T'L) in addition to _____.

54 *Chapter 6. International Parity Relationships and Forecasting Foreign Exchange Rates,*

a. Purchasing
b. 7-Eleven
c. 4-4-5 Calendar
d. 529 plan

21. _____ is the value of goods/services compared to the amount paid with a currency. Currency can be either a commodity money, like gold or silver, or fiat currency like US dollars which are the world reserve currency. As Adam Smith noted, having money gives one the ability to 'command' others' labor, so _____ to some extent is power over other people, to the extent that they are willing to trade their labor or goods for money or currency.
a. Purchasing power
b. 529 plan
c. 7-Eleven
d. 4-4-5 Calendar

22. The _____ theory uses the long-term equilibrium exchange rate of two currencies to equalize their purchasing power. Developed by Gustav Cassel in 1920, it is based on the law of one price: the theory states that, in ideally efficient markets, identical goods should have only one price.

This purchasing power SEM rate equalizes the purchasing power of different currencies in their home countries for a given basket of goods.

a. TED spread
b. Gross national product
c. Purchasing power parity
d. 4-4-5 Calendar

23. In finance, a _____ is a forward contract in which one party pays a fixed interest rate, and receives a floating interest rate equal to a reference rate (the underlying rate.) The payments are calculated over a notional amount over a certain period, and netted, i.e. only the differential is paid. It is paid on the effective date.
a. Forward rate agreement
b. PAUG
c. Local volatility
d. Triple witching hour

24. The _____ is published by The Economist as an informal way of measuring the purchasing power parity (PPP) between two currencies and provides a test of the extent to which market exchange rates result in goods costing the same in different countries. It 'seeks to make exchange-rate theory a bit more digestible'.
a. 4-4-5 Calendar
b. 529 plan
c. Divisia index
d. Big Mac index

25. The _____ or Plaza Agreement was an agreement between the governments of France, West Germany, Japan, the United States and the United Kingdom, agreeing to depreciate the US dollar in relation to the Japanese yen and German Deutsche Mark by intervening in currency markets. The five governments signed the accord on September 22, 1985 at the Plaza Hotel in New York City.

The exchange rate value of the dollar versus the yen declined by 51% from 1985 to 1987.

a. 7-Eleven
b. 4-4-5 Calendar
c. 529 plan
d. Plaza Accord

26. In finance, the _____ is the global financial market for short-term borrowing and lending. It provides short-term liquidity funding for the global financial system. The _____ is where short-term obligations such as Treasury bills, commercial paper and bankers' acceptances are bought and sold.

Chapter 6. International Parity Relationships and Forecasting Foreign Exchange Rates,

a. Debt-for-equity swap
b. Consumer debt
c. Cramdown
d. Money market

27. Gross domestic product (GDP) is defined as the 'value of all final goods and services produced in a country in one year'. On the other hand, _____ is defined as the 'value of all (final) goods and services produced in a country in one year, plus income earned by its citizens abroad, minus income earned by foreigners in the country'. The key difference between the two is that GDP is the total output of a region, eg.

a. TED spread
b. 4-4-5 Calendar
c. Purchasing power parity
d. Gross national product

28. In business and accounting, _____s are everything of value that is owned by a person or company. The balance sheet of a firm records the monetary value of the _____s owned by the firm. The two major _____ classes are tangible _____s and intangible _____s.

a. Income
b. Asset
c. Accounts payable
d. EBITDA

29. In economics, the _____ is the proposition by Irving Fisher that the real interest rate is independent of monetary measures, especially the nominal interest rate. The Fisher equation is

$r_r = r_n - \pi^e$.

This means, the real interest rate (r_r) equals the nominal interest rate (r_n) minus expected rate of inflation (π^e.) Here all the rates are continuously compounded.

a. 529 plan
b. 7-Eleven
c. 4-4-5 Calendar
d. Fisher hypothesis

30. The _____ is a hypothesis in international finance that says that the difference in the nominal interest rates between two countries determines the movement of the nominal exchange rate between their currencies, with the value of the currency of the country with the lower nominal interest rate increasing. This is also known as the assumption of Uncovered Interest Parity.

The Fisher hypothesis says that the real interest rate in an economy is independent of monetary variables.

a. A Random Walk Down Wall Street
b. Official bank rate
c. Interest rate risk
d. International Fisher effect

31. _____ is the branch of economics that studies the dynamics of exchange rates, foreign investment, and how these affect international trade. It also studies international projects, international investments and capital flows, and trade deficits. It includes the study of futures, options and currency swaps.

a. ABN Amro
b. International finance
c. A Random Walk Down Wall Street
d. AAB

32. A _____, is a mathematical formalization of a trajectory that consists of taking successive random steps. The results of _____ analysis have been applied to computer science, physics, ecology, economics and a number of other fields as a fundamental model for random processes in time. For example, the path traced by a molecule as it travels in a liquid or a gas, the search path of a foraging animal, the price of a fluctuating stock and the financial status of a gambler can all be modeled as _____s.

    a. 529 plan
    b. 7-Eleven
    c. 4-4-5 Calendar
    d. Random walk

33. The _____ is a financial theory stating that stock market prices evolve according to a random walk and thus the prices of the stock market cannot be predicted. It has been described as 'jibing' with the efficient market hypothesis. Economists have historically accepted the _____. They have run several tests and continue to believe that stock prices are completely random because of the efficiency of the market.

    a. Cox-Ingersoll-Ross model
    b. Hull-White model
    c. Rendleman-Bartter model
    d. Random walk hypothesis

34. _____ is the removal or simplification of government rules and regulations that constrain the operation of market forces. _____ does not mean elimination of laws against fraud, but eliminating or reducing government control of how business is done, thereby moving toward a more free market.

The stated rationale for '_____' is often that fewer and simpler regulations will lead to a raised level of competitiveness, therefore higher productivity, more efficiency and lower prices overall.

    a. Supply shock
    b. Value added
    c. Demand shock
    d. Deregulation

35. The _____ is the over-the-counter financial market in contracts for future delivery, so called forward contracts. Forward contracts are personalized between parties. The _____ is a general term used to describe the informal market by which these contracts are entered into.

    a. Spot rate
    b. Delta hedging
    c. Limits to arbitrage
    d. Forward market

36. The _____ or spot rate of a commodity, a security or a currency is the price that is quoted for immediate (spot) settlement (payment and delivery.) Spot settlement is normally one or two business days from trade date. This is in contrast with the forward price established in a forward contract or futures contract, where contract terms (price) are set now, but delivery and payment will occur at a future date.

    a. Central Securities Depository
    b. Market price
    c. Spot price
    d. Cost of carry

37. The _____ or cash market is a commodities or securities market in which goods are sold for cash and delivered immediately. Contracts bought and sold on these markets are immediately effective. _____s can operate wherever the infrastructure exists to conduct the transaction.

    a. Foreign exchange controls
    b. Spot market
    c. Currency swap
    d. Non-deliverable forward

Chapter 6. International Parity Relationships and Forecasting Foreign Exchange Rates,

38. In statistics, a _____, is a type of finite impulse response filter used to analyze a set of data points by creating a series of averages of different subsets of the full data set. A _____ is not a single number, but it is a set of numbers, each of which is the average of the corresponding subset of a larger set of data points. A _____ may also use unequal weights for each data value in the subset to emphasize particular values in the subset.
   a. Gordon growth model
   b. Loans and interest, in Judaism
   c. Voluntary Emissions Reductions
   d. Moving average

39. _____ is a security analysis discipline for forecasting the future direction of prices through the study of past market data, primarily price and volume. In its purest form, _____ considers only the actual price and volume behavior of the market or instrument. Technical analysts may employ models and trading rules based on price and volume transformations, such as the relative strength index, moving averages, regressions, inter-market and intra-market price correlations, cycles or, classically, through recognition of chart patterns.
   a. Dow theory
   b. Support and resistance
   c. Point and figure
   d. Technical analysis

40. In economic models, the _____ time frame assumes no fixed factors of production. Firms can enter or leave the marketplace, and the cost (and availability) of land, labor, raw materials, and capital goods can be assumed to vary. In contrast, in the short-run time frame, certain factors are assumed to be fixed, because there is not sufficient time for them to change.
   a. 529 plan
   b. Long-run
   c. Short-run
   d. 4-4-5 Calendar

41. In economics, the concept of the _____ refers to the decision-making time frame of a firm in which at least one factor of production is fixed. Costs which are fixed in the _____ have no impact on a firms decisions. For example a firm can raise output by increasing the amount of labour through overtime.
   a. Long-run
   b. 4-4-5 Calendar
   c. 529 plan
   d. Short-run

42. _____ is concerned with the tasks of developing and applying quantitative or statistical methods to the study and elucidation of economic principles. _____ combines economic theory with statistics to analyze and test economic relationships. Theoretical _____ considers questions about the statistical properties of estimators and tests, while applied _____ is concerned with the application of econometric methods to assess economic theories.
   a. Econometrics
   b. ABN Amro
   c. A Random Walk Down Wall Street
   d. AAB

43. A _____ secures the proper functioning of money by regulating economic agents, transaction types, and money supply.

They are traditionally formed by the policy decisions of individual governments and administrated as a domestic economic issue.

The current trend, however, is to use international trade and investment to alter the policy and legislation of individual governments.

58 *Chapter 6. International Parity Relationships and Forecasting Foreign Exchange Rates,*

a. Payback period
c. Pattern day trader
b. Bond credit rating
d. Monetary system

44. In economics, _____ is the total amount of money available in an economy at a particular point in time. There are several ways to define 'money', but each includes currency in circulation and demand deposits.

_____ data are recorded and published.

a. Money supply
c. 4-4-5 Calendar
b. 7-Eleven
d. 529 plan

45. In economics, the _____ is a theory emphasizing the positive relationship of overall prices or the nominal value of expenditures to the quantity of money.

It is the mainstream economic theory of the price level. Alternative theories include the real bills doctrine and the more recent fiscal theory of the price level.

a. Supply shock
c. Deregulation
b. Value added
d. Quantity theory of money

Chapter 7. Futures and Options on Foreign Exchange,

1. In finance, the _____ between two currencies specifies how much one currency is worth in terms of the other. For example an _____ of 102 Japanese yen to the United States dollar means that JPY 102 is worth the same as USD 1. The foreign exchange market is one of the largest markets in the world.

   a. ABN Amro
   b. AAB
   c. A Random Walk Down Wall Street
   d. Exchange rate

2. _____ is the discipline of identifying, monitoring and limiting risks. In some cases the acceptable risk may be near zero. Risks can come from accidents, natural causes and disasters as well as deliberate attacks from an adversary.

   a. Risk management
   b. Penny stock
   c. 4-4-5 Calendar
   d. FIFO

3. In finance, a _____ is a standardized contract, to buy or sell a specified commodity of standardized quality at a certain date in the future, at a market determined price (the futures price.)

   The price is determined by the instantaneous equilibrium between the forces of supply and demand among competing buy and sell orders on the exchange at the time of the purchase or sale of the contract.

   In many cases, the items may be such non-traditional 'commodities' as foreign currencies, commercial or government paper [e.g., bonds], or 'baskets' of corporate equity ['stock indices'] or other financial instruments.

   a. Repurchase agreement
   b. Financial future
   c. Heston model
   d. Futures contract

4. An _____ is a contract written by a seller that conveys to the buyer the right -- but not the obligation -- to buy (in the case of a call _____) or to sell (in the case of a put _____) a particular asset, such as a piece of property such as, among others, a futures contract. In return for granting the _____, the seller collects a payment (the premium) from the buyer.

   For example, buying a call _____ provides the right to buy a specified quantity of a security at a set strike price at some time on or before expiration, while buying a put _____ provides the right to sell.

   a. Option
   b. Amortization
   c. Annuity
   d. AT'T Mobility LLC

5. A _____ is an exchange of promises between two or more parties to do an act which is enforceable in a court of law. It is where an unqualified offer meets a qualified acceptance and the parties reach Consensus ad Idem. The parties must have the necessary capacity to _____ and the _____ must not be either trifling, indeterminate, impossible or illegal.

   a. Contract
   b. 7-Eleven
   c. 4-4-5 Calendar
   d. 529 plan

6. A _____ is a financial contract whose value is derived from the value of something else (known as the underlying.) The underlying on which a _____ is based can be an asset, weather conditions bonds or other forms of credit.

   a. Derivative
   b. 7-Eleven
   c. 529 plan
   d. 4-4-5 Calendar

Chapter 7. Futures and Options on Foreign Exchange,

7. _____s are deposits denominated in United States dollars at banks outside the United States, and thus are not under the jurisdiction of the Federal Reserve. Consequently, such deposits are subject to much less regulation than similar deposits within the United States, allowing for higher margins. There is nothing 'European' about _____ deposits; a US dollar-denominated deposit in Tokyo or Caracas would likewise be deemed _____ deposits.

   a. A Random Walk Down Wall Street   b. AAB
   c. ABN Amro   d. Eurodollar

8. In finance, a _____ in a security, such as a stock or a bond means the holder of the position owns the security and will profit if the price of the security goes up.

Similarly, a _____ in a futures contract or similar derivative, means the holder of the position will profit if the price of the underlying security goes up. Going long is the more conventional practice of investing and is contrasted with going short

- Short (finance)

   a. Forward market   b. Central Securities Depository
   c. Long position   d. Delta hedging

9. In finance, a _____ is collateral that the holder of a position in securities, options, or futures contracts has to deposit to cover the credit risk of his counterparty (most often his broker.) This risk can arise if the holder has done any of the following:

- borrowed cash from the counterparty to buy securities or options,
- sold securities or options short, or
- entered into a futures contract.

The collateral can be in the form of cash or securities, and it is deposited in a _____ account. On U.S. futures exchanges, '_____' was formally called performance bond.

_____ buying is buying securities with cash borrowed from a broker, using other securities as collateral.

   a. Margin   b. Share
   c. Procter ' Gamble   d. Credit

10. _____ is a life of security. It may also refer to the final payment date of a loan or other financial instrument, at which point all remaining interest and principal is due to be paid.

1, 3, 6 months _____ band can be calculated by using 30-day per month periods.

   a. Replacement cost   b. False billing
   c. Primary market   d. Maturity

Chapter 7. Futures and Options on Foreign Exchange,

11. _____ is the value on a given date of a future payment or series of future payments, discounted to reflect the time value of money and other factors such as investment risk. _____ calculations are widely used in business and economics to provide a means to compare cash flows at different times on a meaningful 'like to like' basis.

The most commonly applied model of the time value of money is compound interest.

a. Present value of benefits
b. Negative gearing
c. Present value
d. Net present value

12. Days to Cover (DTC) is a numerical term that describes the relationship between the amount of shares in a given equity that have been short sold and the number of days of typical trading that it would require to 'cover' all _____ outstanding. For example, if there are ten million shares of XYZ Inc. that are currently short sold and the average daily volume of XYZ shares traded each day is one million, it would require ten days of trading for all _____ to be covered (10 million / 1 million.)

a. Stock or scrip dividends
b. Guaranteed investment contracts
c. Cash budget
d. Short positions

13. The concept was first developed in game theory and consequently zero-sum situations are often called _____s though this does not imply that the concept applies only to what are commonly referred to as games.

For 2-player finite _____s, the different game theoretic Solution concepts of Nash equilibrium, minimax, and maximin all give the same solution. In the solution, players play a mixed strategy.

a. Zero-sum game
b. 4-4-5 Calendar
c. 7-Eleven
d. 529 plan

14. In finance, a _____ is a debt security, in which the authorized issuer owes the holders a debt and, depending on the terms of the _____, is obliged to pay interest (the coupon) and/or to repay the principal at a later date, termed maturity.

Thus a _____ is a loan: the issuer is the borrower, the _____ holder is the lender, and the coupon is the interest. _____s provide the borrower with external funds to finance long-term investments, or, in the case of government _____s, to finance current expenditure.

a. Bond
b. Puttable bond
c. Catastrophe bonds
d. Convertible bond

15. The _____ is where currency trading takes place. It is where banks and other official institutions facilitate the buying and selling of foreign currencies. FX transactions typically involve one party purchasing a quantity of one currency in exchange for paying a quantity of another.

a. Foreign exchange market
b. Foreign exchange option
c. Spot market
d. Floating exchange rate

16. _____ is a fee paid on borrowed assets. It is the price paid for the use of borrowed money , or, money earned by deposited funds . Assets that are sometimes lent with _____ include money, shares, consumer goods through hire purchase, major assets such as aircraft, and even entire factories in finance lease arrangements.

a. AAB
b. Interest
c. Insolvency
d. A Random Walk Down Wall Street

17. An _____ is the price a borrower pays for the use of money they do not own, and the return a lender receives for deferring the use of funds, by lending it to the borrower. _____s are normally expressed as a percentage rate over the period of one year.

_____s targets are also a vital tool of monetary policy and are used to control variables like investment, inflation, and unemployment.

a. A Random Walk Down Wall Street
b. AAB
c. ABN Amro
d. Interest rate

18. An _____ is a futures contract with an interest-bearing instrument as the underlying asset.

Examples include Treasury-bill futures, Treasury-bond futures and Eurodollar futures.

The global market for exchange-traded _____s is notionally valued by the Bank for International Settlements at $5,794,200 million in 2005.

a. Interest rate future
b. Interest rate derivative
c. Open interest
d. Equity swap

19. A _____ is a fungible, negotiable instrument representing financial value. They are broadly categorized into debt securities (such as banknotes, bonds and debentures), and equity securities; e.g., common stocks. The company or other entity issuing the _____ is called the issuer.

a. Security
b. Tracking stock
c. Book entry
d. Securities lending

20. _____ refers to the various forms of financial support and financial transactions used in international trade. _____ uses a range of instruments to provide finance to exporters and importers, including documentary credits such as letters of credit.

While a seller (the exporter) can require the purchaser (an importer) to prepay for goods shipped, the purchaser (importer) may wish to reduce risk by requiring the seller to document that the goods have been shipped.

a. Free cash flow
b. Debtor-in-possession financing
c. Forfaiting
d. Trade finance

21. In economics and finance, _____ is the practice of taking advantage of a price differential between two or more markets: striking a combination of matching deals that capitalize upon the imbalance, the profit being the difference between the market prices. When used by academics, an _____ is a transaction that involves no negative cash flow at any probabilistic or temporal state and a positive cash flow in at least one state; in simple terms, a risk-free profit.

a. Issuer
b. Efficient-market hypothesis
c. Initial margin
d. Arbitrage

Chapter 7. Futures and Options on Foreign Exchange, 63

22. A _____, also FX future or foreign exchange future, is a futures contract to exchange one currency for another at a specified date in the future at a price (exchange rate) that is fixed on the purchase date. Typically, one of the currencies is the US dollar. The price of a future is then in terms of US dollars per unit of other currency.
   a. Foreign exchange controls
   b. Non-deliverable forward
   c. Currency swap
   d. Currency future

23. In finance, a _____ is a position established in one market in an attempt to offset exposure to the price risk of an equal but opposite obligation or position in another market -- usually, but not always, in the context of one's commercial activity. Hedging is a strategy designed to minimize exposure to such business risks as a sharp contraction in demand for one's inventory, while still allowing the business to profit from producing and maintaining that inventory. A typical hedger might be a farmer with 2000 acres of unharvested wheat in the ground, who would rather tend his crop without the distraction of uncertain prices.
   a. Hedge
   b. 4-4-5 Calendar
   c. 7-Eleven
   d. 529 plan

24. The _____ is an American financial and commodity derivative exchange based in Chicago. The _____ was founded in 1898 as the Chicago Butter and Egg Board. Originally, the exchange was a non-profit organization.
   a. Financial Crimes Enforcement Network
   b. Public Company Accounting Oversight Board
   c. Chicago Mercantile Exchange
   d. Gamelan Council

25. In banking and finance, _____ denotes all activities from the time a commitment is made for a transaction until it is settled. _____ is necessary because the speed of trades is much faster than the cycle time for completing the underlying transaction.

In its widest sense _____ involves the management of post-trading, pre-settlement credit exposures, to ensure that trades are settled in accordance with market rules, even if a buyer or seller should become insolvent prior to settlement.

   a. Clearing
   b. Procter ' Gamble
   c. Share
   d. Clearing house

26. A _____ is a financial services company that provides clearing and settlement services for financial transactions, usually on a futures exchange, and often acts as central counterparty (the payor actually pays the _____, which then pays the payee). A _____ may also offer novation, the substitution of a new contract or debt for an old, or other credit enhancement services to its members.

The term is also used for banks like Suffolk Bank that acted as a restraint on the over-issuance of private bank notes.

   a. Warrant
   b. Valuation
   c. Bucket shop
   d. Clearing house

27. A _____ is an international bond that is denominated in a currency not native to the country where it is issued. It can be categorised according to the currency in which it is issued. London is one of the centers of the _____ market, but _____s may be traded throughout the world - for example in Singapore or Tokyo.

Chapter 7. Futures and Options on Foreign Exchange,

a. Eurobond
b. Interest rate option
c. Education production function
d. Economic entity

28. _____ is defined by The Wall Street Journal, as a form of barter that involves a company selling 'an unused asset to another company while at the same time agreeing to buy back the same or similar assets at about the same price.' Round trips are characteristic of the New Economy companies. They played a crucial part in temporarily inflating the market capitalization of energy traders such as Enron, CMS Energy, Reliant Energy, and Dynegy.

Other companies making unconventional _____ deals include AOL with Sun Microsystems and Global Crossing with Qwest Communications.

a. Residual value
b. Net pay
c. Round-tripping
d. Days Sales Outstanding

29. The _____ , largely the creation of Leo Melamed, is part of the Chicago Mercantile Exchange (CME), the largest futures exchange in the United States and the second largest in the world after Eurex, for the trading of futures contracts and options on futures. The _____ was started on May 16, 1972. Two of the more prevalent contracts traded are currency futures and interest rate futures.

a. AAB
b. ABN Amro
c. A Random Walk Down Wall Street
d. International Monetary Market

30. A _____, securities exchange or (in Europe) bourse is a corporation or mutual organization which provides 'trading' facilities for stock brokers and traders, to trade stocks and other securities. _____s also provide facilities for the issue and redemption of securities as well as other financial instruments and capital events including the payment of income and dividends. The securities traded on a _____ include: shares issued by companies, unit trusts and other pooled investment products and bonds.

a. 7-Eleven
b. 529 plan
c. 4-4-5 Calendar
d. Stock Exchange

31. A _____ is something for which there is demand, but which is supplied without qualitative differentiation across a market. It is a product that is the same no matter who produces it, such as petroleum, notebook paper, or milk. In other words, copper is copper.

a. 529 plan
b. 4-4-5 Calendar
c. 7-Eleven
d. Commodity

32. A _____ is a central financial exchange where people can trade standardized futures contracts; that is, a contract to buy specific quantities of a commodity or financial instrument at a specified price with delivery set at a specified time in the future.

Though the origins of futures trading can supposedly be traced to Ancient Greek or Phoenician times, the first modern organized _____ began in 1710 at the Dojima Rice Exchange in Osaka, Japan.

The United States followed in the early 1800s.

Chapter 7. Futures and Options on Foreign Exchange, 65

a. 4-4-5 Calendar
c. 7-Eleven
b. Futures Exchange
d. 529 plan

33. _____ denotes the total number of derivative contracts, like futures and options, that are currently active on a specific underlying security, having specific terms.

Namely, the total contracts for a specific strike price and expiration date, that have been traded, but have not yet expired, have not yet been closed through a closing transaction, or have not yet been terminated via early exercise. A closing transaction occurs when a counterparty that longs the contract sells, or, conversely, when a counterparty that shorts the contract buys.

a. Open Interest
c. Equity derivative
b. International Swaps and Derivatives Association
d. Equity swap

34. The _____ process is the process of determining the price of an asset in the marketplace through the interactions of buyers and sellers.

_____ is different from valuation. _____ process involves buyers and sellers arriving at a transaction price for a specific item at a given time.

a. Pecking order theory
c. Return on capital employed
b. Seed round
d. Price discovery

35. The _____ was a period of financial crisis that gripped much of Asia beginning in July 1997, and raised fears of a worldwide economic meltdown (financial contagion).

The crisis started in Thailand with the financial collapse of the Thai baht caused by the decision of the Thai government to float the baht, cutting its peg to the USD, after exhaustive efforts to support it in the face of a severe financial overextension that was in part real estate driven. At the time, Thailand had acquired a burden of foreign debt that made the country effectively bankrupt even before the collapse of its currency.

a. OTC Bulletin Board
c. International trade
b. Asian Financial Crisis
d. Internal control

36. _____ is the term used to describe deposits residing in banks that are located outside the borders of the country that issues the currency the deposit is denominated in. For example a deposit denominated in US dollars residing in a Japanese bank is a _____ deposit, or more specifically a Eurodollar deposit.

Key points are the location of the bank and the denomination of the currency, not the nationality of the bank or the owner of the deposit/loan.

a. A Random Walk Down Wall Street
c. AAB
b. Eurocurrency
d. ABN Amro

37. A _____ is a financial contract between two parties, the buyer and the seller of this type of option. Often it is simply labeled a 'call'. The buyer of the option has the right, but not the obligation to buy an agreed quantity of a particular commodity or financial instrument (the underlying instrument) from the seller of the option at a certain time (the expiration date) for a certain price (the strike price.)
   a. Bear call spread
   b. Bull spread
   c. Bear spread
   d. Call option

38. In options, the _____ is a key variable in a derivatives contract between two parties. Where the contract requires delivery of the underlying instrument, the trade will be at the _____, regardless of the spot price (market price) of the underlying instrument at that time.

Definition - The fixed price at which the owner of an option can purchase, in the case of a call in the case of a put, the underlying security or commodity.

   a. Naked put
   b. Moneyness
   c. Swaption
   d. Strike price

39. A _____ is a financial contract between two parties, the seller (writer) and the buyer of the option. The put allows its buyer the right but not the obligation to sell a commodity or financial instrument (the underlying instrument) to the writer (seller) of the option at a certain time for a certain price (the strike price.) The writer (seller) has the obligation to purchase the underlying asset at that strike price, if the buyer exercises the option.
   a. Debit spread
   b. Put option
   c. Bear spread
   d. Bear call spread

40. _____ N.V. is a pan-European stock exchange based in Paris and with subsidiaries in Belgium, France, Netherlands, Luxembourg, Portugal and the United Kingdom. In addition to equities and derivatives markets, the _____ group provides clearing and information services. As of 31 January 2006, markets run by _____ had a market capitalization of US$2.9 trillion, making it the 5th largest exchange on the planet.
   a. AAB
   b. Euronext
   c. ABN Amro
   d. A Random Walk Down Wall Street

41. An _____ option has no intrinsic value. A call option is _____ when the strike price is above the spot price of the underlying security. A put option is _____ when the strike price is below the spot price.
   a. A Random Walk Down Wall Street
   b. ABN Amro
   c. AAB
   d. Out-of-the-money

42. In finance, _____ refers to the value of a security which is intrinsic to or contained in the security itself. It is also frequently called fundamental value. It is ordinarily calculated by summing the future income generated by the asset, and discounting it to the present value.
   a. Alpha
   b. Intrinsic value
   c. Amortization
   d. Accretion

43. In finance, the value of an option consists of two components, its intrinsic value and its _____. Time value is simply the difference between option value and intrinsic value. _____ is also known as theta, extrinsic value, or instrumental value.

a. Global Squeeze
c. Conservatism
b. Debt buyer
d. Time value

44. _____ most frequently refers to the standard deviation of the continuously compounded returns of a financial instrument with a specific time horizon. It is often used to quantify the risk of the instrument over that time period. _____ is typically expressed in annualized terms, and it may either be an absolute number ($5) or a fraction of the mean (5%).
a. Portfolio insurance
c. Currency swap
b. Seasoned equity offering
d. Volatility

Chapter 8. Management of Transaction Exposure,

1. _____ is the balance of the amounts of cash being received and paid by a business during a defined period of time, sometimes tied to a specific project. Measurement of _____ can be used

- to evaluate the state or performance of a business or project.
- to determine problems with liquidity. Being profitable does not necessarily mean being liquid. A company can fail because of a shortage of cash, even while profitable.
- to generate project rate of returns. The time of _____s into and out of projects are used as inputs to financial models such as internal rate of return, and net present value.
- to examine income or growth of a business when it is believed that accrual accounting concepts do not represent economic realities. Alternately, _____ can be used to 'validate' the net income generated by accrual accounting.

_____ as a generic term may be used differently depending on context, and certain _____ definitions may be adapted by analysts and users for their own uses. Common terms include operating _____ and free _____.

_____s can be classified into:

1. Operational _____s: Cash received or expended as a result of the company's core business activities.
2. Investment _____s: Cash received or expended through capital expenditure, investments or acquisitions.
3. Financing _____s: Cash received or expended as a result of financial activities, such as interests and dividends.

All three together - the net _____ - are necessary to reconcile the beginning cash balance to the ending cash balance. Loan draw downs or equity injections, that is just shifting of capital but no expenditure as such, are not considered in the net _____.

    a. Corporate finance   b. Cash flow
    c. Shareholder value   d. Real option

2. A _____, reserve bank, or monetary authority is the entity responsible for the monetary policy of a country or of a group of member states. It is a bank that can lend money to other banks in times of need. Its primary responsibility is to maintain the stability of the national currency and money supply, but more active duties include controlling subsidized-loan interest rates, and acting as a lender of last resort to the banking sector during times of financial crisis (private banks often being integral to the national financial system.)

    a. Central Bank   b. 7-Eleven
    c. 4-4-5 Calendar   d. 529 plan

3. In banking and finance, _____ denotes all activities from the time a commitment is made for a transaction until it is settled. _____ is necessary because the speed of trades is much faster than the cycle time for completing the underlying transaction.

In its widest sense _____ involves the management of post-trading, pre-settlement credit exposures, to ensure that trades are settled in accordance with market rules, even if a buyer or seller should become insolvent prior to settlement.

a. Clearing
b. Share
c. Clearing house
d. Procter ' Gamble

4. A _____ is a financial services company that provides clearing and settlement services for financial transactions, usually on a futures exchange, and often acts as central counterparty (the payor actually pays the _____, which then pays the payee). A _____ may also offer novation, the substitution of a new contract or debt for an old, or other credit enhancement services to its members.

The term is also used for banks like Suffolk Bank that acted as a restraint on the over-issuance of private bank notes.

a. Bucket shop
b. Clearing House
c. Warrant
d. Valuation

5. _____ is the provision of resources (such as granting a loan) by one party to another party where that second party does not reimburse the first party immediately, thereby generating a debt, and instead arranges either to repay or return those resources (or material(s) of equal value) at a later date. The first party is called a creditor, also known as a lender, while the second party is called a debtor, also known as a borrower.

Movements of financial capital are normally dependent on either _____ or equity transfers.

a. Clearing house
b. Comparable
c. Credit
d. Warrant

6. _____ is a business valuation method. _____ is the net present value of a project if financed solely by ownership equity plus the present value of all the benefits of financing. Usually, the main benefit is a tax shield resulted from tax deductibility of interest payments. Another one can be a subsidized borrowing.
a. ABN Amro
b. Adjusted present value
c. A Random Walk Down Wall Street
d. AAB

7. _____ is the value on a given date of a future payment or series of future payments, discounted to reflect the time value of money and other factors such as investment risk. _____ calculations are widely used in business and economics to provide a means to compare cash flows at different times on a meaningful 'like to like' basis.

The most commonly applied model of the time value of money is compound interest.

a. Present value of benefits
b. Negative gearing
c. Net present value
d. Present value

8. _____ or amalgamation is the act of merging many things into one. In business, it often refers to the mergers or acquisitions of many smaller companies into much larger ones. The financial accounting term of _____ refers to the aggregated financial statements of a group company as consolidated account.
a. Retained earnings
b. Write-off
c. Cost of goods sold
d. Consolidation

9. _____ are formal records of a business' financial activities.

Chapter 8. Management of Transaction Exposure,

_____ provide an overview of a business' financial condition in both short and long term. There are four basic _____:

1. **Balance sheet**: also referred to as statement of financial position or condition, reports on a company's assets, liabilities, and net equity as of a given point in time.
2. **Income statement**: also referred to as Profit and Loss statement (or a 'P'L'), reports on a company's income, expenses, and profits over a period of time.
3. **Statement of retained earnings**: explains the changes in a company's retained earnings over the reporting period.
4. **Statement of cash flows**: reports on a company's cash flow activities, particularly its operating, investing and financing activities.

a. Statement on Auditing Standards No. 70: Service Organizations
b. Financial statements
c. Notes to the Financial Statements
d. Statement of retained earnings

10. The _____ is the over-the-counter financial market in contracts for future delivery, so called forward contracts. Forward contracts are personalized between parties. The _____ is a general term used to describe the informal market by which these contracts are entered into.
    a. Limits to arbitrage
    b. Delta hedging
    c. Spot rate
    d. Forward market

11. In finance, a _____ is a position established in one market in an attempt to offset exposure to the price risk of an equal but opposite obligation or position in another market -- usually, but not always, in the context of one's commercial activity. Hedging is a strategy designed to minimize exposure to such business risks as a sharp contraction in demand for one's inventory, while still allowing the business to profit from producing and maintaining that inventory. A typical hedger might be a farmer with 2000 acres of unharvested wheat in the ground, who would rather tend his crop without the distraction of uncertain prices.
    a. 4-4-5 Calendar
    b. 529 plan
    c. 7-Eleven
    d. Hedge

12. A _____, also FX future or foreign exchange future, is a futures contract to exchange one currency for another at a specified date in the future at a price (exchange rate) that is fixed on the purchase date. Typically, one of the currencies is the US dollar. The price of a future is then in terms of US dollars per unit of other currency.
    a. Currency swap
    b. Non-deliverable forward
    c. Currency future
    d. Foreign exchange controls

13. In finance, the _____ is the global financial market for short-term borrowing and lending. It provides short-term liquidity funding for the global financial system. The _____ is where short-term obligations such as Treasury bills, commercial paper and bankers' acceptances are bought and sold.
    a. Consumer debt
    b. Cramdown
    c. Debt-for-equity swap
    d. Money market

14. In finance, a _____ is a standardized contract, to buy or sell a specified commodity of standardized quality at a certain date in the future, at a market determined price (the futures price.)

Chapter 8. Management of Transaction Exposure, 71

The price is determined by the instantaneous equilibrium between the forces of supply and demand among competing buy and sell orders on the exchange at the time of the purchase or sale of the contract.

In many cases, the items may be such non-traditional 'commodities' as foreign currencies, commercial or government paper [e.g., bonds], or 'baskets' of corporate equity ['stock indices'] or other financial instruments.

a. Financial future
b. Futures contract
c. Heston model
d. Repurchase agreement

15. In economics, the _____ is the proposition by Irving Fisher that the real interest rate is independent of monetary measures, especially the nominal interest rate. The Fisher equation is

$r_r = r_n >- >\pi^e$.

This means, the real interest rate (r_r) equals the nominal interest rate (r_n) minus expected rate of inflation ($>\pi^e$.) Here all the rates are continuously compounded.

a. 4-4-5 Calendar
b. 7-Eleven
c. 529 plan
d. Fisher hypothesis

16. An _____ is a contract written by a seller that conveys to the buyer the right -- but not the obligation -- to buy (in the case of a call _____) or to sell (in the case of a put _____) a particular asset, such as a piece of property such as, among others, a futures contract. In return for granting the _____, the seller collects a payment (the premium) from the buyer.

For example, buying a call _____ provides the right to buy a specified quantity of a security at a set strike price at some time on or before expiration, while buying a put _____ provides the right to sell.

a. Amortization
b. AT'T Mobility LLC
c. Option
d. Annuity

17. A _____ is an exchange of promises between two or more parties to do an act which is enforceable in a court of law. It is where an unqualified offer meets a qualified acceptance and the parties reach Consensus ad Idem. The parties must have the necessary capacity to _____ and the _____ must not be either trifling, indeterminate, impossible or illegal.

a. 529 plan
b. 7-Eleven
c. 4-4-5 Calendar
d. Contract

18. _____s are deposits denominated in United States dollars at banks outside the United States, and thus are not under the jurisdiction of the Federal Reserve. Consequently, such deposits are subject to much less regulation than similar deposits within the United States, allowing for higher margins. There is nothing 'European' about _____ deposits; a US dollar-denominated deposit in Tokyo or Caracas would likewise be deemed _____ deposits.

a. Eurodollar
b. AAB
c. ABN Amro
d. A Random Walk Down Wall Street

19. A _____ is an agreement between two parties to buy or sell an asset at a specified point of time in the future. The price of the underlying instrument, in whatever form, is paid before control of the instrument changes. This is one of the many forms of buy/sell orders where the time of trade is not the time where the securities themselves are exchanged.
   a. Derivatives markets
   b. Forward contract
   c. Loan Credit Default Swap Index
   d. Constant maturity credit default swap

20. A _____ is something for which there is demand, but which is supplied without qualitative differentiation across a market. It is a product that is the same no matter who produces it, such as petroleum, notebook paper, or milk. In other words, copper is copper.
   a. 7-Eleven
   b. 529 plan
   c. Commodity
   d. 4-4-5 Calendar

21. In finance, a _____ is a derivative in which two counterparties agree to exchange one stream of cash flows against another stream. These streams are called the legs of the _____.

The cash flows are calculated over a notional principal amount, which is usually not exchanged between counterparties.

   a. Local volatility
   b. Volatility swap
   c. Volatility arbitrage
   d. Swap

22. In finance, the _____ between two currencies specifies how much one currency is worth in terms of the other. For example an _____ of 102 Japanese yen to the United States dollar means that JPY 102 is worth the same as USD 1. The foreign exchange market is one of the largest markets in the world.
   a. AAB
   b. A Random Walk Down Wall Street
   c. ABN Amro
   d. Exchange rate

23. The _____ is where currency trading takes place. It is where banks and other official institutions facilitate the buying and selling of foreign currencies. FX transactions typically involve one party purchasing a quantity of one currency in exchange for paying a quantity of another.
   a. Foreign exchange market
   b. Spot market
   c. Floating exchange rate
   d. Foreign exchange option

24. An _____ or bill is a commercial document issued by a seller to the buyer, indicating the products, quantities, and agreed prices for products or services the seller has provided the buyer. An _____ indicates the buyer must pay the seller, according to the payment terms.

In the rental industry, an _____ must include a specific reference to the duration of the time being billed, so rather than quantity, price and discount the invoicing amount is based on quantity, price, discount and duration.

   a. A Random Walk Down Wall Street
   b. AAB
   c. Invoice
   d. ABN Amro

Chapter 8. Management of Transaction Exposure, 73

25. The _____ was a basket of the currencies of the European Community member states, used as the unit of account of the European Community before being replaced by the euro on January 1, 1999, at parity. The _____ itself replaced the European Unit of Account, also at parity, on March 13, 1979. The European Exchange Rate Mechanism attempted to minimize fluctuations between member state currencies and the _____.

a. Outsourcing
b. Electronic communication network
c. OTC Bulletin Board
d. European Currency Unit

26. A standard, commercial _____ is a document issued mostly by a financial institution, used primarily in trade finance, which usually provides an irrevocable payment undertaking.

The _____ can also be the source of payment for a transaction, meaning that redeeming the _____ will pay an exporter. Letters of credit are used primarily in international trade transactions of significant value, for deals between a supplier in one country and a customer in another.

a. Bond indenture
b. McFadden Act
c. Letter of credit
d. Duty of loyalty

27. A _____ occurs when a financial sponsor acquires a controlling interest in a company's equity and where a significant percentage of the purchase price is financed through leverage (borrowing.) The assets of the acquired company are used as collateral for the borrowed capital, sometimes with assets of the acquiring company. The bonds or other paper issued for _____s are commonly considered not to be investment grade because of the significant risks involved.

a. Pension fund
b. Leverage
c. Limited partnership
d. Leveraged buyout

28. In general, _____ means to allow a positive value and a negative value to set-off and partially or entirely cancel each other out.

In the context of credit risk, there are at least three specific types of _____:

- Close-out _____

- _____ by novation

- Settlement or payment _____

_____ decreases credit exposure, increases business with existing counterparties, and reduces both operational and settlement risk and operational costs.

a. Forward price
b. Reinvestment risk
c. Moneylender
d. Netting

29. The _____ is a private, not-for-profit organization whose primary purpose is to develop generally accepted accounting principles (GAAP) within the United States in the public's interest. The Securities and Exchange Commission (SEC) designated the _____ as the organization responsible for setting accounting standards for public companies in the U.S. It was created in 1973, replacing the Accounting Principles Board and the Committee on Accounting Procedure of the American Institute of Certified Public Accountants. The _____'s mission is 'to establish and improve standards of financial accounting and reporting for the guidance and education of the public, including issuers, auditors, and users of financial information.'

The _____ is not a governmental body.

a. MRU Holdings
b. Credit karma
c. PlaNet Finance
d. FASB

30. In economics and contract theory, _____ deals with the study of decisions in transactions where one party has more or better information than the other. This creates an imbalance of power in transactions which can sometimes cause the transactions to go awry. Examples of this problem are adverse selection and moral hazard.

a. AAB
b. A Random Walk Down Wall Street
c. ABN Amro
d. Information asymmetry

31. In economics and related disciplines, a _____ is a cost incurred in making an economic exchange. For example, most people, when buying or selling a stock, must pay a commission to their broker; that commission is a _____ of doing the stock deal. Or consider buying a banana from a store; to purchase the banana, your costs will be not only the price of the banana itself, but also the energy and effort it requires to find out which of the various banana products you prefer, where to get them and at what price, the cost of traveling from your house to the store and back, the time waiting in line, and the effort of the paying itself; the costs above and beyond the cost of the banana are the _____s.

a. Marginal cost
b. Variable costs
c. Fixed costs
d. Transaction cost

32. In economics, business, and accounting, a _____ is the value of money that has been used up to produce something, and hence is not available for use anymore. In business, the _____ may be one of acquisition, in which case the amount of money expended to acquire it is counted as _____. In this case, money is the input that is gone in order to acquire the thing.

a. Cost
b. Sliding scale fees
c. Marginal cost
d. Fixed costs

33. _____ refers to a tax levied by various jurisdictions on the profits made by companies or associations. It is a tax on the value of the corporation's profits.

The measure of taxable profits varies from country to country.

a. Corporate tax
b. First-mover advantage
c. Proxy fight
d. Trade finance

Chapter 8. Management of Transaction Exposure,

34. In finance, _____ occurs when a debtor has not met its legal obligations according to the debt contract, e.g. it has not made a scheduled payment, or has violated a loan covenant (condition) of the debt contract. _____ may occur if the debtor is either unwilling or unable to pay their debt. This can occur with all debt obligations including bonds, mortgages, loans, and promissory notes.
   a. Vendor finance
   b. Debt validation
   c. Credit crunch
   d. Default

35. A _____ is a financial contract whose value is derived from the value of something else (known as the underlying.) The underlying on which a _____ is based can be an asset, weather conditions bonds or other forms of credit.
   a. 529 plan
   b. 7-Eleven
   c. Derivative
   d. 4-4-5 Calendar

36. Procter is a surname, and may also refer to:

   - Bryan Waller Procter (pseud. Barry Cornwall), English poet
   - Goodwin Procter, American law firm
   - _____, consumer products multinational

   a. Valuation
   b. Procter ' Gamble
   c. Clearing house
   d. Bucket shop

37. _____ is a Fortune 500, American multinational corporation headquartered in Cincinnati, Ohio, that manufactures a wide range of consumer goods. As of 2008, P'G is the 8th largest corporation in the world by market capitalization and 14th largest US company by profit.
   a. 4-4-5 Calendar
   b. 529 plan
   c. 7-Eleven
   d. Procter ' Gamble Co.

38. _____ is one of the authors of the Black-Scholes equation. In 1997 he was awarded the Nobel Memorial Prize in Economic Sciences for 'a new method to determine the value of derivatives'. The model provides the fundamental conceptual framework for valuing options, such as calls or puts, and is referred to as the Black-Scholes model, which has become the standard in financial markets globally.
   a. Adolph Coors
   b. Robert James Shiller
   c. Andrew Tobias
   d. Myron Samuel Scholes

39. A _____ is a foreign exchange agreement between two parties to exchange principal and fixed rate interest payments on a loan in one currency for principal and fixed rate interest payments on an equal (regarding net present value) loan in another currency. They are motivated by comparative advantage.
   a. Forex swap
   b. Foreign exchange market
   c. Currency swap
   d. Currency pair

40. The _____ are a type of exotic options with path dependency, among many other kind of options. The payoff depends on the optimal (maximum or minimum) underlying asset's price occurring over the life of the option. The option allows the holder to 'look back' over time to determine the payoff.

a. Database auditing
b. Help desk and incident reporting auditing
c. Weighted mean
d. Lookback options

41. _____ is the discipline of identifying, monitoring and limiting risks. In some cases the acceptable risk may be near zero. Risks can come from accidents, natural causes and disasters as well as deliberate attacks from an adversary.
   a. FIFO
   b. Penny stock
   c. 4-4-5 Calendar
   d. Risk management

42. In financial accounting, a _____ or statement of financial position is a summary of a person's or organization's balances. Assets, liabilities and ownership equity are listed as of a specific date, such as the end of its financial year. A _____ is often described as a snapshot of a company's financial condition.
   a. Statement on Auditing Standards No. 70: Service Organizations
   b. Balance sheet
   c. Statement of retained earnings
   d. Financial statements

43. The _____ is an American financial and commodity derivative exchange based in Chicago. The _____ was founded in 1898 as the Chicago Butter and Egg Board. Originally, the exchange was a non-profit organization.
   a. Public Company Accounting Oversight Board
   b. Gamelan Council
   c. Financial Crimes Enforcement Network
   d. Chicago Mercantile Exchange

44. A _____ is a futures contract on a short term interest rate (STIR.) Contracts vary, but are often defined on an interest rate index such as 3-month sterling or US dollar LIBOR.

They are traded across a wide range of currencies, including the G12 country currencies and many others.

   a. Real estate derivatives
   b. Dual currency deposit
   c. Financial Future
   d. Notional amount

45. A _____ is a central financial exchange where people can trade standardized futures contracts; that is, a contract to buy specific quantities of a commodity or financial instrument at a specified price with delivery set at a specified time in the future.

Though the origins of futures trading can supposedly be traced to Ancient Greek or Phoenician times, the first modern organized _____ began in 1710 at the Dojima Rice Exchange in Osaka, Japan.

The United States followed in the early 1800s.

   a. 529 plan
   b. 4-4-5 Calendar
   c. 7-Eleven
   d. Futures Exchange

46. The _____ started life on September 30, 1982, to take advantage of the removal of currency controls in the UK in 1979. The exchange modelled itself after the Chicago Board of Trade and the Chicago Mercantile Exchange. It initially offered futures contracts and options linked to short term interest rates.
   a. 7-Eleven
   b. 4-4-5 Calendar
   c. 529 plan
   d. London International Financial Futures Exchange

Chapter 8. Management of Transaction Exposure, 77

47. A _____, securities exchange or (in Europe) bourse is a corporation or mutual organization which provides 'trading' facilities for stock brokers and traders, to trade stocks and other securities. _____s also provide facilities for the issue and redemption of securities as well as other financial instruments and capital events including the payment of income and dividends. The securities traded on a _____ include: shares issued by companies, unit trusts and other pooled investment products and bonds.

a. Stock Exchange
b. 4-4-5 Calendar
c. 529 plan
d. 7-Eleven

48. The role of the _____ is to issue accounting standards in the United Kingdom. It is recognised for that purpose under the Companies Act 1985. It took over the task of setting accounting standards from the Accounting Standards Committee (ASC) in 1990.

a. A Random Walk Down Wall Street
b. ABN Amro
c. Accounting Standards Board
d. AAB

49. The term _____ refers to three closely related concepts:

- The _____ model is a mathematical model of the market for an equity, in which the equity's price is a stochastic process.
- The _____ PDE is a partial differential equation which (in the model) must be satisfied by the price of a derivative on the equity.
- The _____ formula is the result obtained by solving the _____ PDE for a European call option.

Fischer Black and Myron Scholes first articulated the _____ formula in their 1973 paper, 'The Pricing of Options and Corporate Liabilities.' The foundation for their research relied on work developed by scholars such as Jack L. Treynor, Paul Samuelson, A. James Boness, Sheen T. Kassouf, and Edward O. Thorp. The fundamental insight of _____ is that the option is implicitly priced if the stock is traded.

Robert C. Merton was the first to publish a paper expanding the mathematical understanding of the options pricing model and coined the term '_____' options pricing model.

a. Modified Internal Rate of Return
b. Stochastic volatility
c. Perpetuity
d. Black-Scholes

50. _____ is the field of accountancy concerned with the preparation of financial statements for decision makers, such as stockholders, suppliers, banks, employees, government agencies, owners, and other stakeholders. The fundamental need for _____ is to reduce principal-agent problem by measuring and monitoring agents' performance and reporting the results to interested users.

_____ is used to prepare accounting information for people outside the organization or not involved in the day to day running of the company.

a. 7-Eleven
b. 529 plan
c. 4-4-5 Calendar
d. Financial Accounting

Chapter 8. Management of Transaction Exposure,

51. The _____ is a private, not-for-profit organization whose primary purpose is to develop generally accepted accounting principles (GAAP) within the United States in the public's interest. The Securities and Exchange Commission (SEC) designated the _____ as the organization responsible for setting accounting standards for public companies in the U.S. It was created in 1973, replacing the Accounting Principles Board and the Committee on Accounting Procedure of the American Institute of Certified Public Accountants. The _____'s mission is 'to establish and improve standards of financial accounting and reporting for the guidance and education of the public, including issuers, auditors, and users of financial information.'

The _____ is not a governmental body.

a. KPMG
c. Federal Deposit Insurance Corporation
b. World Congress of Accountants
d. Financial Accounting Standards Board

52. A _____ or directed economy is an economic system in which the government or workers' councils manages the economy. It is an economic system in which the central government makes all decisions on the production and consumption of goods and services. Its most extensive form is referred to as a command economy, centrally _____, or command and control economy.

a. 4-4-5 Calendar
c. 7-Eleven
b. 529 plan
d. Planned economy

Chapter 9. Management of Economic Exposure,

1. _____ is a business valuation method. _____ is the net present value of a project if financed solely by ownership equity plus the present value of all the benefits of financing. Usually, the main benefit is a tax shield resulted from tax deductibility of interest payments. Another one can be a subsidized borrowing.

   a. ABN Amro
   b. A Random Walk Down Wall Street
   c. AAB
   d. Adjusted present value

2. A _____, reserve bank, or monetary authority is the entity responsible for the monetary policy of a country or of a group of member states. It is a bank that can lend money to other banks in times of need. Its primary responsibility is to maintain the stability of the national currency and money supply, but more active duties include controlling subsidized-loan interest rates, and acting as a lender of last resort to the banking sector during times of financial crisis (private banks often being integral to the national financial system.)

   a. 7-Eleven
   b. 529 plan
   c. 4-4-5 Calendar
   d. Central Bank

3. In banking and finance, _____ denotes all activities from the time a commitment is made for a transaction until it is settled. _____ is necessary because the speed of trades is much faster than the cycle time for completing the underlying transaction.

   In its widest sense _____ involves the management of post-trading, pre-settlement credit exposures, to ensure that trades are settled in accordance with market rules, even if a buyer or seller should become insolvent prior to settlement.

   a. Procter ' Gamble
   b. Clearing house
   c. Share
   d. Clearing

4. A _____ is a financial services company that provides clearing and settlement services for financial transactions, usually on a futures exchange, and often acts as central counterparty (the payor actually pays the _____, which then pays the payee). A _____ may also offer novation, the substitution of a new contract or debt for an old, or other credit enhancement services to its members.

   The term is also used for banks like Suffolk Bank that acted as a restraint on the over-issuance of private bank notes.

   a. Warrant
   b. Bucket shop
   c. Valuation
   d. Clearing House

5. _____ is the provision of resources (such as granting a loan) by one party to another party where that second party does not reimburse the first party immediately, thereby generating a debt, and instead arranges either to repay or return those resources (or material(s) of equal value) at a later date. The first party is called a creditor, also known as a lender, while the second party is called a debtor, also known as a borrower.

   Movements of financial capital are normally dependent on either _____ or equity transfers.

   a. Credit
   b. Comparable
   c. Warrant
   d. Clearing house

6. In finance, the _____ between two currencies specifies how much one currency is worth in terms of the other. For example an _____ of 102 Japanese yen to the United States dollar means that JPY 102 is worth the same as USD 1. The foreign exchange market is one of the largest markets in the world.
   a. ABN Amro
   b. AAB
   c. A Random Walk Down Wall Street
   d. Exchange rate

7. The _____ is where currency trading takes place. It is where banks and other official institutions facilitate the buying and selling of foreign currencies. FX transactions typically involve one party purchasing a quantity of one currency in exchange for paying a quantity of another.
   a. Foreign exchange option
   b. Spot market
   c. Floating exchange rate
   d. Foreign exchange market

8. _____ is a term used in accounting relating to the increase in value of an asset. In this sense it is the reverse of depreciation, which measures the fall in value of assets over their normal life-time.

   _____ is a rise of a currency in a floating exchange rate.

   a. A Random Walk Down Wall Street
   b. Operating cash flow
   c. Other Comprehensive Basis of Accounting
   d. Appreciation

9. While the full name of the Swiss verein is Deloitte Touche Tohmatsu, in 1989 it initially branded itself _____ and then simply Deloitte. In 2003 the rebranding campaign was commissioned by Bill Parrett, the then CEO of DTT, and led by Jerry Leamon, the global Clients and Markets leader.

Deloitte member firms offer services in the following functions, with country-specific variations on their legal implementation (i.e. all operating within a single company or through separate legal entities operating as subsidiaries of an umbrella legal entity for the country.)

   a. Rate of return
   b. Deloitte ' Touche
   c. Monte Carlo methods
   d. Fixed income

10. In economics, the _____, measures the payments that flow between any individual country and all other countries. It is used to summarize all international economic transactions for that country during a specific time period, usually a year. The _____ is determined by the country's exports and imports of goods, services, and financial capital, as well as financial transfers.
   a. 4-4-5 Calendar
   b. Gross national product
   c. Purchasing power parity
   d. Balance of payments

Chapter 9. Management of Economic Exposure, 81

11. _____ is a form of risk that arises from the change in price of one currency against another. Whenever investors or companies have assets or business operations across national borders, they face _____ if their positions are not hedged.

- Transaction risk is the risk that exchange rates will change unfavourably over time. It can be hedged against using forward currency contracts;
- Translation risk is an accounting risk, proportional to the amount of assets held in foreign currencies. Changes in the exchange rate over time will render a report inaccurate, and so assets are usually balanced by borrowings in that currency.

The exchange risk associated with a foreign denominated instrument is a key element in foreign investment. This risk flows from differential monetary policy and growth in real productivity, which results in differential inflation rates.

a. Currency risk
b. Credit risk
c. Tracking error
d. Market risk

12. In financial accounting, a _____ or statement of financial position is a summary of a person's or organization's balances. Assets, liabilities and ownership equity are listed as of a specific date, such as the end of its financial year. A _____ is often described as a snapshot of a company's financial condition.

a. Statement on Auditing Standards No. 70: Service Organizations
b. Financial statements
c. Statement of retained earnings
d. Balance sheet

13. In finance, a _____ is a position established in one market in an attempt to offset exposure to the price risk of an equal but opposite obligation or position in another market -- usually, but not always, in the context of one's commercial activity. Hedging is a strategy designed to minimize exposure to such business risks as a sharp contraction in demand for one's inventory, while still allowing the business to profit from producing and maintaining that inventory. A typical hedger might be a farmer with 2000 acres of unharvested wheat in the ground, who would rather tend his crop without the distraction of uncertain prices.

a. 4-4-5 Calendar
b. 529 plan
c. 7-Eleven
d. Hedge

14. _____ is the balance of the amounts of cash being received and paid by a business during a defined period of time, sometimes tied to a specific project. Measurement of _____ can be used

- to evaluate the state or performance of a business or project.
- to determine problems with liquidity. Being profitable does not necessarily mean being liquid. A company can fail because of a shortage of cash, even while profitable.
- to generate project rate of returns. The time of _____s into and out of projects are used as inputs to financial models such as internal rate of return, and net present value.
- to examine income or growth of a business when it is believed that accrual accounting concepts do not represent economic realities. Alternately, _____ can be used to 'validate' the net income generated by accrual accounting.

Chapter 9. Management of Economic Exposure,

_____ as a generic term may be used differently depending on context, and certain _____ definitions may be adapted by analysts and users for their own uses. Common terms include operating _____ and free _____.

_____s can be classified into:

1. Operational _____s: Cash received or expended as a result of the company's core business activities.
2. Investment _____s: Cash received or expended through capital expenditure, investments or acquisitions.
3. Financing _____s: Cash received or expended as a result of financial activities, such as interests and dividends.

All three together - the net _____ - are necessary to reconcile the beginning cash balance to the ending cash balance. Loan draw downs or equity injections, that is just shifting of capital but no expenditure as such, are not considered in the net _____.

a. Shareholder value
c. Real option
b. Corporate finance
d. Cash flow

15. _____ is the value on a given date of a future payment or series of future payments, discounted to reflect the time value of money and other factors such as investment risk. _____ calculations are widely used in business and economics to provide a means to compare cash flows at different times on a meaningful 'like to like' basis.

The most commonly applied model of the time value of money is compound interest.

a. Present value of benefits
c. Net present value
b. Negative gearing
d. Present value

16. A _____ is an exchange of promises between two or more parties to do an act which is enforceable in a court of law. It is where an unqualified offer meets a qualified acceptance and the parties reach Consensus ad Idem. The parties must have the necessary capacity to _____ and the _____ must not be either trifling, indeterminate, impossible or illegal.
a. 529 plan
c. 7-Eleven
b. Contract
d. 4-4-5 Calendar

17. _____s are deposits denominated in United States dollars at banks outside the United States, and thus are not under the jurisdiction of the Federal Reserve. Consequently, such deposits are subject to much less regulation than similar deposits within the United States, allowing for higher margins. There is nothing 'European' about _____ deposits; a US dollar-denominated deposit in Tokyo or Caracas would likewise be deemed _____ deposits.
a. Eurodollar
c. A Random Walk Down Wall Street
b. ABN Amro
d. AAB

18. A _____ is an agreement between two parties to buy or sell an asset at a specified point of time in the future. The price of the underlying instrument, in whatever form, is paid before control of the instrument changes. This is one of the many forms of buy/sell orders where the time of trade is not the time where the securities themselves are exchanged.
   a. Derivatives markets
   b. Forward contract
   c. Loan Credit Default Swap Index
   d. Constant maturity credit default swap

19. The _____ or cash market is a commodities or securities market in which goods are sold for cash and delivered immediately. Contracts bought and sold on these markets are immediately effective. _____s can operate wherever the infrastructure exists to conduct the transaction.
   a. Currency swap
   b. Non-deliverable forward
   c. Foreign exchange controls
   d. Spot market

20. In finance, a _____ is a standardized contract, to buy or sell a specified commodity of standardized quality at a certain date in the future, at a market determined price (the futures price.)

The price is determined by the instantaneous equilibrium between the forces of supply and demand among competing buy and sell orders on the exchange at the time of the purchase or sale of the contract.

In many cases, the items may be such non-traditional 'commodities' as foreign currencies, commercial or government paper [e.g., bonds], or 'baskets' of corporate equity ['stock indices'] or other financial instruments.

   a. Repurchase agreement
   b. Financial future
   c. Heston model
   d. Futures contract

21. In business and accounting, _____s are everything of value that is owned by a person or company. The balance sheet of a firm records the monetary value of the _____s owned by the firm. The two major _____ classes are tangible _____s and intangible _____s.
   a. Income
   b. EBITDA
   c. Accounts payable
   d. Asset

22. An _____ represents the ownership in the shares of a foreign company trading on US financial markets. The stock of many non-US companies trades on US exchanges through the use of _____s. _____s enable US investors to buy shares in foreign companies without undertaking cross-border transactions.
   a. American depository receipt
   b. ABN Amro
   c. A Random Walk Down Wall Street
   d. AAB

23. _____ is a term used in accounting, economics and finance to spread the cost of an asset over the span of several years.

In simple words we can say that _____ is the reduction in the value of an asset due to usage, passage of time, wear and tear, technological outdating or obsolescence, depletion or other such factors.

In accounting, _____ is a term used to describe any method of attributing the historical or purchase cost of an asset across its useful life, roughly corresponding to normal wear and tear.

Chapter 9. Management of Economic Exposure,

a. Matching principle
b. Deferred financing costs
c. Bottom line
d. Depreciation

24. A _____ is a certificate issued by a depository bank, which purchases shares of foreign companies and deposits it on the account. _____s represent ownership of an underlying number of shares.

They facilitate trade of shares, and are commonly used to invest in companies from developing or emerging markets.

a. Short positions
b. The Security Industry Association
c. Special journals
d. Global depository receipt

25. The phrase _____ refers to the aspect of corporate strategy, corporate finance and management dealing with the buying, selling and combining of different companies that can aid, finance, or help a growing company in a given industry grow rapidly without having to create another business entity.

An acquisition, also known as a takeover, is the buying of one company (the 'target') by another. An acquisition may be friendly or hostile.

a. 4-4-5 Calendar
b. 529 plan
c. 7-Eleven
d. Mergers and acquisitions

26. In economics, business, and accounting, a _____ is the value of money that has been used up to produce something, and hence is not available for use anymore. In business, the _____ may be one of acquisition, in which case the amount of money expended to acquire it is counted as _____. In this case, money is the input that is gone in order to acquire the thing.

a. Marginal cost
b. Sliding scale fees
c. Cost
d. Fixed costs

27. In business, _____ is income that a company receives from its normal business activities, usually from the sale of goods and services to customers. Some companies also receive _____ from interest, dividends or royalties paid to them by other companies. _____ may refer to business income in general, or it may refer to the amount, in a monetary unit, received during a period of time, as in 'Last year, Company X had _____ of $32 million.'

In many countries, including the UK, _____ is referred to as turnover.

a. Furniture, Fixtures and Equipment
b. Bottom line
c. Revenue
d. Matching principle

28. _____ in finance is a risk management technique, related to hedging, that mixes a wide variety of investments within a portfolio. Because the fluctuations of a single security have less impact on a diverse portfolio, _____ minimizes the risk from any one investment.

A simple example of _____ is the following: On a particular island the entire economy consists of two companies: one that sells umbrellas and another that sells sunscreen.

a. Diversification
c. 7-Eleven
b. 4-4-5 Calendar
d. 529 plan

29. In marketing, _____ is the process of distinguishing the differences of a product or offering from others, to make it more attractive to a particular target market. This involves differentiating it from competitors' products as well as one's own product offerings.

_____ is a source of competitive advantage. Although research in a niche market may result in changing your product in order to improve differentiation, the changes themselves are not differentiation.

a. Product differentiation
c. 7-Eleven
b. 4-4-5 Calendar
d. 529 plan

30. The phrase _____ according to the Organization for Economic Co-operation and Development, refers to 'creative work undertaken on a systematic basis in order to increase the stock of knowledge, including knowledge of (hu)man, culture and society, and the use of this stock of knowledge to devise new applications'.

New product design and development is more than often a crucial factor in the survival of a company. In an industry that is fast changing, firms must continually revise their design and range of products. This is necessary due to continuous technology change and development as well as other competitors and the changing preference of customers.

a. Research and development
c. 7-Eleven
b. 4-4-5 Calendar
d. 529 plan

31. In finance, a _____ is a debt security, in which the authorized issuer owes the holders a debt and, depending on the terms of the _____, is obliged to pay interest (the coupon) and/or to repay the principal at a later date, termed maturity.

Thus a _____ is a loan: the issuer is the borrower, the _____ holder is the lender, and the coupon is the interest. _____s provide the borrower with external funds to finance long-term investments, or, in the case of government _____s, to finance current expenditure.

a. Bond
c. Convertible bond
b. Puttable bond
d. Catastrophe bonds

32. _____ is a political organization established in 2002 and dedicated to the protection of children from abuse, exploitation and neglect. It is a nonprofit, 501(c)(4) membership association with members in every U.S. state and 10 nations. _____ achieved great success in its first three years, winning legislative victories in eight state legislatures.

a. Ford Foundation
c. First Prudential Markets
b. The Depository Trust ' Clearing Corporation
d. Protect

33. _____ is an organization's process of defining its strategy and making decisions on allocating its resources to pursue this strategy, including its capital and people. Various business analysis techniques can be used in _____, including SWOT analysis (Strengths, Weaknesses, Opportunities, and Threats) and PEST analysis (Political, Economic, Social, and Technological analysis) or STEER analysis involving Socio-cultural, Technological, Economic, Ecological, and Regulatory factors and EPISTEL (Environment, Political, Informatic, Social, Technological, Economic and Legal)

_____ is the formal consideration of an organization's future course. All _____ deals with at least one of three key questions:

1. 'What do we do?'
2. 'For whom do we do it?'
3. 'How do we excel?'

In business _____, the third question is better phrased 'How can we beat or avoid competition?'. (Bradford and Duncan, page 1.)

   a. Strategic planning   b. 529 plan
   c. 7-Eleven   d. 4-4-5 Calendar

34. A _____, also FX future or foreign exchange future, is a futures contract to exchange one currency for another at a specified date in the future at a price (exchange rate) that is fixed on the purchase date. Typically, one of the currencies is the US dollar. The price of a future is then in terms of US dollars per unit of other currency.
   a. Foreign exchange controls   b. Non-deliverable forward
   c. Currency swap   d. Currency future

35. An _____ is a contract written by a seller that conveys to the buyer the right -- but not the obligation -- to buy (in the case of a call _____) or to sell (in the case of a put _____) a particular asset, such as a piece of property such as, among others, a futures contract. In return for granting the _____, the seller collects a payment (the premium) from the buyer.

For example, buying a call _____ provides the right to buy a specified quantity of a security at a set strike price at some time on or before expiration, while buying a put _____ provides the right to sell.

   a. Amortization   b. Option
   c. AT'T Mobility LLC   d. Annuity

Chapter 9. Management of Economic Exposure,

36. An _____ is a document a company presents at an annual general meeting for approval by its shareholders, or a charitable organization presents its trustees. The report is made up of reports, which may include the following:

- Chairman's report
- CEO's report
- Auditor's report on corporate governance
- Mission statement
- Corporate governance statement of compliance
- Statement of directors' responsibilities
- Invitation to the company's AGM

as well as financial statements including:

- Auditor's report on the financial statements
- Balance sheet
- Statement of retained earnings
- Income statement
- Cash flow statement
- Notes to the financial statements
- Accounting policies

Other information deemed relevant to stakeholders may be included, such as a report on operations for manufacturing firms. In the case of larger companies, it is usually a sleek, colorful, high gloss publication.

The details provided in the report are of use to investors to understand the company's financial position and future direction.

a. Outstanding balance
c. Accrued liabilities
b. Amortization schedule
d. Annual Report

37. A _____ is a bond issued by a corporation. The term is usually applied to longer-term debt instruments, generally with a maturity date falling at least a year after their issue date. (The term 'commercial paper' is sometimes used for instruments with a shorter maturity.)
a. Government bond
c. Brady bonds
b. Serial bond
d. Corporate bond

38. _____ is the discipline of identifying, monitoring and limiting risks. In some cases the acceptable risk may be near zero. Risks can come from accidents, natural causes and disasters as well as deliberate attacks from an adversary.
a. FIFO
c. Penny stock
b. 4-4-5 Calendar
d. Risk management

39. The _____ Options Exchange is a futures exchange based in London. _____ is now part of NYSE Euronext following its takeover by Euronext in January 2002 and Euronext's merger with New York Stock Exchange in April 2007.

The _____ started life on September 30, 1982, to take advantage of the removal of currency controls in the UK in 1979.

a. 4-4-5 Calendar
c. 7-Eleven
b. LIFFE
d. 529 plan

Chapter 10. Management of Translation Exposure,

1. In financial accounting, a _____ or statement of financial position is a summary of a person's or organization's balances. Assets, liabilities and ownership equity are listed as of a specific date, such as the end of its financial year. A _____ is often described as a snapshot of a company's financial condition.

   a. Statement on Auditing Standards No. 70: Service Organizations
   b. Statement of retained earnings
   c. Balance sheet
   d. Financial statements

2. In finance, the _____ between two currencies specifies how much one currency is worth in terms of the other. For example an _____ of 102 Japanese yen to the United States dollar means that JPY 102 is worth the same as USD 1. The foreign exchange market is one of the largest markets in the world.

   a. AAB
   b. A Random Walk Down Wall Street
   c. ABN Amro
   d. Exchange rate

3. The _____ is a private, not-for-profit organization whose primary purpose is to develop generally accepted accounting principles (GAAP) within the United States in the public's interest. The Securities and Exchange Commission (SEC) designated the _____ as the organization responsible for setting accounting standards for public companies in the U.S. It was created in 1973, replacing the Accounting Principles Board and the Committee on Accounting Procedure of the American Institute of Certified Public Accountants. The _____'s mission is 'to establish and improve standards of financial accounting and reporting for the guidance and education of the public, including issuers, auditors, and users of financial information.'

   The _____ is not a governmental body.

   a. MRU Holdings
   b. Credit karma
   c. PlaNet Finance
   d. FASB

4. The _____ is where currency trading takes place. It is where banks and other official institutions facilitate the buying and selling of foreign currencies. FX transactions typically involve one party purchasing a quantity of one currency in exchange for paying a quantity of another.

   a. Foreign exchange market
   b. Foreign exchange option
   c. Spot market
   d. Floating exchange rate

5. _____, refers to consumption opportunity gained by an entity within a specified time frame, which is generally expressed in monetary terms. However, for households and individuals, '_____ is the sum of all the wages, salaries, profits, interests payments, rents and other forms of earnings received... in a given period of time.' For firms, _____ generally refers to net-profit: what remains of revenue after expenses have been subtracted.

   a. Accrual
   b. OIBDA
   c. Income
   d. Annual report

6. An _____ is a financial statement for companies that indicates how Revenue is transformed into net income The purpose of the _____ is to show managers and investors whether the company made or lost money during the period being reported.

   The important thing to remember about an _____ is that it represents a period of time.

a. ABN Amro
b. Income statement
c. A Random Walk Down Wall Street
d. AAB

7. _____, in bookkeeping, refers to assets, liabilities, income, and expenses recorded on individual pages of the so called book of final entry or ledger. Changes in _____ value are made by chronologically posting debit (DR) and credit (CR) entries to its page. Examples of _____s are cash, _____s receivable, mortgages, loans, land and buildings, common stock, sales, services provided, wages, and payroll overhead.
   a. Alpha
   b. Account
   c. Accretion
   d. Option

8. _____ means regulating, adapting or settling in a variety of contexts:

In commercial law, _____ means the settlement of a loss incurred on insured goods. The calculation of the amounts of compensation to be paid by or to the several interests is a complicated matter. It involves much detail and arithmetic, and requires a full and accurate knowledge of the principles of the subject.

   a. Intelligent investor
   b. Asset recovery
   c. Equity method
   d. Adjustment

9. An _____ represents the ownership in the shares of a foreign company trading on US financial markets. The stock of many non-US companies trades on US exchanges through the use of _____s. _____s enable US investors to buy shares in foreign companies without undertaking cross-border transactions.
   a. ABN Amro
   b. A Random Walk Down Wall Street
   c. American depository receipt
   d. AAB

10. _____ is a term used in accounting relating to the increase in value of an asset. In this sense it is the reverse of depreciation, which measures the fall in value of assets over their normal life-time.

_____ is a rise of a currency in a floating exchange rate.

   a. Operating cash flow
   b. Appreciation
   c. A Random Walk Down Wall Street
   d. Other Comprehensive Basis of Accounting

11. _____ is a term used in accounting, economics and finance to spread the cost of an asset over the span of several years.

In simple words we can say that _____ is the reduction in the value of an asset due to usage, passage of time, wear and tear, technological outdating or obsolescence, depletion or other such factors.

In accounting, _____ is a term used to describe any method of attributing the historical or purchase cost of an asset across its useful life, roughly corresponding to normal wear and tear.

   a. Bottom line
   b. Matching principle
   c. Deferred financing costs
   d. Depreciation

12. A _____ is a certificate issued by a depository bank, which purchases shares of foreign companies and deposits it on the account. _____s represent ownership of an underlying number of shares.

They facilitate trade of shares, and are commonly used to invest in companies from developing or emerging markets.

a. The Security Industry Association
b. Special journals
c. Short positions
d. Global depository receipt

13. The role of the _____ is to issue accounting standards in the United Kingdom. It is recognised for that purpose under the Companies Act 1985. It took over the task of setting accounting standards from the Accounting Standards Committee (ASC) in 1990.

a. ABN Amro
b. A Random Walk Down Wall Street
c. AAB
d. Accounting Standards Board

14. _____ is the monetary unit of account of the principal economic environment in which an economic entity operates.

Statement of Financial Standards No. 52 (SFAS 52) is the primary source of GAAP for translation of foreign currency financial statements.

a. Currency board
b. Devaluation
c. Reserve currency
d. Functional currency

15. The _____ founded on April 1, 2001 is the successor of the International Accounting Standards Committee (IASC) founded in June 1973 in London. It is responsible for developing the International Financial Reporting Standards (new name for the International Accounting Standards issued after 2001), and promoting the use and application of these standards.

The _____ is an independent, privately-funded accounting standard-setter based in London, UK.

a. International Federation of Accountants
b. American Accounting Association
c. Association of Certified Public Accountants
d. International Accounting Standards Board

16. _____ is the balance of the amounts of cash being received and paid by a business during a defined period of time, sometimes tied to a specific project. Measurement of _____ can be used

- to evaluate the state or performance of a business or project.
- to determine problems with liquidity. Being profitable does not necessarily mean being liquid. A company can fail because of a shortage of cash, even while profitable.
- to generate project rate of returns. The time of _____s into and out of projects are used as inputs to financial models such as internal rate of return, and net present value.
- to examine income or growth of a business when it is believed that accrual accounting concepts do not represent economic realities. Alternately, _____ can be used to 'validate' the net income generated by accrual accounting.

Chapter 10. Management of Translation Exposure,

_____ as a generic term may be used differently depending on context, and certain _____ definitions may be adapted by analysts and users for their own uses. Common terms include operating _____ and free _____.

_____s can be classified into:

1. Operational _____s: Cash received or expended as a result of the company's core business activities.
2. Investment _____s: Cash received or expended through capital expenditure, investments or acquisitions.
3. Financing _____s: Cash received or expended as a result of financial activities, such as interests and dividends.

All three together - the net _____ - are necessary to reconcile the beginning cash balance to the ending cash balance. Loan draw downs or equity injections, that is just shifting of capital but no expenditure as such, are not considered in the net _____.

a. Cash flow
c. Shareholder value
b. Real option
d. Corporate finance

17. _____ or financing is to provide capital (funds), which means money for a project, a person, a business or any other private or public institutions.

Those funds can be allocated for either short term or long term purposes. The health fund is a new way of _____ private healthcare centers.

a. Product life cycle
c. Proxy fight
b. Synthetic CDO
d. Funding

18. The _____ is published by The Economist as an informal way of measuring the purchasing power parity (PPP) between two currencies and provides a test of the extent to which market exchange rates result in goods costing the same in different countries. It 'seeks to make exchange-rate theory a bit more digestible'.
    a. Divisia index
    c. 529 plan
    b. Big Mac index
    d. 4-4-5 Calendar

19. In economics, _____ is a rise in the general level of prices of goods and services in an economy over a period of time. The term '_____' once referred to increases in the money supply (monetary _____); however, economic debates about the relationship between money supply and price levels have led to its primary use today in describing price _____.
    _____ can also be described as a decline in the real value of money--a loss of purchasing power in the medium of exchange which is also the monetary unit of account.
    a. Inflation
    c. ABN Amro
    b. A Random Walk Down Wall Street
    d. AAB

20. _____ is a fee paid on borrowed assets. It is the price paid for the use of borrowed money, or, money earned by deposited funds. Assets that are sometimes lent with _____ include money, shares, consumer goods through hire purchase, major assets such as aircraft, and even entire factories in finance lease arrangements.
   a. Insolvency
   b. A Random Walk Down Wall Street
   c. AAB
   d. Interest

21. _____ was a domestic tax measure implemented by U.S. President John F. Kennedy in July 1963. It was meant to make it less profitable for U.S. investors to invest abroad by taxing the interest on foreign securities. It was seen by some as retaliation against Canadian attempts to repatriate their economy one month earlier under the direction of Finance Minister Walter Gordon.
   a. A Random Walk Down Wall Street
   b. AAB
   c. ABN Amro
   d. Interest Equalization Tax

22. _____ is the loss of value of a country's currency with respect to one or more foreign reference currencies, typically in a floating exchange rate system. It is most often used for the unofficial increase of the exchange rate due to market forces, though sometimes it appears interchangeably with devaluation. Its opposite is called appreciation.
   a. 4-4-5 Calendar
   b. Currency depreciation
   c. 7-Eleven
   d. 529 plan

23. Realization is generally understood in financial circles as the point at which revenue is recognized, typically through a transaction which involves the exchange of an asset, product, or service for cash or its equivalents.

This approach gives the accounting division a strictly objective basis for changing the books. For example, a homeowner may believe that his house has grown in value during a strong market, or fallen in value during a weak market, but until the house is actually sold for a specific price to a specific buyer, the change in value can only be estimated and is considered _____.

   a. AAB
   b. A Random Walk Down Wall Street
   c. ABN Amro
   d. Unrealized

24. In economics, the _____, measures the payments that flow between any individual country and all other countries. It is used to summarize all international economic transactions for that country during a specific time period, usually a year. The _____ is determined by the country's exports and imports of goods, services, and financial capital, as well as financial transfers.
   a. Balance of payments
   b. 4-4-5 Calendar
   c. Purchasing power parity
   d. Gross national product

25. In economics, _____ is a monetary standard in which the value of the monetary unit is defined as equivalent either to a certain quantity of gold or to a certain quantity of silver. Such a system effectively establishes a fixed rate of exchange for the two metals. The merits of the system were the subject of debate in the late 19th century.
   a. 529 plan
   b. 7-Eleven
   c. 4-4-5 Calendar
   d. Bimetallism

26. _____ or amalgamation is the act of merging many things into one. In business, it often refers to the mergers or acquisitions of many smaller companies into much larger ones. The financial accounting term of _____ refers to the aggregated financial statements of a group company as consolidated account.

a. Retained earnings
b. Cost of goods sold
c. Write-off
d. Consolidation

27. _____ is a type of trade policy that allows traders to act and transact without interference from government. Thus, the policy permits trading partners mutual gains from trade, with goods and services produced according to the theory of comparative advantage.

Under a _____ policy, prices are a reflection of true supply and demand, and are the sole determinant of resource allocation.

a. Yield spread
b. Free Trade
c. Monte Carlo methods
d. Seasoned equity offering

28. The _____ is a trilateral trade bloc in North America created by the governments of the United States, Canada, and Mexico. The agreement creating the trade bloc came into force on January 1, 1994. It superseded the Canada-United States Free Trade Agreement between the U.S. and Canada.

a. North American Free Trade Agreement
b. 529 plan
c. 7-Eleven
d. 4-4-5 Calendar

29. In finance, a _____ is a position established in one market in an attempt to offset exposure to the price risk of an equal but opposite obligation or position in another market -- usually, but not always, in the context of one's commercial activity. Hedging is a strategy designed to minimize exposure to such business risks as a sharp contraction in demand for one's inventory, while still allowing the business to profit from producing and maintaining that inventory. A typical hedger might be a farmer with 2000 acres of unharvested wheat in the ground, who would rather tend his crop without the distraction of uncertain prices.

a. 529 plan
b. 7-Eleven
c. 4-4-5 Calendar
d. Hedge

30. A _____ is an exchange of promises between two or more parties to do an act which is enforceable in a court of law. It is where an unqualified offer meets a qualified acceptance and the parties reach Consensus ad Idem. The parties must have the necessary capacity to _____ and the _____ must not be either trifling, indeterminate, impossible or illegal.

a. 7-Eleven
b. 529 plan
c. 4-4-5 Calendar
d. Contract

31. A _____ is a financial contract whose value is derived from the value of something else (known as the underlying.) The underlying on which a _____ is based can be an asset, weather conditions bonds or other forms of credit.

a. 529 plan
b. 7-Eleven
c. Derivative
d. 4-4-5 Calendar

32. _____s are deposits denominated in United States dollars at banks outside the United States, and thus are not under the jurisdiction of the Federal Reserve. Consequently, such deposits are subject to much less regulation than similar deposits within the United States, allowing for higher margins. There is nothing 'European' about _____ deposits; a US dollar-denominated deposit in Tokyo or Caracas would likewise be deemed _____ deposits.

a. AAB
b. ABN Amro
c. A Random Walk Down Wall Street
d. Eurodollar

33. A _____ is an agreement between two parties to buy or sell an asset at a specified point of time in the future. The price of the underlying instrument, in whatever form, is paid before control of the instrument changes. This is one of the many forms of buy/sell orders where the time of trade is not the time where the securities themselves are exchanged.

a. Forward contract
b. Derivatives markets
c. Loan Credit Default Swap Index
d. Constant maturity credit default swap

34. In finance, a _____ is a standardized contract, to buy or sell a specified commodity of standardized quality at a certain date in the future, at a market determined price (the futures price.)

The price is determined by the instantaneous equilibrium between the forces of supply and demand among competing buy and sell orders on the exchange at the time of the purchase or sale of the contract.

In many cases, the items may be such non-traditional 'commodities' as foreign currencies, commercial or government paper [e.g., bonds], or 'baskets' of corporate equity ['stock indices'] or other financial instruments.

a. Futures contract
b. Repurchase agreement
c. Heston model
d. Financial future

35. _____ is a form of risk that arises from the change in price of one currency against another. Whenever investors or companies have assets or business operations across national borders, they face _____ if their positions are not hedged.

- Transaction risk is the risk that exchange rates will change unfavourably over time. It can be hedged against using forward currency contracts;
- Translation risk is an accounting risk, proportional to the amount of assets held in foreign currencies. Changes in the exchange rate over time will render a report inaccurate, and so assets are usually balanced by borrowings in that currency.

The exchange risk associated with a foreign denominated instrument is a key element in foreign investment. This risk flows from differential monetary policy and growth in real productivity, which results in differential inflation rates.

a. Currency risk
b. Credit risk
c. Tracking error
d. Market risk

Chapter 11. International Banking and Money Market,

1. _____ is the term used to describe deposits residing in banks that are located outside the borders of the country that issues the currency the deposit is denominated in. For example a deposit denominated in US dollars residing in a Japanese bank is a _____ deposit, or more specifically a Eurodollar deposit.

Key points are the location of the bank and the denomination of the currency, not the nationality of the bank or the owner of the deposit/loan.

a. A Random Walk Down Wall Street
b. AAB
c. ABN Amro
d. Eurocurrency

2. The _____ or forward rate is the agreed upon price of an asset in a forward contract. Using the rational pricing assumption, we can express the _____ in terms of the spot price and any dividends etc., so that there is no possibility for arbitrage.

The _____ is given by:

where

$\quad$ F is the _____ to be paid at time T
$\quad$ e^x is the exponential function
$\quad$ r is the risk-free interest rate
$\quad$ q is the cost-of-carry
$\quad$ S_0 is the spot price of the asset (i.e. what it would sell for at time 0)
$\quad$ D_i is a dividend which is guaranteed to be paid at time t_i where $0 < t_i < T$.

The two questions here are what price the short position (the seller of the asset) should offer to maximize his gain, and what price the long position (the buyer of the asset) should accept to maximize his gain?

At the very least we know that both do not want to lose any money in the deal.

a. Financial Gerontology
b. Biweekly Mortgage
c. Security interest
d. Forward price

3. In finance, a _____ is a forward contract in which one party pays a fixed interest rate, and receives a floating interest rate equal to a reference rate (the underlying rate.) The payments are calculated over a notional amount over a certain period, and netted, i.e. only the differential is paid. It is paid on the effective date.

a. Triple witching hour
b. PAUG
c. Local volatility
d. Forward rate agreement

Chapter 11. International Banking and Money Market,

4. The _____ of 1933 established the Federal Deposit Insurance Corporation (FDIC) in the United States and included banking reforms, some of which were designed to control speculation. Some provisions such as Regulation Q, which allowed the Federal Reserve to regulate interest rates in savings accounts, were repealed by the Depository Institutions Deregulation and Monetary Control Act of 1980. Provisions that prohibit a bank holding company from owning other financial companies were repealed on November 12, 1999, by the Gramm-Leach-Bliley Act.
   a. 529 plan
   b. 7-Eleven
   c. 4-4-5 Calendar
   d. Glass-Steagall Act

5. A _____ is an international bond that is denominated in a currency not native to the country where it is issued. It can be categorised according to the currency in which it is issued. London is one of the centers of the _____ market, but _____ s may be traded throughout the world - for example in Singapore or Tokyo.
   a. Education production function
   b. Economic entity
   c. Interest rate option
   d. Eurobond

6. _____ is the branch of economics that studies the dynamics of exchange rates, foreign investment, and how these affect international trade. It also studies international projects, international investments and capital flows, and trade deficits. It includes the study of futures, options and currency swaps.
   a. ABN Amro
   b. A Random Walk Down Wall Street
   c. AAB
   d. International finance

7.

A _____ is a type of financial intermediary and a type of bank. Commercial banking is also known as business banking. It is a bank that provides checking accounts, savings accounts, and money market accounts and that accepts time deposits.

   a. 4-4-5 Calendar
   b. Commercial Bank
   c. 7-Eleven
   d. 529 plan

8. _____ is the provision of resources (such as granting a loan) by one party to another party where that second party does not reimburse the first party immediately, thereby generating a debt, and instead arranges either to repay or return those resources (or material(s) of equal value) at a later date. The first party is called a creditor, also known as a lender, while the second party is called a debtor, also known as a borrower.

Movements of financial capital are normally dependent on either _____ or equity transfers.

   a. Clearing house
   b. Credit
   c. Warrant
   d. Comparable

9. _____ consists of the sale of goods or merchandise from a fixed location, such as a department store, boutique or kiosk in small or individual lots for direct consumption by the purchaser. _____ may include subordinated services, such as delivery. Purchasers may be individuals or businesses.
   a. 529 plan
   b. 7-Eleven
   c. 4-4-5 Calendar
   d. Retailing

Chapter 11. International Banking and Money Market,

10. _____ is a diversified financial services company with operations around the world. Wells Fargo is the fourth largest bank in the US by assets and the second largest bank by market cap.

   a. Holding company
   b. Wells Fargo ' Co.
   c. Federal Deposit Insurance Corporation
   d. Gold exchange-traded fund

11. In finance, a _____ is a debt security, in which the authorized issuer owes the holders a debt and, depending on the terms of the _____, is obliged to pay interest (the coupon) and/or to repay the principal at a later date, termed maturity.

Thus a _____ is a loan: the issuer is the borrower, the _____ holder is the lender, and the coupon is the interest. _____s provide the borrower with external funds to finance long-term investments, or, in the case of government _____s, to finance current expenditure.

   a. Convertible bond
   b. Catastrophe bonds
   c. Puttable bond
   d. Bond

12. The _____ is a financial market where participants buy and sell debt securities, usually in the form of bonds. As of 2006, the size of the international _____ is an estimated $45 trillion, of which the size of the outstanding U.S. _____ debt was $25.2 trillion.

Nearly all of the $923 billion average daily trading volume in the U.S. _____ takes place between broker-dealers and large institutions in a decentralized, over-the-counter market.

   a. 4-4-5 Calendar
   b. Fixed income
   c. 529 plan
   d. Bond market

13. The _____ is a private, not-for-profit organization whose primary purpose is to develop generally accepted accounting principles (GAAP) within the United States in the public's interest. The Securities and Exchange Commission (SEC) designated the _____ as the organization responsible for setting accounting standards for public companies in the U.S. It was created in 1973, replacing the Accounting Principles Board and the Committee on Accounting Procedure of the American Institute of Certified Public Accountants. The _____'s mission is 'to establish and improve standards of financial accounting and reporting for the guidance and education of the public, including issuers, auditors, and users of financial information.'

The _____ is not a governmental body.

   a. MRU Holdings
   b. Credit karma
   c. PlaNet Finance
   d. FASB

14. In financial accounting, the term _____ is most commonly used to describe any part of shareholders' equity, except for basic share capital. Sometimes, the term is used instead of the term provision; such a use, however, is inconsistent with the terminology suggested by International Accounting Standards Board. For more information about provisions, see provision (accounting.)

   a. Closing entries
   b. FIFO and LIFO accounting
   c. Treasury stock
   d. Reserve

15. The institution most often referenced by the word '_____' is a public or publicly traded _____, the shares of which are traded on a public stock exchange (e.g., the New York Stock Exchange or Nasdaq in the United States) where shares of stock of _____s are bought and sold by and to the general public. Most of the largest businesses in the world are publicly traded _____s. However, the majority of _____s are said to be closely held, privately held or close _____s, meaning that no ready market exists for the trading of shares.
   a. Protect
   b. Federal Home Loan Mortgage Corporation
   c. Depository Trust Company
   d. Corporation

16. Explicit _____ is a measure implemented in many countries to protect bank depositors, in full or in part, from losses caused by a bank's inability to pay its debts when due. _____ systems are one component of a financial system safety net that promotes financial stability.
   a. Reserve requirement
   b. Time deposit
   c. Banking panic
   d. Deposit Insurance

17. The _____ is a United States government corporation created by the Glass-Steagall Act of 1933. It provides deposit insurance, which guarantees the safety of checking and savings deposits in member banks, currently up to $250,000 per depositor per bank. Insured deposits are backed by the full faith and credit of the United States.
   a. NYSE Group
   b. Federal Deposit Insurance Corporation
   c. FASB
   d. Ford Foundation

18. _____ in its classic form is defined as a company from one country making a physical investment into building a factory in another country. It is the establishment of an enterprise by a foreigner. Its definition can be extended to include investments made to acquire lasting interest in enterprises operating outside of the economy of the investor.
   a. Dow Jones ' Company
   b. Foreign direct investment
   c. MicroPlace
   d. Public company

19. A _____, in business matters, is an entity that is controlled by a bigger and more powerful entity. The controlled entity is called a company, corporation, or limited liability company, and the controlling entity is called its parent (or the parent company.) The reason for this distinction is that a lone company cannot be a _____ of any organization; only an entity representing a legal fiction as a separate entity can be a _____.
   a. 529 plan
   b. Subsidiary
   c. Joint stock company
   d. 4-4-5 Calendar

20. _____s are deposits denominated in United States dollars at banks outside the United States, and thus are not under the jurisdiction of the Federal Reserve. Consequently, such deposits are subject to much less regulation than similar deposits within the United States, allowing for higher margins. There is nothing 'European' about _____ deposits; a US dollar-denominated deposit in Tokyo or Caracas would likewise be deemed _____ deposits.
   a. Eurodollar
   b. A Random Walk Down Wall Street
   c. ABN Amro
   d. AAB

21. In business and accounting, _____s are everything of value that is owned by a person or company. The balance sheet of a firm records the monetary value of the _____s owned by the firm. The two major _____ classes are tangible _____s and intangible _____s.
   a. Income
   b. Accounts payable
   c. Asset
   d. EBITDA

Chapter 11. International Banking and Money Market,

22. The _____ refers to the banking supervision Accords (recommendations on banking laws and regulations), Basel I and Basel II issued by the Basel Committee on Banking Supervision (BCBS.) They are called the _____s as the BCBS maintains its secretariat at the Bank of International Settlements in Basel, Switzerland and the committee normally meets there.

The Basel Committee consists of representatives from central banks and regulatory authorities of the Group of Ten (economic) countries, plus others (specifically Luxembourg and Spain).

a. Variable rate mortgage
b. Banking panic
c. Private money
d. Basel Accord

23. _____ is the risk of loss due to a debtor's non-payment of a loan or other line of credit (either the principal or interest (coupon) or both)

Most lenders employ their own models (credit scorecards) to rank potential and existing customers according to risk, and then apply appropriate strategies. With products such as unsecured personal loans or mortgages, lenders charge a higher price for higher risk customers and vice versa. With revolving products such as credit cards and overdrafts, risk is controlled through careful setting of credit limits.

a. Liquidity risk
b. Market risk
c. Transaction risk
d. Credit risk

24. _____ is that which is owed; usually referencing assets owed, but the term can cover other obligations. In the case of assets, _____ is a means of using future purchasing power in the present before a summation has been earned. Some companies and corporations use _____ as a part of their overall corporate finance strategy.

a. Credit cycle
b. Partial Payment
c. Debt
d. Cross-collateralization

25. _____ is the capital that a business raises by taking out a loan. It is a loan made to a company that is normally repaid at some future date. _____ differs from equity or share capital because subscribers to _____ do not become part owners of the business, but are merely creditors, and the suppliers of _____ usually receive a contractually fixed annual percentage return on their loan, and this is known as the coupon rate.

a. Risk-return spectrum
b. Debt capital
c. Financial assistance
d. Floating charge

26. In finance, the _____ is the global financial market for short-term borrowing and lending. It provides short-term liquidity funding for the global financial system. The _____ is where short-term obligations such as Treasury bills, commercial paper and bankers' acceptances are bought and sold.

a. Cramdown
b. Debt-for-equity swap
c. Consumer debt
d. Money market

27. An _____ is a risk arising from execution of a company's business functions. As such, it is a very broad concept including e.g. fraud risks, legal risks, physical or environmental risks, etc. The term _____ is most commonly found in risk management programs of financial institutions that must organize their risk management program according to Basel II.

Chapter 11. International Banking and Money Market,

a. AAB
c. Operational risk
b. A Random Walk Down Wall Street
d. ABN Amro

28. A _____ is a financial contract whose value is derived from the value of something else (known as the underlying.) The underlying on which a _____ is based can be an asset, weather conditions bonds or other forms of credit.
  a. 529 plan
  c. Derivative
  b. 4-4-5 Calendar
  d. 7-Eleven

29. _____ is the risk that the value of an investment will decrease due to moves in market factors. The five standard _____ factors are:

- Equity risk, the risk that stock prices will change.
- Interest rate risk, the risk that interest rates will change.
- Currency risk, the risk that foreign exchange rates will change.
- Commodity risk, the risk that commodity prices (e.g. grains, metals) will change.

As with other forms of risk, _____ may be measured in a number of ways. Traditionally, this is done using a Value at Risk methodology. Value at risk is well established as a risk management technique, but it contains a number of limiting assumptions that constrain its accuracy.

  a. Tracking error
  c. Transaction risk
  b. Currency risk
  d. Market risk

30. _____ is a structured finance process that involves pooling and repackaging of cash-flow-producing financial assets into securities, which are then sold to investors. The term '_____' is derived from the fact that the form of financial instruments used to obtain funds from the investors are securities. As a portfolio risk backed by amortizing cash flows - and unlike general corporate debt - the credit quality of securitized debt is non-stationary due to changes in volatility that are time- and structure-dependent.
  a. The Glass-Steagall Act of 1933
  c. Reputational risk
  b. Special journals
  d. Securitization

31. A _____ is a fungible, negotiable instrument representing financial value. They are broadly categorized into debt securities (such as banknotes, bonds and debentures), and equity securities; e.g., common stocks. The company or other entity issuing the _____ is called the issuer.
  a. Securities lending
  c. Security
  b. Book entry
  d. Tracking stock

32. The _____ is where currency trading takes place. It is where banks and other official institutions facilitate the buying and selling of foreign currencies. FX transactions typically involve one party purchasing a quantity of one currency in exchange for paying a quantity of another.
  a. Floating exchange rate
  c. Foreign exchange option
  b. Spot market
  d. Foreign exchange market

33. The _____ is a daily reference rate based on the interest rates at which banks borrow unsecured funds from banks in the London wholesale money market (or interbank market.) It is roughly comparable to the U.S. Federal funds rate.

During 1984 it became apparent that an increasing number of banks were trading actively in a variety of relatively new market instruments, notably interest rate swaps, foreign currency options and forward rate agreements.

a. Risk-free interest rate
b. Shanghai Interbank Offered Rate
c. Fixed interest
d. London Interbank Offered Rate

34. A _____ s a time deposit, a financial product commonly offered to consumers by banks, thrift institutions, and credit unions.

They are similar to savings accounts in that they are insured and thus virtually risk-free; they are 'money in the bank'. They are different from savings accounts in that they have a specific, fixed term (often three months, six months, or one to five years), and, usually, a fixed interest rate.

a. Time deposit
b. Variable rate mortgage
c. Reserve requirement
d. Certificate of deposit

35. The _____ (or Euribor) is a daily reference rate based on the averaged interest rates at which banks offer to lend unsecured funds to other banks in the euro wholesale money market (or interbank market.)

Euribor rates are used as a reference rate for euro-denominated forward rate agreements, short term interest rate futures contracts and interest rate swaps, in very much the same way as LIBOR rates are commonly used for Sterling and US dollar-denominated instruments. They thus provide the basis for some of the world's most liquid and active interest rate markets.

a. European Monetary System
b. Exchange Rate Mechanism
c. A Random Walk Down Wall Street
d. Euro Interbank Offered Rate

36. An _____ is a single market with a common currency. It is to be distinguished from a mere currency union, which does not involve a single market. This is the fifth stage of economic integration.
a. A Random Walk Down Wall Street
b. ABN Amro
c. AAB
d. Economic and Monetary Union

37. _____ is a fee paid on borrowed assets. It is the price paid for the use of borrowed money, or, money earned by deposited funds. Assets that are sometimes lent with _____ include money, shares, consumer goods through hire purchase, major assets such as aircraft, and even entire factories in finance lease arrangements.
a. A Random Walk Down Wall Street
b. Insolvency
c. AAB
d. Interest

38. An _____ is the price a borrower pays for the use of money they do not own, and the return a lender receives for deferring the use of funds, by lending it to the borrower. _____s are normally expressed as a percentage rate over the period of one year.

_____s targets are also a vital tool of monetary policy and are used to control variables like investment, inflation, and unemployment.

a. Interest rate
b. ABN Amro
c. A Random Walk Down Wall Street
d. AAB

39. _____ is the value on a given date of a future payment or series of future payments, discounted to reflect the time value of money and other factors such as investment risk. _____ calculations are widely used in business and economics to provide a means to compare cash flows at different times on a meaningful 'like to like' basis.

The most commonly applied model of the time value of money is compound interest.

a. Present value of benefits
b. Net present value
c. Negative gearing
d. Present value

40. _____ is a term applied in many countries to a reference interest rate used by banks. The term originally indicated the rate of interest at which banks lent to favored customers, i.e., those with high credibility, though this is no longer always the case. Some variable interest rates may be expressed as a percentage above or below _____.

a. Time deposit
b. Reserve requirement
c. Credit bureau
d. Prime rate

41. _____ is a business valuation method. _____ is the net present value of a project if financed solely by ownership equity plus the present value of all the benefits of financing. Usually, the main benefit is a tax shield resulted from tax deductibility of interest payments. Another one can be a subsidized borrowing.

a. AAB
b. Adjusted present value
c. ABN Amro
d. A Random Walk Down Wall Street

42. In finance, the _____ between two currencies specifies how much one currency is worth in terms of the other. For example an _____ of 102 Japanese yen to the United States dollar means that JPY 102 is worth the same as USD 1. The foreign exchange market is one of the largest markets in the world.

a. ABN Amro
b. Exchange rate
c. AAB
d. A Random Walk Down Wall Street

43. _____ are dollar-denominated bonds, issued mostly by Latin American countries in the 1980s, named after U.S. Treasury Secretary Nicholas Brady.

_____ were created in March 1989 in order to convert bonds issued by mostly Latin American countries into a variety or 'menu' of new bonds after many of those countries defaulted on their debt in the 1980's. At that time, the market for sovereign debt was small and illiquid, and the standardization of emerging-market debt facilitated risk-spreading and trading.

a. Municipal bond
b. Coupon rate
c. Nominal yield
d. Brady bonds

44. In economics and finance, _____ represents passive holdings of securities such as foreign stocks, bonds, or other financial assets, none of which entails active management or control of the securities' issuer by the investor; where such control exists, it is known as foreign direct investment. Generally, this means the investor holds less than 10% of the total shares or less than the amount needed to hold the majority vote.

Some examples of _____ are:

- purchase of shares in a foreign company.
- purchase of bonds issued by a foreign government.
- acquisition of assets in a foreign country.

Factors affecting international _____:

- tax rates on interest or dividends (investors will normally prefer countries where the tax rates are relatively low)
- interest rates (money tends to flow to countries with high interest rates)
- exchange rates (foreign investors may be attracted if the local currency is expected to strengthen)

_____ is part of the capital account on the balance of payments statistics.

a. Tactical asset allocation
c. Divestment
b. Portable alpha
d. Portfolio investment

45. In economics, the _____, measures the payments that flow between any individual country and all other countries. It is used to summarize all international economic transactions for that country during a specific time period, usually a year. The _____ is determined by the country's exports and imports of goods, services, and financial capital, as well as financial transfers.

a. 4-4-5 Calendar
c. Gross national product
b. Purchasing power parity
d. Balance of payments

46. _____ refers to the phenomenon of major oil-producing states mainly from OPEC earning more money from the export of oil than they could usefully invest in their own economies. It was a phenomenon of the late 1970s and early 1980s with the peak years for petrodollar surpluses.

During this period, states such as Saudi Arabia, Kuwait and Qatar amassed large surpluses of petrodollars which they could not invest in their own countries.

a. Reserve currency
c. Functional currency
b. Devaluation
d. Petrodollar recycling

47. In a _____, a company's creditors generally agree to cancel some or all of the debt in exchange for equity in the company.

These deals often occur when large companies run into serious financial trouble, and often result in these companies being taken over by their principal creditors. This is because both the debt and the remaining assets in these companies are so large that there is no advantage for the creditors to drive the company into bankruptcy.

a. Financial Gerontology
b. Covestor
c. Debt restructuring
d. Debt-for-equity swap

48. In finance, a _____ is a derivative in which two counterparties agree to exchange one stream of cash flows against another stream. These streams are called the legs of the _____.

The cash flows are calculated over a notional principal amount, which is usually not exchanged between counterparties.

a. Swap
b. Local volatility
c. Volatility swap
d. Volatility arbitrage

49. The phrase _____ refers to the aspect of corporate strategy, corporate finance and management dealing with the buying, selling and combining of different companies that can aid, finance, or help a growing company in a given industry grow rapidly without having to create another business entity.

An acquisition, also known as a takeover, is the buying of one company (the 'target') by another. An acquisition may be friendly or hostile.

a. 4-4-5 Calendar
b. 529 plan
c. 7-Eleven
d. Mergers and acquisitions

50. A _____ is a firm that quotes both a buy and a sell price in a financial instrument or commodity, hoping to make a profit on the bid/offer spread, or turn.

In foreign exchange trading, where most deals are conducted over-the-counter and are, therefore, completely virtual, the _____ sells to and buys from its clients. Hence, the client's loss and the spread is the _____ firm's profit, which gets thus compensated for the effort of providing liquidity in a competitive market.

a. 529 plan
b. 7-Eleven
c. Market maker
d. 4-4-5 Calendar

51. A _____ is a private or public market for the trading of company stock and derivatives of company stock at an agreed price; these are securities listed on a stock exchange as well as those only traded privately.

The size of the world _____ is estimated at about $36.6 trillion US at the beginning of October 2008. The world derivatives market has been estimated at about $480 trillion face or nominal value, 12 times the size of the entire world economy.

a. Adolph Coors
b. Andrew Tobias
c. Anton Gelonkin
d. Stock market

Chapter 11. International Banking and Money Market,

52. A _____ is a financial crisis that occurs when many banks suffer runs at the same time. A systemic banking crisis is one where all or almost all of the banking capital in a country is wiped out. The resulting chain of bankruptcies can cause a long economic recession. Much of the Great Depression's economic damage was caused directly by bank runs. The cost of cleaning up a systemic banking crisis can be huge, with fiscal costs averaging 13% of GDP and economic output losses averaging 20% of GDP for important crises from 1970 to 2007.

a. Credit bureau
b. Probability of default
c. Deposit insurance
d. Banking panic

53. A _____ is a set of companies with interlocking business relationships and shareholdings. It is a type of business group.

The prototypical _____ are those which appeared in Japan during the 'economic miracle' following World War II.

a. Zero-coupon bond
b. Relative strength Index
c. Stock split
d. Keiretsu

54. The _____ was a period of financial crisis that gripped much of Asia beginning in July 1997, and raised fears of a worldwide economic meltdown (financial contagion).

The crisis started in Thailand with the financial collapse of the Thai baht caused by the decision of the Thai government to float the baht, cutting its peg to the USD, after exhaustive efforts to support it in the face of a severe financial overextension that was in part real estate driven. At the time, Thailand had acquired a burden of foreign debt that made the country effectively bankrupt even before the collapse of its currency.

a. OTC Bulletin Board
b. Asian Financial Crisis
c. Internal control
d. International trade

55. _____ is a type of risk faced by investors, corporations, and governments. It is a risk that can be understood and managed with proper aforethought and investment.

Broadly, _____ refers to the complications businesses and governments may face as a result of what are commonly referred to as political decisions--or 'any political change that alters the expected outcome and value of a given economic action by changing the probability of achieving business objectives.' .

a. Political risk
b. Single-index model
c. Capital asset
d. Mid price

Chapter 12. International Bond Market,

1. In finance, a _____ is a debt security, in which the authorized issuer owes the holders a debt and, depending on the terms of the _____, is obliged to pay interest (the coupon) and/or to repay the principal at a later date, termed maturity.

Thus a _____ is a loan: the issuer is the borrower, the _____ holder is the lender, and the coupon is the interest. _____s provide the borrower with external funds to finance long-term investments, or, in the case of government _____s, to finance current expenditure.

a. Convertible bond
b. Catastrophe bonds
c. Puttable bond
d. Bond

2. The _____ is a financial market where participants buy and sell debt securities, usually in the form of bonds. As of 2006, the size of the international _____ is an estimated $45 trillion, of which the size of the outstanding U.S. _____ debt was $25.2 trillion.

Nearly all of the $923 billion average daily trading volume in the U.S. _____ takes place between broker-dealers and large institutions in a decentralized, over-the-counter market.

a. 4-4-5 Calendar
b. Fixed income
c. 529 plan
d. Bond market

3. A _____ is an international bond that is denominated in a currency not native to the country where it is issued. It can be categorised according to the currency in which it is issued. London is one of the centers of the _____ market, but _____s may be traded throughout the world - for example in Singapore or Tokyo.

a. Economic entity
b. Interest rate option
c. Education production function
d. Eurobond

4. The _____ was a period of financial crisis that gripped much of Asia beginning in July 1997, and raised fears of a worldwide economic meltdown (financial contagion).

The crisis started in Thailand with the financial collapse of the Thai baht caused by the decision of the Thai government to float the baht, cutting its peg to the USD, after exhaustive efforts to support it in the face of a severe financial overextension that was in part real estate driven. At the time, Thailand had acquired a burden of foreign debt that made the country effectively bankrupt even before the collapse of its currency.

a. International trade
b. OTC Bulletin Board
c. Internal control
d. Asian Financial Crisis

5. In probability theory and statistics, the _____ of a random variable, probability distribution averaging the squared distance of its possible values from the expected value (mean.) Whereas the mean is a way to describe the location of a distribution, the _____ is a way to capture its scale or degree of being spread out. The unit of _____ is the square of the unit of the original variable.

a. Variance
b. Monte Carlo methods
c. Semivariance
d. Harmonic mean

6. _____s are deposits denominated in United States dollars at banks outside the United States, and thus are not under the jurisdiction of the Federal Reserve. Consequently, such deposits are subject to much less regulation than similar deposits within the United States, allowing for higher margins. There is nothing 'European' about _____ deposits; a US dollar-denominated deposit in Tokyo or Caracas would likewise be deemed _____ deposits.
   a. A Random Walk Down Wall Street
   b. AAB
   c. ABN Amro
   d. Eurodollar

7. In financial accounting, the term _____ is most commonly used to describe any part of shareholders' equity, except for basic share capital. Sometimes, the term is used instead of the term provision; such a use, however, is inconsistent with the terminology suggested by International Accounting Standards Board. For more information about provisions, see provision (accounting.)
   a. Closing entries
   b. FIFO and LIFO accounting
   c. Treasury stock
   d. Reserve

8. A _____ is a fungible, negotiable instrument representing financial value. They are broadly categorized into debt securities (such as banknotes, bonds and debentures), and equity securities; e.g., common stocks. The company or other entity issuing the _____ is called the issuer.
   a. Security
   b. Book entry
   c. Securities lending
   d. Tracking stock

9. Congress enacted the _____, in the aftermath of the stock market crash of 1929 and during the ensuing Great Depression. It requires that any offer or sale of securities using the means and instrumentalities of interstate commerce be registered pursuant to the 1933 Act, unless an exemption from registration exists under the law.
   a. Securities Act of 1933
   b. 529 plan
   c. 4-4-5 Calendar
   d. 7-Eleven

10. The _____ of 1934 is a law governing the secondary trading of securities (stocks, bonds, and debentures) in the United States of America. The Act, 48 Stat. 881 (enacted June 6, 1934), codified at 15 U.S.C. § 78a et seq., was a sweeping piece of legislation. The Act and related statutes form the basis of regulation of the financial markets and their participants in the United States.
    a. Securities Exchange Act
    b. 4-4-5 Calendar
    c. 7-Eleven
    d. 529 plan

11. The U.S. _____ is an independent agency of the United States government which holds primary responsibility for enforcing the federal securities laws and regulating the securities industry, the nation's stock and options exchanges, and other electronic securities markets. The SEC was created by section 4 of the SEC of 1934 (now codified as 15 U.S.C. § 78d and commonly referred to as the 1934 Act.)
    a. 4-4-5 Calendar
    b. Securities and Exchange Commission
    c. 529 plan
    d. 7-Eleven

12. _____ generally refers to two kinds of taxes: Taxes which employers are required to withhold from employees' pay Pay-As-You-Earn or Pay-As-You-Go tax; and taxes which are paid from the employer's own funds and which are directly related to employing a worker, which may be either fixed charges or proportionally linked to an employee's pay.

In China, the _____ is a specific tax which is paid to states and territories by employers, not by employees. The tax is not deducted from the worker's pay.

Chapter 12. International Bond Market,

a. Capital gain
b. Withholding tax
c. Tax brackets
d. Payroll tax

13. _____ is an amount withheld by the party making a payment to another (payee) and paid to the taxation authorities. The amount the payer deducts may vary, depending on the nature of the product or service being paid for. The payee is assessed on the gross amount, and the tax to be withheld (the _____) is computed in that assessment.
a. Capital gain
b. Capital gains tax
c. Tax holiday
d. Withholding tax

14. A _____ is a document that indicates that the bearer of the document has title to property, such as shares or bonds. They differ from normal registered instruments, in that no records are kept of who owns the underlying property, or of the transactions involving transfer of ownership. Whoever physically holds the bearer bond papers owns the property.
a. Bearer instrument
b. Securities lending
c. Marketable
d. Book entry

15. _____ is an arrangement with the U.S. Securities and Exchange Commission that allows a single registration document to be filed that permits the issuance of multiple securities.

_____ is a registration of a new issue which can be prepared up to two years in advance, so that the issue can be offered quickly as soon as funds are needed or market conditions are favorable.

For example, current market conditions in the housing market are not favorable for a specific firm to issue a public offering.

a. Shelf registration
b. Black Sea Trade and Development Bank
c. Bought deal
d. 4-4-5 Calendar

16. _____ is the set of processes, customs, policies, laws and institutions affecting the way a corporation is directed, administered or controlled. _____ also includes the relationships among the many stakeholders involved and the goals for which the corporation is governed. The principal stakeholders are the shareholders, management and the board of directors.
a. Corporate governance
b. Patent
c. Foreign Corrupt Practices Act
d. Due diligence

17. _____ are government bonds issued by the United States Department of the Treasury through the Bureau of the Public Debt. They are the debt financing instruments of the U.S. Federal government, and they are often referred to simply as Treasuries or Treasurys. There are four types of marketable _____: Treasury bills, Treasury notes, Treasury bonds, and Treasury Inflation Protected Securities (TIPS.)
a. Treasury Inflation-Protected Securities
b. 4-4-5 Calendar
c. Treasury Inflation Protected Securities
d. Treasury securities

18. The coupon or _____ of a bond is the amount of interest paid per year expressed as a percentage of the face value of the bond.

For example if you hold $10,000 nominal of a bond described as a 4.5% loan stock, you will receive $450 in interest each year (probably in two installments of $225 each.)

Not all bonds have coupons.

a. Revenue bonds
c. Zero-coupon bond
b. Puttable bond
d. Coupon rate

19. _____ is the term used to describe deposits residing in banks that are located outside the borders of the country that issues the currency the deposit is denominated in. For example a deposit denominated in US dollars residing in a Japanese bank is a _____ deposit, or more specifically a Eurodollar deposit.

Key points are the location of the bank and the denomination of the currency, not the nationality of the bank or the owner of the deposit/loan.

a. A Random Walk Down Wall Street
c. ABN Amro
b. AAB
d. Eurocurrency

20. The _____ is a daily reference rate based on the interest rates at which banks borrow unsecured funds from banks in the London wholesale money market (or interbank market.) It is roughly comparable to the U.S. Federal funds rate.

During 1984 it became apparent that an increasing number of banks were trading actively in a variety of relatively new market instruments, notably interest rate swaps, foreign currency options and forward rate agreements.

a. Shanghai Interbank Offered Rate
c. Risk-free interest rate
b. Fixed interest
d. London Interbank Offered Rate

21. Accrual, in accounting, describes the accounting method known as _____, whereby revenues and expenses are recognized when they are accrued, i.e. accumulated (earned or incurred), regardless when the actual cash is received or paid out.

E.g. a company delivers a product to a customer who will pay for it 30 days later in the next fiscal year starting a week after the delivery. The company recognizes the proceeds as a revenue in its current income statement still for the fiscal year of the delivery, even though it will get paid in cash during the following accounting period.

a. AAB
c. A Random Walk Down Wall Street
b. ABN Amro
d. Accrual basis

22. A _____ is a financial contract between two parties, the buyer and the seller of this type of option. Often it is simply labeled a 'call'. The buyer of the option has the right, but not the obligation to buy an agreed quantity of a particular commodity or financial instrument (the underlying instrument) from the seller of the option at a certain time (the expiration date) for a certain price (the strike price.)

a. Bear spread
c. Bear call spread
b. Call option
d. Bull spread

Chapter 12. International Bond Market, 111

23. A _____ is a profit that results from investments into a capital asset, such as stocks, bonds or real estate, which exceeds the purchase price. It is the difference between a higher selling price and a lower purchase price, resulting in a financial gain for the seller. Conversely, a capital loss arises if the proceeds from the sale of a capital asset are less than the purchase price.
  - a. Capital gains tax
  - b. Payroll tax
  - c. Tax brackets
  - d. Capital gain

24. In finance, a _____ is a type of bond that can be converted into shares of stock in the issuing company, usually at some pre-announced ratio. It is a hybrid security with debt- and equity-like features. Although it typically has a low coupon rate, the holder is compensated with the ability to convert the bond to common stock, usually at a substantial discount to the stock's market value.
  - a. Gilts
  - b. Corporate bond
  - c. Bond fund
  - d. Convertible bond

25. _____ is a fee paid on borrowed assets. It is the price paid for the use of borrowed money , or, money earned by deposited funds . Assets that are sometimes lent with _____ include money, shares, consumer goods through hire purchase, major assets such as aircraft, and even entire factories in finance lease arrangements.
  - a. Insolvency
  - b. A Random Walk Down Wall Street
  - c. Interest
  - d. AAB

26. A _____ is a bond bought at a price lower than its face value, with the face value repaid at the time of maturity. It does not make periodic interest payments, or have so-called 'coupons,' hence the term _____. Investors earn return from the compounded interest all paid at maturity plus the difference between the discounted price of the bond and its par value.
  - a. Bond fund
  - b. Corporate bond
  - c. Clean price
  - d. Zero-coupon bond

27. An _____ is a contract written by a seller that conveys to the buyer the right -- but not the obligation -- to buy (in the case of a call _____) or to sell (in the case of a put _____) a particular asset, such as a piece of property such as, among others, a futures contract. In return for granting the _____, the seller collects a payment (the premium) from the buyer.

For example, buying a call _____ provides the right to buy a specified quantity of a security at a set strike price at some time on or before expiration, while buying a put _____ provides the right to sell.

  - a. Annuity
  - b. Amortization
  - c. AT'T Mobility LLC
  - d. Option

28. In finance, a _____ is a security that entitles the holder to buy stock of the company that issued it at a specified price, which is usually higher than the stock price at time of issue.

_____s are frequently attached to bonds or preferred stock as a sweetener, allowing the issuer to pay lower interest rates or dividends. They can be used to enhance the yield of the bond, and make them more attractive to potential buyers.

a. Credit
b. Clearing
c. Clearing house
d. Warrant

29. In economics and finance, _____ represents passive holdings of securities such as foreign stocks, bonds, or other financial assets, none of which entails active management or control of the securities' issuer by the investor; where such control exists, it is known as foreign direct investment. Generally, this means the investor holds less than 10% of the total shares or less than the amount needed to hold the majority vote.

Some examples of _____ are:

- purchase of shares in a foreign company.
- purchase of bonds issued by a foreign government.
- acquisition of assets in a foreign country.

Factors affecting international _____:

- tax rates on interest or dividends (investors will normally prefer countries where the tax rates are relatively low)
- interest rates (money tends to flow to countries with high interest rates)
- exchange rates (foreign investors may be attracted if the local currency is expected to strengthen)

_____ is part of the capital account on the balance of payments statistics.

a. Tactical asset allocation
b. Portfolio investment
c. Divestment
d. Portable alpha

30. In economics, the _____, measures the payments that flow between any individual country and all other countries. It is used to summarize all international economic transactions for that country during a specific time period, usually a year. The _____ is determined by the country's exports and imports of goods, services, and financial capital, as well as financial transfers.

a. Balance of payments
b. Gross national product
c. 4-4-5 Calendar
d. Purchasing power parity

31. _____ is the provision of resources (such as granting a loan) by one party to another party where that second party does not reimburse the first party immediately, thereby generating a debt, and instead arranges either to repay or return those resources (or material(s) of equal value) at a later date. The first party is called a creditor, also known as a lender, while the second party is called a debtor, also known as a borrower.

Movements of financial capital are normally dependent on either _____ or equity transfers.

a. Clearing house
b. Warrant
c. Comparable
d. Credit

32. A _____ assesses the credit worthiness of an individual, corporation, or even a country. _____s are calculated from financial history and current assets and liabilities. Typically, a _____ tells a lender or investor the probability of the subject being able to pay back a loan.

a. Debenture
b. Credit cycle
c. Credit report monitoring
d. Credit rating

33. In finance, _____ occurs when a debtor has not met its legal obligations according to the debt contract, e.g. it has not made a scheduled payment, or has violated a loan covenant (condition) of the debt contract. _____ may occur if the debtor is either unwilling or unable to pay their debt. This can occur with all debt obligations including bonds, mortgages, loans, and promissory notes.

   a. Vendor finance
   b. Default
   c. Credit crunch
   d. Debt validation

34. A bond is considered _____ if its credit rating is BBB- or higher by Standard and Poor's or Baa3 or higher by Moody's or BBB(low) or higher by DBRS. Generally they are bonds that are judged by the rating agency as likely enough to meet payment obligations that banks are allowed to invest in them.

Ratings play a critical role in determining how much companies and other entities that issue debt, including sovereign governments, have to pay to access credit markets, i.e., the amount of interest they pay on their issued debt.

   a. A Random Walk Down Wall Street
   b. AAB
   c. Investment grade
   d. ABN Amro

35. The _____ is the difference between the amount paid by the underwriting group in a new issue of securities and the price at which securities are offered for sale to the public. It is the underwriter's gross profit margin, usually expressed in points per unit of sale (bond or stock.) Spreads may vary widely and are influenced by the underwriter's expectation of market demand for the securities offered for sale, interest rates, and so on.

   a. A Random Walk Down Wall Street
   b. AAB
   c. Underwriting spread
   d. ABN Amro

36. In economics, _____ describes the state of a market with respect to competition.

   - Perfect competition, in which the market consists of a very large number of firms producing a homogeneous product.
   - Monopolistic competition where there are a large number of independent firms which have a very small proportion of the market share.
   - Oligopoly, in which a market is dominated by a small number of firms which own more than 40% of the market share.
   - Oligopsony, a market dominated by many sellers and a few buyers.
   - Monopoly, where there is only one provider of a product or service.
   - Natural monopoly, a monopoly in which economies of scale cause efficiency to increase continuously with the size of the firm. A firm is a natural monopoly if it is able to serve the entire market demand at a lower cost than any combination of two or more smaller, more specialized firms.
   - Monopsony, when there is only one buyer in a market.

The imperfectly competitive structure is quite identical to the realistic market conditions where some monopolistic competitors, monopolists, oligopolists, and duopolists exist and dominate the market conditions. The elements of _____ include the number and size distribution of firms, entry conditions, and the extent of differentiation.

Chapter 12. International Bond Market,

These somewhat abstract concerns tend to determine some but not all details of a specific concrete market system where buyers and sellers actually meet and commit to trade.

a. Fixed exchange rate
c. Market structure
b. Gross domestic product
d. Human capital

37. _____ offer, asking price is a price a seller of a good is willing to accept for that particular good.

In bid and ask, the term _____ is used in contrast to the term bid price. The difference between the _____ and the bid price is called the spread.

a. Ask price
c. Interest rate parity
b. AAB
d. A Random Walk Down Wall Street

38. In banking and finance, _____ denotes all activities from the time a commitment is made for a transaction until it is settled. _____ is necessary because the speed of trades is much faster than the cycle time for completing the underlying transaction.

In its widest sense _____ involves the management of post-trading, pre-settlement credit exposures, to ensure that trades are settled in accordance with market rules, even if a buyer or seller should become insolvent prior to settlement.

a. Procter ' Gamble
c. Share
b. Clearing
d. Clearing house

39. A _____ is a firm that quotes both a buy and a sell price in a financial instrument or commodity, hoping to make a profit on the bid/offer spread, or turn.

In foreign exchange trading, where most deals are conducted over-the-counter and are, therefore, completely virtual, the _____ sells to and buys from its clients. Hence, the client's loss and the spread is the _____ firm's profit, which gets thus compensated for the effort of providing liquidity in a competitive market.

a. 7-Eleven
c. 4-4-5 Calendar
b. 529 plan
d. Market maker

40. _____ is the value on a given date of a future payment or series of future payments, discounted to reflect the time value of money and other factors such as investment risk. _____ calculations are widely used in business and economics to provide a means to compare cash flows at different times on a meaningful 'like to like' basis.

The most commonly applied model of the time value of money is compound interest.

a. Present value
c. Negative gearing
b. Present value of benefits
d. Net present value

41. The institution most often referenced by the word '_____' is a public or publicly traded _____, the shares of which are traded on a public stock exchange (e.g., the New York Stock Exchange or Nasdaq in the United States) where shares of stock of _____s are bought and sold by and to the general public. Most of the largest businesses in the world are publicly traded _____s. However, the majority of _____s are said to be closely held, privately held or close _____s, meaning that no ready market exists for the trading of shares.
   a. Protect
   b. Federal Home Loan Mortgage Corporation
   c. Depository Trust Company
   d. Corporation

42. A _____ is a bond issued by a national government denominated in the country's own currency. Bonds issued by national governments in foreign currencies are normally referred to as sovereign bonds. The first ever _____ was issued by the British government in 1693 to raise money to fund a war against France.
   a. Collateralized debt obligations
   b. Municipal bond
   c. Zero-coupon bond
   d. Government Bond

43. A _____ is a listing of bonds or fixed income instruments and a statistic reflecting the composite value of its components. It is used as a tool to represent the characteristics of its component fixed income instruments. They differ from stock market indices in their complexity.
   a. 4-4-5 Calendar
   b. 529 plan
   c. Bond market Index
   d. 7-Eleven

44. _____, also called fair price (in a commonplace conflation of the two distinct concepts), is a concept used in finance and economics, defined as a rational and unbiased estimate of the potential market price of a good, service, or asset, taking into account such objective factors as:

   - acquisition/production/distribution costs, replacement costs, or costs of close substitutes
   - actual utility at a given level of development of social productive capability
   - supply vs. demand

and subjective factors such as

   - risk characteristics
   - cost of capital
   - individually perceived utility

In accounting, _____ is used as an estimate of the market value of an asset (or liability) for which a market price cannot be determined (usually because there is no established market for the asset.) Under GAAP (FAS 157), _____ is the amount at which the asset could be bought or sold in a current transaction between willing parties, or transferred to an equivalent party, other than in a liquidation sale. This is used for assets whose carrying value is based on mark-to-market valuations; for assets carried at historical cost, the _____ of the asset is not used. One example of where _____ is an issue is a College kitchen with a cost of $2 million which was built 5 years ago.

   a. 7-Eleven
   b. 529 plan
   c. 4-4-5 Calendar
   d. Fair Value

45. A _____ is a bond issued by a corporation. The term is usually applied to longer-term debt instruments, generally with a maturity date falling at least a year after their issue date. (The term 'commercial paper' is sometimes used for instruments with a shorter maturity.)

 a. Government bond
 b. Serial bond
 c. Brady bonds
 d. Corporate bond

Chapter 13. International Equity Markets,

1. A _____ is a private or public market for the trading of company stock and derivatives of company stock at an agreed price; these are securities listed on a stock exchange as well as those only traded privately.

The size of the world _____ is estimated at about $36.6 trillion US at the beginning of October 2008 . The world derivatives market has been estimated at about $480 trillion face or nominal value, 12 times the size of the entire world economy.

a. Andrew Tobias
b. Adolph Coors
c. Stock market
d. Anton Gelonkin

2. The _____ is an American stock exchange. It is the largest electronic screen-based equity securities trading market in the United States. With approximately 3,200 companies, it has more trading volume per day than any other stock exchange in the world.

a. 529 plan
b. NASDAQ
c. 4-4-5 Calendar
d. 7-Eleven

3. In economics and finance, _____ represents passive holdings of securities such as foreign stocks, bonds, or other financial assets, none of which entails active management or control of the securities' issuer by the investor; where such control exists, it is known as foreign direct investment. Generally, this means the investor holds less than 10% of the total shares or less than the amount needed to hold the majority vote.

Some examples of _____ are:

- purchase of shares in a foreign company.
- purchase of bonds issued by a foreign government.
- acquisition of assets in a foreign country.

Factors affecting international _____:

- tax rates on interest or dividends (investors will normally prefer countries where the tax rates are relatively low)
- interest rates (money tends to flow to countries with high interest rates)
- exchange rates (foreign investors may be attracted if the local currency is expected to strengthen)

_____ is part of the capital account on the balance of payments statistics.

a. Divestment
b. Portable alpha
c. Tactical asset allocation
d. Portfolio investment

4. _____ is a measurement of corporate or economic size equal to the share price times the number of shares outstanding of a public company. As owning stock represents owning the company, including all its equity, capitalization could represent the public opinion of a company's net worth and is a determining factor in stock valuation. Likewise, the capitalization of stock markets or economic regions may be compared to other economic indicators.

a. Synthetic CDO
b. Just-in-time
c. Proxy fight
d. Market capitalization

Chapter 13. International Equity Markets,

5. The term _____ is used to describe a nation's social, or business activity in the process of rapid industrialization. _____ are generally less-wealthy than the developed world, and are wealthier (or the wealthiest of) the developing world. According to The Economist many people find the term dated, but a new term has yet to gain much traction.
   a. AAB
   b. A Random Walk Down Wall Street
   c. ABN Amro
   d. Emerging Markets

6. _____ is that which is owed; usually referencing assets owed, but the term can cover other obligations. In the case of assets, _____ is a means of using future purchasing power in the present before a summation has been earned. Some companies and corporations use _____ as a part of their overall corporate finance strategy.
   a. Credit cycle
   b. Debt
   c. Cross-collateralization
   d. Partial Payment

7. An _____ is a company whose main business is holding securities of other companies purely for investment purposes. The _____ invests money on behalf of its shareholders who in turn share in the profits and losses.
   a. A Random Walk Down Wall Street
   b. Investment company
   c. Unit investment trust
   d. AAB

8. _____ is a measure of the ability of a debtor to pay their debts as and when they fall due. It is usually expressed as a ratio or a percentage of current liabilities.

For a corporation with a published balance sheet there are various ratios used to calculate a measure of liquidity.

   a. Accounting liquidity
   b. Invested capital
   c. Operating profit margin
   d. Operating leverage

9. _____ in finance is a risk management technique, related to hedging, that mixes a wide variety of investments within a portfolio. Because the fluctuations of a single security have less impact on a diverse portfolio, _____ minimizes the risk from any one investment.

A simple example of _____ is the following: On a particular island the entire economy consists of two companies: one that sells umbrellas and another that sells sunscreen.

   a. 7-Eleven
   b. 529 plan
   c. 4-4-5 Calendar
   d. Diversification

10. _____ generally refers to the buying and holding of shares of stock on a stock market by individuals and funds in anticipation of income from dividends and capital gain as the value of the stock rises. It also sometimes refers to the acquisition of equity (ownership) participation in a private (unlisted) company or a startup (a company being created or newly created.) When the investment is in infant companies, it is referred to as venture capital investing and is generally understood to be higher risk than investment in listed going-concern situations.
    a. Open outcry
    b. Insider trading
    c. Intellidex
    d. Equity investment

11. In economics, _____ is a function of the number of firms and their respective shares of the total production (alternatively, total capacity or total reserves) in a market. Alternative terms are Industry concentration and Seller concentration.

Chapter 13. International Equity Markets,

_____ is related to the concept of industrial concentration, which concerns the distribution of production within an industry, as opposed to a market.

a. 7-Eleven
b. 4-4-5 Calendar
c. Market concentration
d. 529 plan

12. In business, _____ is income that a company receives from its normal business activities, usually from the sale of goods and services to customers. Some companies also receive _____ from interest, dividends or royalties paid to them by other companies. _____ may refer to business income in general, or it may refer to the amount, in a monetary unit, received during a period of time, as in 'Last year, Company X had _____ of $32 million.'

In many countries, including the UK, _____ is referred to as turnover.

a. Matching principle
b. Revenue
c. Furniture, Fixtures and Equipment
d. Bottom line

13. _____ offer, asking price is a price a seller of a good is willing to accept for that particular good.

In bid and ask, the term _____ is used in contrast to the term bid price. The difference between the _____ and the bid price is called the spread.

a. AAB
b. Interest rate parity
c. A Random Walk Down Wall Street
d. Ask price

14. A _____ is an international bond that is denominated in a currency not native to the country where it is issued. It can be categorised according to the currency in which it is issued. London is one of the centers of the _____ market, but _____s may be traded throughout the world - for example in Singapore or Tokyo.

a. Eurobond
b. Education production function
c. Interest rate option
d. Economic entity

15. A _____ is a member of an exchange who is an employee of a member firm and executes orders, as agent, on the floor of the exchange for clients. The _____ receives an order via teletype machine from his firm's trading department and then proceeds to the appropriate trading post on the exchange floor. There he joins other brokers and the specialist in the security being bought or sold and executes the trade at the best competitive price available.

a. Business valuation standards
b. Multivariate normal distribution
c. Case-Shiller Home Price Indices
d. Floor broker

16. A _____ is an order to buy a security at no more (or sell at no less) than a specific price. This gives the customer some control over the price at which the trade is executed, but may prevent the order from being executed ('filled'.)

A buy _____ can only be executed by the broker at the limit price or lower.

a. Limit order
b. Block premium
c. Commercial mortgage-backed securities
d. Common stock

Chapter 13. International Equity Markets,

17. A _____ is a buy or sell order to be executed by the broker immediately at current market prices. As long as there are willing sellers and buyers, _____s are filled.

A _____ is the simplest of the order types.

a. Trading curb
c. Stockholder
b. Block premium
d. Market order

18. _____ is an economic concept with commonplace familiarity. It is the price that a good or service is offered at, or will fetch, in the marketplace. It is of interest mainly in the study of microeconomics.

a. Central Securities Depository
c. Market price
b. Convertible arbitrage
d. Delta hedging

19. _____ is the value on a given date of a future payment or series of future payments, discounted to reflect the time value of money and other factors such as investment risk. _____ calculations are widely used in business and economics to provide a means to compare cash flows at different times on a meaningful 'like to like' basis.

The most commonly applied model of the time value of money is compound interest.

a. Present value
c. Negative gearing
b. Present value of benefits
d. Net present value

20. The _____ is that part of the capital markets that deals with the issuance of new securities. Companies, governments or public sector institutions can obtain funding through the sale of a new stock or bond issue. This is typically done through a syndicate of securities dealers.

a. Sector rotation
c. Primary market
b. Peer group analysis
d. Volatility clustering

21. The U.S. _____ is an independent agency of the United States government which holds primary responsibility for enforcing the federal securities laws and regulating the securities industry, the nation's stock and options exchanges, and other electronic securities markets. The SEC was created by section 4 of the SEC of 1934 (now codified as 15 U.S.C. Â§ 78d and commonly referred to as the 1934 Act.)

a. 7-Eleven
c. 529 plan
b. 4-4-5 Calendar
d. Securities and Exchange Commission

22. A _____ is a fungible, negotiable instrument representing financial value. They are broadly categorized into debt securities (such as banknotes, bonds and debentures), and equity securities; e.g., common stocks. The company or other entity issuing the _____ is called the issuer.

a. Book entry
c. Tracking stock
b. Securities lending
d. Security

23. A _____, securities exchange or (in Europe) bourse is a corporation or mutual organization which provides 'trading' facilities for stock brokers and traders, to trade stocks and other securities. _____s also provide facilities for the issue and redemption of securities as well as other financial instruments and capital events including the payment of income and dividends. The securities traded on a _____ include: shares issued by companies, unit trusts and other pooled investment products and bonds.

Chapter 13. International Equity Markets,

a. Stock Exchange
c. 529 plan
b. 7-Eleven
d. 4-4-5 Calendar

24. In economics, business, and accounting, a _____ is the value of money that has been used up to produce something, and hence is not available for use anymore. In business, the _____ may be one of acquisition, in which case the amount of money expended to acquire it is counted as _____. In this case, money is the input that is gone in order to acquire the thing.
a. Cost
c. Marginal cost
b. Sliding scale fees
d. Fixed costs

25. In economics, _____ describes the state of a market with respect to competition.

- Perfect competition, in which the market consists of a very large number of firms producing a homogeneous product.
- Monopolistic competition where there are a large number of independent firms which have a very small proportion of the market share.
- Oligopoly, in which a market is dominated by a small number of firms which own more than 40% of the market share.
- Oligopsony, a market dominated by many sellers and a few buyers.
- Monopoly, where there is only one provider of a product or service.
- Natural monopoly, a monopoly in which economies of scale cause efficiency to increase continuously with the size of the firm. A firm is a natural monopoly if it is able to serve the entire market demand at a lower cost than any combination of two or more smaller, more specialized firms.
- Monopsony, when there is only one buyer in a market.

The imperfectly competitive structure is quite identical to the realistic market conditions where some monopolistic competitors, monopolists, oligopolists, and duopolists exist and dominate the market conditions. The elements of _____ include the number and size distribution of firms, entry conditions, and the extent of differentiation.

These somewhat abstract concerns tend to determine some but not all details of a specific concrete market system where buyers and sellers actually meet and commit to trade.

a. Gross domestic product
c. Fixed exchange rate
b. Human capital
d. Market structure

26. _____ N.V. is a pan-European stock exchange based in Paris and with subsidiaries in Belgium, France, Netherlands, Luxembourg, Portugal and the United Kingdom. In addition to equities and derivatives markets, the _____ group provides clearing and information services. As of 31 January 2006, markets run by _____ had a market capitalization of US$2.9 trillion, making it the 5th largest exchange on the planet.
a. A Random Walk Down Wall Street
c. Euronext
b. ABN Amro
d. AAB

27. A _____ is a portfolio consisting of a weighted sum of every asset in the market, with weights in the proportions that they exist in the market (with the necessary assumption that these assets are infinitely divisible.)

Neha Tyagi's critique (1977) states that this is only a theoretical concept, as to create a _____ for investment purposes in practice would necessarily include every single possible available asset, including real estate, precious metals, stamp collections, jewelry, and anything with any worth, as the theoretical market being referred to would be the world market. As a result, proxies for the market are used in practice by investors.

   a. Market price
   b. Delta neutral
   c. Central Securities Depository
   d. Market Portfolio

28. The _____ is one of several stock market indices, created by nineteenth-century Wall Street Journal editor and Dow Jones ' Company co-founder Charles Dow. Dow compiled the index to gauge the performance of the industrial sector of the American stock market. It is the second-oldest U.S. market index, after the Dow Jones Transportation Average, which Dow also created.
   a. 7-Eleven
   b. Dow Jones Industrial Average
   c. 4-4-5 Calendar
   d. 529 plan

29. The _____ is a capital budgeting metric used by firms to decide whether they should make investments. It is an indicator of the efficiency or quality of an investment, as opposed to net present value (NPV), which indicates value or magnitude.

The IRR is the annualized effective compounded return rate which can be earned on the invested capital, i.e., the yield on the investment.

   a. ABN Amro
   b. AAB
   c. A Random Walk Down Wall Street
   d. Internal rate of return

30. _____ are units of families of exchange-traded funds (ETFs) managed by Barclays Global Investors. The first _____ were known as WEBS but were since rebranded.

Each _____ fund tracks a bond or stock market index.

   a. IShares
   b. ABN Amro
   c. A Random Walk Down Wall Street
   d. AAB

31. In finance, _____, also known as return on investment is the ratio of money gained or lost on an investment relative to the amount of money invested. The amount of money gained or lost may be referred to as interest, profit/loss, gain/loss, or net income/loss. The money invested may be referred to as the asset, capital, principal, or the cost basis of the investment.
   a. Rate of return
   b. Composiition of Creditors
   c. Stock or scrip dividends
   d. Doctrine of the Proper Law

32. _____ is exchange of capital, goods, and services across international borders or territories. In most countries, it represents a significant share of gross domestic product (GDP.) While _____ has been present throughout much of history , its economic, social, and political importance has been on the rise in recent centuries.

Chapter 13. International Equity Markets, 123

a. Index number
c. International trade
b. OTC Bulletin Board
d. United States Treasury security

33. An _____ represents the ownership in the shares of a foreign company trading on US financial markets. The stock of many non-US companies trades on US exchanges through the use of _____s. _____s enable US investors to buy shares in foreign companies without undertaking cross-border transactions.

a. AAB
c. ABN Amro
b. A Random Walk Down Wall Street
d. American depository receipt

34. In business and finance, a _____ (also referred to as equity _____) of stock means a _____ of ownership in a corporation (company.) In the plural, stocks is often used as a synonym for _____s especially in the United States, but it is less commonly used that way outside of North America.

In the United Kingdom, South Africa, and Australia, stock can also refer to completely different financial instruments such as government bonds or, less commonly, to all kinds of marketable securities.

a. Procter ' Gamble
c. Share
b. Bucket shop
d. Margin

35. In business, a _____ is the purchase of one company (the target) by another (the acquirer or bidder). In the UK the term refers to the acquisition of a public company whose shares are listed on a stock exchange, in contrast to the acquisition of a private company.

Before a bidder makes an offer for another company, it usually first informs that company's board of directors.

a. Takeover
c. 4-4-5 Calendar
b. Stock swap
d. 529 plan

36. A _____ is a payment made by a corporation to its shareholder members. When a corporation earns a profit or surplus, that money can be put to two uses: it can either be re-invested in the business (called retained earnings), or it can be paid to the shareholders as a _____. Many corporations retain a portion of their earnings and pay the remainder as a _____.

a. Dividend yield
c. Special dividend
b. Dividend puzzle
d. Dividend

37. A _____ is a certificate issued by a depository bank, which purchases shares of foreign companies and deposits it on the account. _____s represent ownership of an underlying number of shares.

They facilitate trade of shares, and are commonly used to invest in companies from developing or emerging markets.

a. Special journals
c. Short positions
b. The Security Industry Association
d. Global depository receipt

Chapter 13. International Equity Markets,

38. The phrase _____ refers to the aspect of corporate strategy, corporate finance and management dealing with the buying, selling and combining of different companies that can aid, finance, or help a growing company in a given industry grow rapidly without having to create another business entity.

An acquisition, also known as a takeover, is the buying of one company (the 'target') by another. An acquisition may be friendly or hostile.

- a. Mergers and acquisitions
- b. 4-4-5 Calendar
- c. 7-Eleven
- d. 529 plan

39. The _____ is where currency trading takes place. It is where banks and other official institutions facilitate the buying and selling of foreign currencies. FX transactions typically involve one party purchasing a quantity of one currency in exchange for paying a quantity of another.
- a. Floating exchange rate
- b. Foreign exchange market
- c. Spot market
- d. Foreign exchange option

40. _____ is the standard framework of guidelines for financial accounting used in the United States of America. It includes the standards, conventions, and rules accountants follow in recording and summarizing transactions, and in the preparation of financial statements. _____ are now issued by the Financial Accounting Standards Board (FASB).
- a. Depreciation
- b. Net income
- c. Revenue
- d. Generally Accepted Accounting Principles

41. _____ refers to the various forms of financial support and financial transactions used in international trade. _____ uses a range of instruments to provide finance to exporters and importers, including documentary credits such as letters of credit.

While a seller (the exporter) can require the purchaser (an importer) to prepay for goods shipped, the purchaser (importer) may wish to reduce risk by requiring the seller to document that the goods have been shipped.

- a. Debtor-in-possession financing
- b. Trade finance
- c. Forfaiting
- d. Free cash flow

42. In economics and finance, _____ is the practice of taking advantage of a price differential between two or more markets: striking a combination of matching deals that capitalize upon the imbalance, the profit being the difference between the market prices. When used by academics, an _____ is a transaction that involves no negative cash flow at any probabilistic or temporal state and a positive cash flow in at least one state; in simple terms, a risk-free profit.
- a. Initial margin
- b. Efficient-market hypothesis
- c. Arbitrage
- d. Issuer

43. _____ is a business valuation method. _____ is the net present value of a project if financed solely by ownership equity plus the present value of all the benefits of financing. Usually, the main benefit is a tax shield resulted from tax deductibility of interest payments. Another one can be a subsidized borrowing.
- a. ABN Amro
- b. A Random Walk Down Wall Street
- c. Adjusted present value
- d. AAB

Chapter 13. International Equity Markets, 125

44. In finance, the _____ between two currencies specifies how much one currency is worth in terms of the other. For example an _____ of 102 Japanese yen to the United States dollar means that JPY 102 is worth the same as USD 1. The foreign exchange market is one of the largest markets in the world.

a. ABN Amro
b. AAB
c. A Random Walk Down Wall Street
d. Exchange rate

45. _____, also called fair price (in a commonplace conflation of the two distinct concepts), is a concept used in finance and economics, defined as a rational and unbiased estimate of the potential market price of a good, service, or asset, taking into account such objective factors as:

- acquisition/production/distribution costs, replacement costs, or costs of close substitutes
- actual utility at a given level of development of social productive capability
- supply vs. demand

and subjective factors such as

- risk characteristics
- cost of capital
- individually perceived utility

In accounting, _____ is used as an estimate of the market value of an asset (or liability) for which a market price cannot be determined (usually because there is no established market for the asset.) Under GAAP (FAS 157), _____ is the amount at which the asset could be bought or sold in a current transaction between willing parties, or transferred to an equivalent party, other than in a liquidation sale. This is used for assets whose carrying value is based on mark-to-market valuations; for assets carried at historical cost, the _____ of the asset is not used. One example of where _____ is an issue is a College kitchen with a cost of $2 million which was built 5 years ago.

a. 4-4-5 Calendar
b. 529 plan
c. 7-Eleven
d. Fair Value

Chapter 14. Interest Rate and Currency Swaps,

1. In finance, a _____ is a derivative in which two counterparties agree to exchange one stream of cash flows against another stream. These streams are called the legs of the _____.

The cash flows are calculated over a notional principal amount, which is usually not exchanged between counterparties.

   a. Local volatility
   b. Volatility swap
   c. Volatility arbitrage
   d. Swap

2. _____ is a fee paid on borrowed assets. It is the price paid for the use of borrowed money, or, money earned by deposited funds. Assets that are sometimes lent with _____ include money, shares, consumer goods through hire purchase, major assets such as aircraft, and even entire factories in finance lease arrangements.
   a. AAB
   b. A Random Walk Down Wall Street
   c. Interest
   d. Insolvency

3. An _____ is the price a borrower pays for the use of money they do not own, and the return a lender receives for deferring the use of funds, by lending it to the borrower. _____s are normally expressed as a percentage rate over the period of one year.

_____s targets are also a vital tool of monetary policy and are used to control variables like investment, inflation, and unemployment.

   a. ABN Amro
   b. AAB
   c. Interest rate
   d. A Random Walk Down Wall Street

4. An _____ is a derivative in which one party exchanges a stream of interest payments for another party's stream of cash flows. _____s can be used by hedgers to manage their fixed or floating assets and liabilities. They can also be used by speculators to replicate unfunded bond exposures to profit from changes in interest rates.
   a. Equity swap
   b. Implied volatility
   c. International Swaps and Derivatives Association
   d. Interest rate swap

5. In finance, a _____ is a debt security, in which the authorized issuer owes the holders a debt and, depending on the terms of the _____, is obliged to pay interest (the coupon) and/or to repay the principal at a later date, termed maturity.

Thus a _____ is a loan: the issuer is the borrower, the _____ holder is the lender, and the coupon is the interest. _____s provide the borrower with external funds to finance long-term investments, or, in the case of government _____s, to finance current expenditure.

   a. Bond
   b. Convertible bond
   c. Catastrophe bonds
   d. Puttable bond

6. The _____ is a financial market where participants buy and sell debt securities, usually in the form of bonds. As of 2006, the size of the international _____ is an estimated $45 trillion, of which the size of the outstanding U.S. _____ debt was $25.2 trillion.

Nearly all of the $923 billion average daily trading volume in the U.S. _____ takes place between broker-dealers and large institutions in a decentralized, over-the-counter market.

   a. 4-4-5 Calendar
   c. Fixed income
   b. Bond market
   d. 529 plan

7. The _____ of monetary management established the rules for commercial and financial relations among the world's major industrial states in the mid 20th Century. The _____ was the first example of a fully negotiated monetary order intended to govern monetary relations among independent nation-states.

Preparing to rebuild the international economic system as World War II was still raging, 730 delegates from all 44 Allied nations gathered at the Mount Washington Hotel in Bretton Woods, New Hampshire, United States, for the United Nations Monetary and Financial Conference.

   a. Cash budget
   c. The Hong Kong Securities Institute
   b. Bretton Woods system
   d. Fixed Asset Register

8. A _____ is a foreign exchange agreement between two parties to exchange principal and fixed rate interest payments on a loan in one currency for principal and fixed rate interest payments on an equal (regarding net present value) loan in another currency. They are motivated by comparative advantage.
   a. Foreign exchange market
   c. Currency pair
   b. Forex swap
   d. Currency swap

9. A _____ is an international bond that is denominated in a currency not native to the country where it is issued. It can be categorised according to the currency in which it is issued. London is one of the centers of the _____ market, but _____s may be traded throughout the world - for example in Singapore or Tokyo.
   a. Education production function
   c. Economic entity
   b. Interest rate option
   d. Eurobond

10. A _____ is a firm that quotes both a buy and a sell price in a financial instrument or commodity, hoping to make a profit on the bid/offer spread, or turn.

In foreign exchange trading, where most deals are conducted over-the-counter and are, therefore, completely virtual, the _____ sells to and buys from its clients. Hence, the client's loss and the spread is the _____ firm's profit, which gets thus compensated for the effort of providing liquidity in a competitive market.

   a. 4-4-5 Calendar
   c. 7-Eleven
   b. Market maker
   d. 529 plan

11. The _____ is a bank that provides financial and technical assistance to developing countries for development programs (e.g. bridges, roads, schools, etc.) with the stated goal of reducing poverty.

128 *Chapter 14. Interest Rate and Currency Swaps,*

The _____ differs from the _____ Group, in that the _____ comprises only two institutions:

- International Bank for Reconstruction and Development (IBRD)
- International Development Association (IDA)

Whereas the latter incorporates these two in addition to three more:

- International Finance Corporation (IFC)
- Multilateral Investment Guarantee Agency (MIGA)
- International Centre for Settlement of Investment Disputes (ICSID)

John Maynard Keynes (right) represented the UK at the conference, and Harry Dexter White represented the US.

The _____ was created following the ratification of the United Nations Monetary and Financial Conference | Bretton Woods agreement. The concept was originally conceived in July 1944 at the United Nations Monetary and Financial Conference.

a. World Bank
c. 4-4-5 Calendar
b. 7-Eleven
d. 529 plan

12. In economics, business, and accounting, a _____ is the value of money that has been used up to produce something, and hence is not available for use anymore. In business, the _____ may be one of acquisition, in which case the amount of money expended to acquire it is counted as _____. In this case, money is the input that is gone in order to acquire the thing.
   a. Fixed costs
   c. Sliding scale fees
   b. Marginal cost
   d. Cost

13. _____ is that which is owed; usually referencing assets owed, but the term can cover other obligations. In the case of assets, _____ is a means of using future purchasing power in the present before a summation has been earned. Some companies and corporations use _____ as a part of their overall corporate finance strategy.
   a. Debt
   c. Credit cycle
   b. Cross-collateralization
   d. Partial Payment

14. In business and finance, a _____ (also referred to as equity _____) of stock means a _____ of ownership in a corporation (company.) In the plural, stocks is often used as a synonym for _____ s especially in the United States, but it is less commonly used that way outside of North America.

In the United Kingdom, South Africa, and Australia, stock can also refer to completely different financial instruments such as government bonds or, less commonly, to all kinds of marketable securities.

a. Bucket shop
c. Procter ' Gamble
b. Margin
d. Share

15. _____ is the term used to describe deposits residing in banks that are located outside the borders of the country that issues the currency the deposit is denominated in. For example a deposit denominated in US dollars residing in a Japanese bank is a _____ deposit, or more specifically a Eurodollar deposit.

Key points are the location of the bank and the denomination of the currency, not the nationality of the bank or the owner of the deposit/loan.

a. Eurocurrency
c. AAB

b. A Random Walk Down Wall Street
d. ABN Amro

16. The _____ is a daily reference rate based on the interest rates at which banks borrow unsecured funds from banks in the London wholesale money market (or interbank market.) It is roughly comparable to the U.S. Federal funds rate.

During 1984 it became apparent that an increasing number of banks were trading actively in a variety of relatively new market instruments, notably interest rate swaps, foreign currency options and forward rate agreements.

a. Shanghai Interbank Offered Rate
c. Fixed interest

b. Risk-free interest rate
d. London Interbank Offered Rate

17. _____ arises during an interest rate swap in which two parties of different levels of creditworthiness experience different levels of interest rates of debt obligations. A positive _____ means that a swap is in the interest of both parties.

If Company A can borrow at a fixed rate of 12% or at LIBOR+2%, whilst Company B can borrow at a fixed rate of 10% or at LIBOR+1%, then there is a difference of 2% in fixed rate borrowings, but of only 1% in floating rate borrowings. A difference of 1% therefore exists as the _____, and a swap would benefit both parties. The benefits are experienced as, although Company B has an absolute advantage over Company A, Company A has a comparative advantage at floating borrowing.

a. Risk-neutral measure
c. Quality spread differential

b. Commodity price index
d. Local volatility

18. _____ is the value on a given date of a future payment or series of future payments, discounted to reflect the time value of money and other factors such as investment risk. _____ calculations are widely used in business and economics to provide a means to compare cash flows at different times on a meaningful 'like to like' basis.

The most commonly applied model of the time value of money is compound interest.

a. Present value of benefits
c. Negative gearing

b. Present value
d. Net present value

Chapter 14. Interest Rate and Currency Swaps,

19. _____ is the balance of the amounts of cash being received and paid by a business during a defined period of time, sometimes tied to a specific project. Measurement of _____ can be used

- to evaluate the state or performance of a business or project.
- to determine problems with liquidity. Being profitable does not necessarily mean being liquid. A company can fail because of a shortage of cash, even while profitable.
- to generate project rate of returns. The time of _____s into and out of projects are used as inputs to financial models such as internal rate of return, and net present value.
- to examine income or growth of a business when it is believed that accrual accounting concepts do not represent economic realities. Alternately, _____ can be used to 'validate' the net income generated by accrual accounting.

_____ as a generic term may be used differently depending on context, and certain _____ definitions may be adapted by analysts and users for their own uses. Common terms include operating _____ and free _____.

_____s can be classified into:

1. Operational _____s: Cash received or expended as a result of the company's core business activities.
2. Investment _____s: Cash received or expended through capital expenditure, investments or acquisitions.
3. Financing _____s: Cash received or expended as a result of financial activities, such as interests and dividends.

All three together - the net _____ - are necessary to reconcile the beginning cash balance to the ending cash balance. Loan draw downs or equity injections, that is just shifting of capital but no expenditure as such, are not considered in the net _____.

a. Shareholder value
b. Corporate finance
c. Real option
d. Cash flow

20. _____ is a business valuation method. _____ is the net present value of a project if financed solely by ownership equity plus the present value of all the benefits of financing. Usually, the main benefit is a tax shield resulted from tax deductibility of interest payments. Another one can be a subsidized borrowing.
 a. ABN Amro
 b. A Random Walk Down Wall Street
 c. AAB
 d. Adjusted present value

21. The institution most often referenced by the word '_____' is a public or publicly traded _____, the shares of which are traded on a public stock exchange (e.g., the New York Stock Exchange or Nasdaq in the United States) where shares of stock of _____s are bought and sold by and to the general public. Most of the largest businesses in the world are publicly traded _____s. However, the majority of _____s are said to be closely held, privately held or close _____s, meaning that no ready market exists for the trading of shares.
 a. Federal Home Loan Mortgage Corporation
 b. Depository Trust Company
 c. Corporation
 d. Protect

Chapter 14. Interest Rate and Currency Swaps, 131

22. _____ is the branch of economics that studies the dynamics of exchange rates, foreign investment, and how these affect international trade. It also studies international projects, international investments and capital flows, and trade deficits. It includes the study of futures, options and currency swaps.

a. AAB
b. ABN Amro
c. International Finance
d. A Random Walk Down Wall Street

23. A _____ is a fungible, negotiable instrument representing financial value. They are broadly categorized into debt securities (such as banknotes, bonds and debentures), and equity securities; e.g., common stocks. The company or other entity issuing the _____ is called the issuer.

a. Book entry
b. Tracking stock
c. Securities lending
d. Security

24. A _____ is a private or public market for the trading of company stock and derivatives of company stock at an agreed price; these are securities listed on a stock exchange as well as those only traded privately.

The size of the world _____ is estimated at about $36.6 trillion US at the beginning of October 2008 . The world derivatives market has been estimated at about $480 trillion face or nominal value, 12 times the size of the entire world economy.

a. Anton Gelonkin
b. Andrew Tobias
c. Adolph Coors
d. Stock Market

25. A _____ is a corporation, especially a commercial bank, organized to perform the fiduciary functions of trusts and agencies. It is normally owned by one of three types of structures: an independent partnership, a bank, or a law firm, each of which specializes in being a trustee of various kinds of trusts and in managing estates.

a. Mutual fund
b. Person-to-person lending
c. Trust Company
d. Savings and loan association

26. _____ in finance is the risk associated with imperfect hedging using futures. It could arise because of the difference between the asset whose price is to be hedged and the asset underlying the derivative, or because of a mismatch between the expiration date of the futures and the actual selling date of the asset.

Under these conditions, the spot price of the asset, and the futures price, do not converge on the expiration date of the future.

a. Liquidity risk
b. Basis risk
c. Credit risk
d. Currency risk

27. _____ is the provision of resources (such as granting a loan) by one party to another party where that second party does not reimburse the first party immediately, thereby generating a debt, and instead arranges either to repay or return those resources (or material(s) of equal value) at a later date. The first party is called a creditor, also known as a lender, while the second party is called a debtor, also known as a borrower.

Movements of financial capital are normally dependent on either _____ or equity transfers.

Chapter 14. Interest Rate and Currency Swaps,

a. Credit
c. Comparable
b. Clearing house
d. Warrant

28. _____ is the risk of loss due to a debtor's non-payment of a loan or other line of credit (either the principal or interest (coupon) or both)

Most lenders employ their own models (credit scorecards) to rank potential and existing customers according to risk, and then apply appropriate strategies. With products such as unsecured personal loans or mortgages, lenders charge a higher price for higher risk customers and vice versa. With revolving products such as credit cards and overdrafts, risk is controlled through careful setting of credit limits.

a. Liquidity risk
c. Market risk
b. Transaction risk
d. Credit risk

29. A _____ is a financial contract whose value is derived from the value of something else (known as the underlying.) The underlying on which a _____ is based can be an asset, weather conditions bonds or other forms of credit.
a. 7-Eleven
c. 529 plan
b. Derivative
d. 4-4-5 Calendar

30. The _____ is a trade organization of participants in the market for over-the-counter derivatives. It is headquartered in New York, and has created a standardized contract (Master Agreement) to enter into derivatives transactions. There are currently two versions of the ISDA Master Agreement: the 1992 edition and the 2002 edition.
a. Equity swap
c. Interest rate derivative
b. Open interest
d. International Swaps and Derivatives Association

31. The _____ or Plaza Agreement was an agreement between the governments of France, West Germany, Japan, the United States and the United Kingdom, agreeing to depreciate the US dollar in relation to the Japanese yen and German Deutsche Mark by intervening in currency markets. The five governments signed the accord on September 22, 1985 at the Plaza Hotel in New York City.

The exchange rate value of the dollar versus the yen declined by 51% from 1985 to 1987.

a. Plaza Accord
c. 7-Eleven
b. 529 plan
d. 4-4-5 Calendar

32. _____ is the risk (variability in value) borne by an interest-bearing asset, such as a loan or a bond, due to variability of interest rates. In general, as rates rise, the price of a fixed rate bond will fall, and vice versa. _____ is commonly measured by the bond's duration.
a. A Random Walk Down Wall Street
c. Official bank rate
b. Interest rate risk
d. International Fisher effect

33. _____ mature in one year or less. Like zero-coupon bonds, they do not pay interest prior to maturity; instead they are sold at a discount of the par value to create a positive yield to maturity. Many regard _____ as the least risky investment available to U.S. investors.

a. 4-4-5 Calendar
c. Treasury securities
b. Treasury Inflation Protected Securities
d. Treasury bills

Chapter 15. International Portfolio Investment,

1. The _____ was a period of financial crisis that gripped much of Asia beginning in July 1997, and raised fears of a worldwide economic meltdown (financial contagion).

The crisis started in Thailand with the financial collapse of the Thai baht caused by the decision of the Thai government to float the baht, cutting its peg to the USD, after exhaustive efforts to support it in the face of a severe financial overextension that was in part real estate driven. At the time, Thailand had acquired a burden of foreign debt that made the country effectively bankrupt even before the collapse of its currency.

   a. Internal control
   b. OTC Bulletin Board
   c. International trade
   d. Asian Financial Crisis

2. _____ is the removal or simplification of government rules and regulations that constrain the operation of market forces. _____ does not mean elimination of laws against fraud, but eliminating or reducing government control of how business is done, thereby moving toward a more free market.

The stated rationale for '_____' is often that fewer and simpler regulations will lead to a raised level of competitiveness, therefore higher productivity, more efficiency and lower prices overall.

   a. Supply shock
   b. Value added
   c. Demand shock
   d. Deregulation

3. _____ is the branch of economics that studies the dynamics of exchange rates, foreign investment, and how these affect international trade. It also studies international projects, international investments and capital flows, and trade deficits. It includes the study of futures, options and currency swaps.
   a. A Random Walk Down Wall Street
   b. ABN Amro
   c. International finance
   d. AAB

4. In economics and finance, _____ represents passive holdings of securities such as foreign stocks, bonds, or other financial assets, none of which entails active management or control of the securities' issuer by the investor; where such control exists, it is known as foreign direct investment. Generally, this means the investor holds less than 10% of the total shares or less than the amount needed to hold the majority vote.

Some examples of _____ are:

- purchase of shares in a foreign company.
- purchase of bonds issued by a foreign government.
- acquisition of assets in a foreign country.

Factors affecting international _____:

- tax rates on interest or dividends (investors will normally prefer countries where the tax rates are relatively low)
- interest rates (money tends to flow to countries with high interest rates)
- exchange rates (foreign investors may be attracted if the local currency is expected to strengthen)

_____ is part of the capital account on the balance of payments statistics.

a. Portfolio investment
b. Divestment
c. Portable alpha
d. Tactical asset allocation

5. In economics, the _____, measures the payments that flow between any individual country and all other countries. It is used to summarize all international economic transactions for that country during a specific time period, usually a year. The _____ is determined by the country's exports and imports of goods, services, and financial capital, as well as financial transfers.

a. Gross national product
b. 4-4-5 Calendar
c. Purchasing power parity
d. Balance of payments

6. _____ is the set of processes, customs, policies, laws and institutions affecting the way a corporation is directed, administered or controlled. _____ also includes the relationships among the many stakeholders involved and the goals for which the corporation is governed. The principal stakeholders are the shareholders, management and the board of directors.

a. Patent
b. Due diligence
c. Foreign Corrupt Practices Act
d. Corporate governance

7. In economics, a _____ is a mechanism that allows people to easily buy and sell (trade) financial securities (such as stocks and bonds), commodities (such as precious metals or agricultural goods), and other fungible items of value at low transaction costs and at prices that reflect the efficient-market hypothesis.

_____s have evolved significantly over several hundred years and are undergoing constant innovation to improve liquidity.

Both general markets (where many commodities are traded) and specialized markets (where only one commodity is traded) exist.

a. Delta hedging
b. Financial market
c. Cost of carry
d. Secondary market

8. The _____ or Plaza Agreement was an agreement between the governments of France, West Germany, Japan, the United States and the United Kingdom, agreeing to depreciate the US dollar in relation to the Japanese yen and German Deutsche Mark by intervening in currency markets. The five governments signed the accord on September 22, 1985 at the Plaza Hotel in New York City.

The exchange rate value of the dollar versus the yen declined by 51% from 1985 to 1987.

a. 7-Eleven
b. 529 plan
c. 4-4-5 Calendar
d. Plaza Accord

9. In business, _____ is income that a company receives from its normal business activities, usually from the sale of goods and services to customers. Some companies also receive _____ from interest, dividends or royalties paid to them by other companies. _____ may refer to business income in general, or it may refer to the amount, in a monetary unit, received during a period of time, as in 'Last year, Company X had _____ of $32 million.'

In many countries, including the UK, _____ is referred to as turnover.

a. Revenue
b. Furniture, Fixtures and Equipment
c. Matching principle
d. Bottom line

10. In probability theory and statistics, _____ indicates the strength and direction of a linear relationship between two random variables. That is in contrast with the usage of the term in colloquial speech, which denotes any relationship, not necessarily linear. In general statistical usage, _____ or co-relation refers to the departure of two random variables from independence.
   a. Geometric mean
   b. Probability distribution
   c. Variance
   d. Correlation

11. _____ in finance is a risk management technique, related to hedging, that mixes a wide variety of investments within a portfolio. Because the fluctuations of a single security have less impact on a diverse portfolio, _____ minimizes the risk from any one investment.

A simple example of _____ is the following: On a particular island the entire economy consists of two companies: one that sells umbrellas and another that sells sunscreen.

   a. Diversification
   b. 529 plan
   c. 4-4-5 Calendar
   d. 7-Eleven

12. A _____ is a private or public market for the trading of company stock and derivatives of company stock at an agreed price; these are securities listed on a stock exchange as well as those only traded privately.

The size of the world _____ is estimated at about $36.6 trillion US at the beginning of October 2008. The world derivatives market has been estimated at about $480 trillion face or nominal value, 12 times the size of the entire world economy.

   a. Adolph Coors
   b. Anton Gelonkin
   c. Andrew Tobias
   d. Stock market

13. In finance, _____ is that risk which is common to an entire market and not to any individual entity or component thereof. It should be distinguished from systemic risk which is the risk that the entire financial system will collapse as a result of some catastrophic event.

Risks can be reduced in four main ways: Avoidance, Reduction, Retention and Transfer.

   a. Capital surplus
   b. Conglomerate merger
   c. Primary market
   d. Systematic risk

14. A _____, reserve bank, or monetary authority is the entity responsible for the monetary policy of a country or of a group of member states. It is a bank that can lend money to other banks in times of need. Its primary responsibility is to maintain the stability of the national currency and money supply, but more active duties include controlling subsidized-loan interest rates, and acting as a lender of last resort to the banking sector during times of financial crisis (private banks often being integral to the national financial system.)

Chapter 15. International Portfolio Investment, 137

    a. 4-4-5 Calendar
    b. 529 plan
    c. 7-Eleven
    d. Central bank

15. The institution most often referenced by the word '_____' is a public or publicly traded _____, the shares of which are traded on a public stock exchange (e.g., the New York Stock Exchange or Nasdaq in the United States) where shares of stock of _____s are bought and sold by and to the general public. Most of the largest businesses in the world are publicly traded _____s. However, the majority of _____s are said to be closely held, privately held or close _____s, meaning that no ready market exists for the trading of shares.
    a. Depository Trust Company
    b. Protect
    c. Federal Home Loan Mortgage Corporation
    d. Corporation

16. In financial accounting, the term _____ is most commonly used to describe any part of shareholders' equity, except for basic share capital. Sometimes, the term is used instead of the term provision; such a use, however, is inconsistent with the terminology suggested by International Accounting Standards Board. For more information about provisions, see provision (accounting.)
    a. FIFO and LIFO accounting
    b. Closing entries
    c. Treasury stock
    d. Reserve

17. _____ is a mathematical science pertaining to the collection, analysis, interpretation or explanation, and presentation of data. It also provides tools for prediction and forecasting based on data. It is applicable to a wide variety of academic disciplines, from the natural and social sciences to the humanities, government and business.
    a. Mean
    b. Covariance
    c. Statistics
    d. Sample size

18. _____ most frequently refers to the standard deviation of the continuously compounded returns of a financial instrument with a specific time horizon. It is often used to quantify the risk of the instrument over that time period. _____ is typically expressed in annualized terms, and it may either be an absolute number ($5) or a fraction of the mean (5%).
    a. Currency swap
    b. Portfolio insurance
    c. Seasoned equity offering
    d. Volatility

19. The _____ is an American stock exchange. It is the largest electronic screen-based equity securities trading market in the United States. With approximately 3,200 companies, it has more trading volume per day than any other stock exchange in the world.
    a. 4-4-5 Calendar
    b. 529 plan
    c. 7-Eleven
    d. NASDAQ

20. The _____ is the rate that a company is expected to pay to finance its assets. WACC is the minimum return that a company must earn on existing asset base to satisfy its creditors, owners, and other providers of capital.

Companies raise money from a number of sources: common equity, preferred equity, straight debt, convertible debt, exchangeable debt, warrants, options, pension liabilities, executive stock options, governmental subsidies, and so on.

    a. Capital intensity
    b. Weighted average cost of capital
    c. 4-4-5 Calendar
    d. Cost of capital

21. In economics, business, and accounting, a _____ is the value of money that has been used up to produce something, and hence is not available for use anymore. In business, the _____ may be one of acquisition, in which case the amount of money expended to acquire it is counted as _____. In this case, money is the input that is gone in order to acquire the thing.

a. Sliding scale fees
b. Marginal cost
c. Cost
d. Fixed costs

22. The _____ is an expected return that the provider of capital plans to earn on their investment.

Capital (money) used for funding a business should earn returns for the capital providers who risk their capital. For an investment to be worthwhile, the expected return on capital must be greater than the _____.

a. Capital intensity
b. Weighted average cost of capital
c. 4-4-5 Calendar
d. Cost of capital

23. A _____ is an international bond that is denominated in a currency not native to the country where it is issued. It can be categorised according to the currency in which it is issued. London is one of the centers of the _____ market, but _____s may be traded throughout the world - for example in Singapore or Tokyo.

a. Eurobond
b. Interest rate option
c. Economic entity
d. Education production function

24. In finance, the _____ between two currencies specifies how much one currency is worth in terms of the other. For example an _____ of 102 Japanese yen to the United States dollar means that JPY 102 is worth the same as USD 1. The foreign exchange market is one of the largest markets in the world.

a. A Random Walk Down Wall Street
b. AAB
c. Exchange rate
d. ABN Amro

25. _____ is a form of risk that arises from the change in price of one currency against another. Whenever investors or companies have assets or business operations across national borders, they face _____ if their positions are not hedged.

- Transaction risk is the risk that exchange rates will change unfavourably over time. It can be hedged against using forward currency contracts;
- Translation risk is an accounting risk, proportional to the amount of assets held in foreign currencies. Changes in the exchange rate over time will render a report inaccurate, and so assets are usually balanced by borrowings in that currency.

The exchange risk associated with a foreign denominated instrument is a key element in foreign investment. This risk flows from differential monetary policy and growth in real productivity, which results in differential inflation rates.

a. Tracking error
b. Market risk
c. Credit risk
d. Currency risk

Chapter 15. International Portfolio Investment, 139

26. In finance, a _____ is a debt security, in which the authorized issuer owes the holders a debt and, depending on the terms of the _____, is obliged to pay interest (the coupon) and/or to repay the principal at a later date, termed maturity.

Thus a _____ is a loan: the issuer is the borrower, the _____ holder is the lender, and the coupon is the interest. _____s provide the borrower with external funds to finance long-term investments, or, in the case of government _____s, to finance current expenditure.

a. Convertible bond
c. Catastrophe bonds
b. Puttable bond
d. Bond

27. The _____ is a financial market where participants buy and sell debt securities, usually in the form of bonds. As of 2006, the size of the international _____ is an estimated $45 trillion, of which the size of the outstanding U.S. _____ debt was $25.2 trillion.

Nearly all of the $923 billion average daily trading volume in the U.S. _____ takes place between broker-dealers and large institutions in a decentralized, over-the-counter market.

a. Fixed income
c. 4-4-5 Calendar
b. Bond market
d. 529 plan

28. A _____ is a professionally managed type of collective investment scheme that pools money from many investors and invests it in stocks, bonds, short-term money market instruments, and/or other securities. The _____ will have a fund manager that trades the pooled money on a regular basis. Currently, the worldwide value of all _____s totals more than $26 trillion.

Since 1940, there have been three basic types of investment companies in the United States: open-end funds, also known in the US as _____s; unit investment trusts (UITs); and closed-end funds.

a. Mutual fund
c. Net asset value
b. Financial intermediary
d. Trust company

29. An _____ represents the ownership in the shares of a foreign company trading on US financial markets. The stock of many non-US companies trades on US exchanges through the use of _____s. _____s enable US investors to buy shares in foreign companies without undertaking cross-border transactions.

a. ABN Amro
c. A Random Walk Down Wall Street
b. AAB
d. American depository receipt

30. The _____ is the market for securities, where companies and governments can raise longterm funds. The _____ includes the stock market and the bond market. Financial regulators, such as the U.S. Securities and Exchange Commission, oversee the _____s in their designated countries to ensure that investors are protected against fraud.

a. Capital market
c. Forward market
b. Delta neutral
d. Spot rate

31. _____ proposes how rational investors will use diversification to optimize their portfolios, and how a risky asset should be priced. The basic concepts of the theory are Markowitz diversification, the efficient frontier, capital asset pricing model, the alpha and beta coefficients, the Capital Market Line and the Securities Market Line.

_____ models an asset's return as a random variable, and models a portfolio as a weighted combination of assets so that the return of a portfolio is the weighted combination of the assets' returns.

   a. Payback period
   c. Consumer basket
   b. Market value
   d. Modern portfolio theory

32. In business and finance, a _____ (also referred to as equity _____) of stock means a _____ of ownership in a corporation (company.) In the plural, stocks is often used as a synonym for _____s especially in the United States, but it is less commonly used that way outside of North America.

In the United Kingdom, South Africa, and Australia, stock can also refer to completely different financial instruments such as government bonds or, less commonly, to all kinds of marketable securities.

   a. Margin
   c. Share
   b. Bucket shop
   d. Procter ' Gamble

33. The term _____ is used to describe a nation's social, or business activity in the process of rapid industrialization. _____ are generally less-wealthy than the developed world, and are wealthier (or the wealthiest of) the developing world. According to The Economist many people find the term dated, but a new term has yet to gain much traction.
   a. ABN Amro
   c. Emerging markets
   b. AAB
   d. A Random Walk Down Wall Street

34. _____ is a term used to describe the value of an entity's assets less the value of its liabilities. The term is commonly used in relation to collective investment schemes. It may also be used as a synonym for the book value of a firm.
   a. Financial intermediary
   c. Net asset value
   b. Retail broker
   d. Passive management

35. A _____, securities exchange or (in Europe) bourse is a corporation or mutual organization which provides 'trading' facilities for stock brokers and traders, to trade stocks and other securities. _____s also provide facilities for the issue and redemption of securities as well as other financial instruments and capital events including the payment of income and dividends. The securities traded on a _____ include: shares issued by companies, unit trusts and other pooled investment products and bonds.
   a. 529 plan
   c. 7-Eleven
   b. Stock Exchange
   d. 4-4-5 Calendar

36. In business and accounting, _____s are everything of value that is owned by a person or company. The balance sheet of a firm records the monetary value of the _____s owned by the firm. The two major _____ classes are tangible _____s and intangible _____s.
   a. EBITDA
   c. Asset
   b. Income
   d. Accounts payable

Chapter 15. International Portfolio Investment, 141

37. _____ is the balance of the amounts of cash being received and paid by a business during a defined period of time, sometimes tied to a specific project. Measurement of _____ can be used

- to evaluate the state or performance of a business or project.
- to determine problems with liquidity. Being profitable does not necessarily mean being liquid. A company can fail because of a shortage of cash, even while profitable.
- to generate project rate of returns. The time of _____s into and out of projects are used as inputs to financial models such as internal rate of return, and net present value.
- to examine income or growth of a business when it is believed that accrual accounting concepts do not represent economic realities. Alternately, _____ can be used to 'validate' the net income generated by accrual accounting.

_____ as a generic term may be used differently depending on context, and certain _____ definitions may be adapted by analysts and users for their own uses. Common terms include operating _____ and free _____.

_____s can be classified into:

1. Operational _____s: Cash received or expended as a result of the company's core business activities.
2. Investment _____s: Cash received or expended through capital expenditure, investments or acquisitions.
3. Financing _____s: Cash received or expended as a result of financial activities, such as interests and dividends.

All three together - the net _____ - are necessary to reconcile the beginning cash balance to the ending cash balance. Loan draw downs or equity injections, that is just shifting of capital but no expenditure as such, are not considered in the net _____.

a. Corporate finance
c. Shareholder value
b. Real option
d. Cash flow

38. A '_____' is a 'Charge' that is paid to obtain the right to delay a payment. Essentially, the payer purchases the right to make a given payment in the future instead of in the Present. The '_____', or 'Charge' that must be paid to delay the payment, is simply the difference between what the payment amount would be if it were paid in the present and what the payment amount would be paid if it were paid in the future.
a. Value at risk
c. Risk modeling
b. Risk aversion
d. Discount

39. _____ is a business valuation method. _____ is the net present value of a project if financed solely by ownership equity plus the present value of all the benefits of financing. Usually, the main benefit is a tax shield resulted from tax deductibility of interest payments. Another one can be a subsidized borrowing.
a. AAB
c. A Random Walk Down Wall Street
b. Adjusted present value
d. ABN Amro

40. _____ is the value on a given date of a future payment or series of future payments, discounted to reflect the time value of money and other factors such as investment risk. _____ calculations are widely used in business and economics to provide a means to compare cash flows at different times on a meaningful 'like to like' basis.

The most commonly applied model of the time value of money is compound Interest.

a. Net present value
b. Negative gearing
c. Present value of benefits
d. Present value

41.

A _____ is a type of financial intermediary and a type of bank. Commercial banking is also known as business banking. It is a bank that provides checking accounts, savings accounts, and money market accounts and that accepts time deposits.

a. 529 plan
b. 7-Eleven
c. 4-4-5 Calendar
d. Commercial Bank

42. A _____ is a certificate issued by a depository bank, which purchases shares of foreign companies and deposits it on the account. _____s represent ownership of an underlying number of shares.

They facilitate trade of shares, and are commonly used to invest in companies from developing or emerging markets.

a. Special journals
b. The Security Industry Association
c. Short positions
d. Global depository receipt

43. An _____ is a company whose main business is holding securities of other companies purely for investment purposes. The _____ invests money on behalf of its shareholders who in turn share in the profits and losses.
a. A Random Walk Down Wall Street
b. Unit investment trust
c. Investment Company
d. AAB

44. In finance, a _____ is a position established in one market in an attempt to offset exposure to the price risk of an equal but opposite obligation or position in another market -- usually, but not always, in the context of one's commercial activity. Hedging is a strategy designed to minimize exposure to such business risks as a sharp contraction in demand for one's inventory, while still allowing the business to profit from producing and maintaining that inventory. A typical hedger might be a farmer with 2000 acres of unharvested wheat in the ground, who would rather tend his crop without the distraction of uncertain prices.
a. Hedge
b. 529 plan
c. 4-4-5 Calendar
d. 7-Eleven

45. A _____ is a private investment fund open to a limited range of investors that is permitted by regulators to undertake a wider range of activities than other investment funds and also pays a performance fee to its investment manager. Each fund will have its own strategy which determines the type of investments and the methods of investment it undertakes. _____s as a class invest in a broad range of investments extending over shares, debt, commodities and beyond.
a. 4-4-5 Calendar
b. 529 plan
c. 7-Eleven
d. Hedge fund

Chapter 15. International Portfolio Investment,

46. _____ is a term used in accounting, economics and finance to spread the cost of an asset over the span of several years.

In simple words we can say that _____ is the reduction in the value of an asset due to usage, passage of time, wear and tear, technological outdating or obsolescence, depletion or other such factors.

In accounting, _____ is a term used to describe any method of attributing the historical or purchase cost of an asset across its useful life, roughly corresponding to normal wear and tear.

 a. Matching principle
 b. Depreciation
 c. Deferred financing costs
 d. Bottom line

47. _____ was an arrangement established in 1979 under the Jenkins European Commission where most nations of the European Economic Community (EEC) linked their currencies to prevent large fluctuations relative to one another.

After the collapse of the Bretton Woods system in 1971, most of the EEC countries agreed in 1972 to maintain stable exchange rates by preventing exchange fluctuations of more than 2.25% (the European 'currency snake'.) In March 1979, this system was replaced by the _____, and the European Currency Unit (ECU) was defined.

 a. A Random Walk Down Wall Street
 b. Exchange Rate Mechanism
 c. Euro Interbank Offered Rate
 d. European Monetary System

48. A _____ secures the proper functioning of money by regulating economic agents, transaction types, and money supply.

They are traditionally formed by the policy decisions of individual governments and administrated as a domestic economic issue.

The current trend, however, is to use international trade and investment to alter the policy and legislation of individual governments.

 a. Payback period
 b. Pattern day trader
 c. Bond credit rating
 d. Monetary System

49. _____ is one of the authors of the Black-Scholes equation. In 1997 he was awarded the Nobel Memorial Prize in Economic Sciences for 'a new method to determine the value of derivatives'. The model provides the fundamental conceptual framework for valuing options, such as calls or puts, and is referred to as the Black-Scholes model, which has become the standard in financial markets globally.

 a. Robert James Shiller
 b. Andrew Tobias
 c. Adolph Coors
 d. Myron Samuel Scholes

50. A _____ is a fungible, negotiable instrument representing financial value. They are broadly categorized into debt securities (such as banknotes, bonds and debentures), and equity securities; e.g., common stocks. The company or other entity issuing the _____ is called the issuer.

a. Tracking stock
b. Book entry
c. Securities lending
d. Security

51. _____ in its classic form is defined as a company from one country making a physical investment into building a factory in another country. It is the establishment of an enterprise by a foreigner. Its definition can be extended to include investments made to acquire lasting interest in enterprises operating outside of the economy of the investor.
a. Foreign direct investment
b. Dow Jones ' Company
c. MicroPlace
d. Public company

52. _____ refers to any type of investment that yields a regular (or fixed) return.

For example, if you lend money to a borrower and the borrower has to pay interest once a month, you have been issued a fixed-income security. When a company does this, it is often called a bond or corporate bank debt (although preferred stock is also sometimes considered to be _____).

a. 529 plan
b. 4-4-5 Calendar
c. Bond market
d. Fixed income

53. In finance, a _____ is a standardized contract, to buy or sell a specified commodity of standardized quality at a certain date in the future, at a market determined price (the futures price.)

The price is determined by the instantaneous equilibrium between the forces of supply and demand among competing buy and sell orders on the exchange at the time of the purchase or sale of the contract.

In many cases, the items may be such non-traditional 'commodities' as foreign currencies, commercial or government paper [e.g., bonds], or 'baskets' of corporate equity ['stock indices'] or other financial instruments.

a. Repurchase agreement
b. Heston model
c. Financial future
d. Futures contract

54. _____, refers to consumption opportunity gained by an entity within a specified time frame, which is generally expressed in monetary terms. However, for households and individuals, '_____ is the sum of all the wages, salaries, profits, interests payments, rents and other forms of earnings received... in a given period of time.' For firms, _____ generally refers to net-profit: what remains of revenue after expenses have been subtracted.
a. OIBDA
b. Annual report
c. Accrual
d. Income

55. The _____ is published by The Economist as an informal way of measuring the purchasing power parity (PPP) between two currencies and provides a test of the extent to which market exchange rates result in goods costing the same in different countries. It 'seeks to make exchange-rate theory a bit more digestible'.
a. 4-4-5 Calendar
b. Divisia index
c. 529 plan
d. Big Mac index

Chapter 15. International Portfolio Investment, 145

56. _____s are deposits denominated in United States dollars at banks outside the United States, and thus are not under the jurisdiction of the Federal Reserve. Consequently, such deposits are subject to much less regulation than similar deposits within the United States, allowing for higher margins. There is nothing 'European' about _____ deposits; a US dollar-denominated deposit in Tokyo or Caracas would likewise be deemed _____ deposits.
- a. ABN Amro
- b. A Random Walk Down Wall Street
- c. AAB
- d. Eurodollar

57. The _____ is based on common law stemming from the 1830 Massachusetts court decision - Harvard College v. Armory, 9 Pick. (26 Mass.)
- a. Prudent man rule
- b. SIPC
- c. Rule 144A
- d. Williams Act

58. In economics and related disciplines, a _____ is a cost incurred in making an economic exchange. For example, most people, when buying or selling a stock, must pay a commission to their broker; that commission is a _____ of doing the stock deal. Or consider buying a banana from a store; to purchase the banana, your costs will be not only the price of the banana itself, but also the energy and effort it requires to find out which of the various banana products you prefer, where to get them and at what price, the cost of traveling from your house to the store and back, the time waiting in line, and the effort of the paying itself; the costs above and beyond the cost of the banana are the _____s.
- a. Marginal cost
- b. Variable costs
- c. Fixed costs
- d. Transaction cost

59. A _____ is an exchange of promises between two or more parties to do an act which is enforceable in a court of law. It is where an unqualified offer meets a qualified acceptance and the parties reach Consensus ad Idem. The parties must have the necessary capacity to _____ and the _____ must not be either trifling, indeterminate, impossible or illegal.
- a. 529 plan
- b. 7-Eleven
- c. Contract
- d. 4-4-5 Calendar

60. In economics, _____ is a rise in the general level of prices of goods and services in an economy over a period of time. The term '_____' once referred to increases in the money supply (monetary _____); however, economic debates about the relationship between money supply and price levels have led to its primary use today in describing price _____. _____ can also be described as a decline in the real value of money--a loss of purchasing power in the medium of exchange which is also the monetary unit of account.
- a. AAB
- b. ABN Amro
- c. A Random Walk Down Wall Street
- d. Inflation

61. _____ refers to a business or organization attempting to acquire goods or services to accomplish the goals of the enterprise. Though there are several organizations that attempt to set standards in the _____ process, processes can vary greatly between organizations. Typically the word '_____' is not used interchangeably with the word 'procurement', since procurement typically includes Expediting, Supplier Quality, and Traffic and Logistics (T'L) in addition to _____.
- a. 529 plan
- b. 4-4-5 Calendar
- c. 7-Eleven
- d. Purchasing

62. _____ is the value of goods/services compared to the amount paid with a currency. Currency can be either a commodity money, like gold or silver, or fiat currency like US dollars which are the world reserve currency. As Adam Smith noted, having money gives one the ability to 'command' others' labor, so _____ to some extent is power over other people, to the extent that they are willing to trade their labor or goods for money or currency.

   a. 529 plan   b. 4-4-5 Calendar
   c. 7-Eleven   d. Purchasing power

63. The _____ theory uses the long-term equilibrium exchange rate of two currencies to equalize their purchasing power. Developed by Gustav Cassel in 1920, it is based on the law of one price: the theory states that, in ideally efficient markets, identical goods should have only one price.

This purchasing power SEM rate equalizes the purchasing power of different currencies in their home countries for a given basket of goods.

   a. Gross national product   b. 4-4-5 Calendar
   c. TED spread   d. Purchasing power parity

64. The _____ is where currency trading takes place. It is where banks and other official institutions facilitate the buying and selling of foreign currencies. FX transactions typically involve one party purchasing a quantity of one currency in exchange for paying a quantity of another.

   a. Foreign exchange option   b. Floating exchange rate
   c. Spot market   d. Foreign exchange market

Chapter 16. Foreign Direct Investment and Cross-Border Acquisitions, 147

1. The _____ is a private, not-for-profit organization whose primary purpose is to develop generally accepted accounting principles (GAAP) within the United States in the public's interest. The Securities and Exchange Commission (SEC) designated the _____ as the organization responsible for setting accounting standards for public companies in the U.S. It was created in 1973, replacing the Accounting Principles Board and the Committee on Accounting Procedure of the American Institute of Certified Public Accountants. The _____'s mission is 'to establish and improve standards of financial accounting and reporting for the guidance and education of the public, including issuers, auditors, and users of financial information.'

The _____ is not a governmental body.

   a. FASB
   b. MRU Holdings
   c. Credit karma
   d. PlaNet Finance

2. _____ in its classic form is defined as a company from one country making a physical investment into building a factory in another country. It is the establishment of an enterprise by a foreigner. Its definition can be extended to include investments made to acquire lasting interest in enterprises operating outside of the economy of the investor.
   a. Public company
   b. MicroPlace
   c. Dow Jones ' Company
   d. Foreign direct investment

3. The phrase _____ refers to the aspect of corporate strategy, corporate finance and management dealing with the buying, selling and combining of different companies that can aid, finance, or help a growing company in a given industry grow rapidly without having to create another business entity.

An acquisition, also known as a takeover, is the buying of one company (the 'target') by another. An acquisition may be friendly or hostile.

   a. Mergers and acquisitions
   b. 7-Eleven
   c. 4-4-5 Calendar
   d. 529 plan

4. The _____ was a period of financial crisis that gripped much of Asia beginning in July 1997, and raised fears of a worldwide economic meltdown (financial contagion).

The crisis started in Thailand with the financial collapse of the Thai baht caused by the decision of the Thai government to float the baht, cutting its peg to the USD, after exhaustive efforts to support it in the face of a severe financial overextension that was in part real estate driven. At the time, Thailand had acquired a burden of foreign debt that made the country effectively bankrupt even before the collapse of its currency.

   a. International trade
   b. OTC Bulletin Board
   c. Internal control
   d. Asian Financial Crisis

5. The institution most often referenced by the word '_____' is a public or publicly traded _____, the shares of which are traded on a public stock exchange (e.g., the New York Stock Exchange or Nasdaq in the United States) where shares of stock of _____s are bought and sold by and to the general public. Most of the largest businesses in the world are publicly traded _____s. However, the majority of _____s are said to be closely held, privately held or close _____s, meaning that no ready market exists for the trading of shares.

Chapter 16. Foreign Direct Investment and Cross-Border Acquisitions,

a. Protect
b. Depository Trust Company
c. Federal Home Loan Mortgage Corporation
d. Corporation

6. _____ is the provision of resources (such as granting a loan) by one party to another party where that second party does not reimburse the first party immediately, thereby generating a debt, and instead arranges either to repay or return those resources (or material(s) of equal value) at a later date. The first party is called a creditor, also known as a lender, while the second party is called a debtor, also known as a borrower.

Movements of financial capital are normally dependent on either _____ or equity transfers.

a. Clearing house
b. Credit
c. Comparable
d. Warrant

7. The _____ of 1977 (15 U.S.C. §§ 78dd-1, et seq.) is a United States federal law known primarily for two of its main provisions, one that addresses accounting transparency requirements under the Securities Exchange Act of 1934 and another concerning bribery of foreign officials.

a. Fair debt collection
b. Federal Deposit Insurance Corporation Improvement Act
c. Competition law
d. Foreign Corrupt Practices Act

8. In economics, the _____, measures the payments that flow between any individual country and all other countries. It is used to summarize all international economic transactions for that country during a specific time period, usually a year. The _____ is determined by the country's exports and imports of goods, services, and financial capital, as well as financial transfers.

a. Gross national product
b. 4-4-5 Calendar
c. Purchasing power parity
d. Balance of payments

9. In economics, _____ is a monetary standard in which the value of the monetary unit is defined as equivalent either to a certain quantity of gold or to a certain quantity of silver. Such a system effectively establishes a fixed rate of exchange for the two metals. The merits of the system were the subject of debate in the late 19th century.

a. 4-4-5 Calendar
b. 529 plan
c. 7-Eleven
d. Bimetallism

10. In finance, a _____ is a debt security, in which the authorized issuer owes the holders a debt and, depending on the terms of the _____, is obliged to pay interest (the coupon) and/or to repay the principal at a later date, termed maturity.

Thus a _____ is a loan: the issuer is the borrower, the _____ holder is the lender, and the coupon is the interest. _____s provide the borrower with external funds to finance long-term investments, or, in the case of government _____s, to finance current expenditure.

a. Puttable bond
b. Convertible bond
c. Catastrophe bonds
d. Bond

11. A _____ is a bond issued by a corporation. The term is usually applied to longer-term debt instruments, generally with a maturity date falling at least a year after their issue date. (The term 'commercial paper' is sometimes used for instruments with a shorter maturity.)
   a. Corporate bond
   b. Government bond
   c. Brady bonds
   d. Serial bond

12. In business and finance, a _____ (also referred to as equity _____) of stock means a _____ of ownership in a corporation (company.) In the plural, stocks is often used as a synonym for _____s especially in the United States, but it is less commonly used that way outside of North America.

In the United Kingdom, South Africa, and Australia, stock can also refer to completely different financial instruments such as government bonds or, less commonly, to all kinds of marketable securities.

   a. Share
   b. Procter ' Gamble
   c. Bucket shop
   d. Margin

13. In business and accounting, _____s are everything of value that is owned by a person or company. The balance sheet of a firm records the monetary value of the _____s owned by the firm. The two major _____ classes are tangible _____s and intangible _____s.
   a. Accounts payable
   b. EBITDA
   c. Income
   d. Asset

14. _____ in finance is a risk management technique, related to hedging, that mixes a wide variety of investments within a portfolio. Because the fluctuations of a single security have less impact on a diverse portfolio, _____ minimizes the risk from any one investment.

A simple example of _____ is the following: On a particular island the entire economy consists of two companies: one that sells umbrellas and another that sells sunscreen.

   a. 4-4-5 Calendar
   b. 7-Eleven
   c. 529 plan
   d. Diversification

15. _____ are defined as identifiable non-monetary assets that cannot be seen, touched or physically measured, which are created through time and/or effort and that are identifiable as a separate asset. There are two primary forms of intangibles - legal intangibles (such as trade secrets (e.g., customer lists), copyrights, patents, trademarks, and goodwill) and competitive intangibles (such as knowledge activities (know-how, knowledge), collaboration activities, leverage activities, and structural activities.) Legal intangibles generate legal property rights defensible in a court of law.
   a. A Random Walk Down Wall Street
   b. AAB
   c. ABN Amro
   d. Intangible assets

16. In economics and finance, _____ represents passive holdings of securities such as foreign stocks, bonds, or other financial assets, none of which entails active management or control of the securities' issuer by the investor; where such control exists, it is known as foreign direct investment. Generally, this means the investor holds less than 10% of the total shares or less than the amount needed to hold the majority vote.

Some examples of _____ are:

- purchase of shares in a foreign company.
- purchase of bonds issued by a foreign government.
- acquisition of assets in a foreign country.

Factors affecting international _____:

- tax rates on interest or dividends (investors will normally prefer countries where the tax rates are relatively low)
- interest rates (money tends to flow to countries with high interest rates)
- exchange rates (foreign investors may be attracted if the local currency is expected to strengthen)

_____ is part of the capital account on the balance of payments statistics.

a. Portfolio investment
c. Tactical asset allocation
b. Divestment
d. Portable alpha

17. _____ or product life cycle is the course of a product's sales and profits over time. The five stages of each _____ are product development, introduction, growth, maturity and decline.

Product Life Cycle deals with the life of a product in the market with respect to business or commercial costs and sales measures.

a. 529 plan
c. 4-4-5 Calendar
b. 7-Eleven
d. Product lifecycle

18. _____ refers to the various forms of financial support and financial transactions used in international trade. _____ uses a range of instruments to provide finance to exporters and importers, including documentary credits such as letters of credit.

While a seller (the exporter) can require the purchaser (an importer) to prepay for goods shipped, the purchaser (importer) may wish to reduce risk by requiring the seller to document that the goods have been shipped.

a. Forfaiting
c. Debtor-in-possession financing
b. Free cash flow
d. Trade finance

19. In microeconomics and management, the term _____ describes a style of management control. Vertically integrated companies are united through a hierarchy with a common owner. Usually each member of the hierarchy produces a different product or (market-specific) service, and the products combine to satisfy a common need.

a. 529 plan
c. 4-4-5 Calendar
b. 7-Eleven
d. Vertical integration

Chapter 16. Foreign Direct Investment and Cross-Border Acquisitions, 151

20. In economics, _____ refers to the ability of a party to produce a good or service using fewer real resources than another entity producing the same good or service. A party has an _____ when using the same input as another party, it can produce a greater output. Since _____ is determined by a simple comparison of labor productivities, it is possible for a a party to have no _____ in anything. It can be contrasted with the concept of comparative advantage which refers to the ability to produce a particular good at a lower opportunity cost.
   a. AAB
   b. A Random Walk Down Wall Street
   c. Economic depreciation
   d. Absolute advantage

21. A _____, reserve bank, or monetary authority is the entity responsible for the monetary policy of a country or of a group of member states. It is a bank that can lend money to other banks in times of need. Its primary responsibility is to maintain the stability of the national currency and money supply, but more active duties include controlling subsidized-loan interest rates, and acting as a lender of last resort to the banking sector during times of financial crisis (private banks often being integral to the national financial system.)
   a. Central bank
   b. 529 plan
   c. 7-Eleven
   d. 4-4-5 Calendar

22. In financial accounting, the term _____ is most commonly used to describe any part of shareholders' equity, except for basic share capital. Sometimes, the term is used instead of the term provision; such a use, however, is inconsistent with the terminology suggested by International Accounting Standards Board. For more information about provisions, see provision (accounting.)
   a. Closing entries
   b. Treasury stock
   c. FIFO and LIFO accounting
   d. Reserve

23. A _____ is a general term that describes any government policy or regulation that restricts international trade. The barriers can take many forms, including the following terms that include many restrictions in international trade within multiple countries that import and export any items of trade.

   - Import duty
   - Import licenses
   - Export licenses
   - Import quotas
   - Tariffs
   - Subsidies
   - Non-tariff barriers to trade
   - Voluntary Export Restraints
   - Local Content Requirements
   - Embargo

   a. Foreign exchange reserves
   b. World Trade Organization
   c. Median
   d. Trade barrier

24. In economics, business, and accounting, a _____ is the value of money that has been used up to produce something, and hence is not available for use anymore. In business, the _____ may be one of acquisition, in which case the amount of money expended to acquire it is counted as _____. In this case, money is the input that is gone in order to acquire the thing.

a. Marginal cost
c. Fixed costs
b. Cost
d. Sliding scale fees

25. Accrual, in accounting, describes the accounting method known as _____, whereby revenues and expenses are recognized when they are accrued, i.e. accumulated (earned or incurred), regardless when the actual cash is received or paid out.

E.g. a company delivers a product to a customer who will pay for it 30 days later in the next fiscal year starting a week after the delivery. The company recognizes the proceeds as a revenue in its current income statement still for the fiscal year of the delivery, even though it will get paid in cash during the following accounting period.

a. ABN Amro
c. A Random Walk Down Wall Street
b. Accrual basis
d. AAB

26. In economics, _____ refers to the ability of a person or a country to produce a particular good at a lower marginal cost and opportunity cost than another person or country. It is the ability to produce a product most efficiently given all the other products that could be produced. It can be contrasted with absolute advantage which refers to the ability of a person or a country to produce a particular good at a lower absolute cost than another.

a. Case-Shiller Home Price Indices
c. Loans and interest, in Judaism
b. Reputational risk
d. Comparative advantage

27. _____ is the set of processes, customs, policies, laws and institutions affecting the way a corporation is directed, administered or controlled. _____ also includes the relationships among the many stakeholders involved and the goals for which the corporation is governed. The principal stakeholders are the shareholders, management and the board of directors.

a. Due diligence
c. Patent
b. Foreign Corrupt Practices Act
d. Corporate governance

28. A _____ is a fungible, negotiable instrument representing financial value. They are broadly categorized into debt securities (such as banknotes, bonds and debentures), and equity securities; e.g., common stocks. The company or other entity issuing the _____ is called the issuer.

a. Tracking stock
c. Book entry
b. Securities lending
d. Security

29. _____ are government bonds issued by the United States Department of the Treasury through the Bureau of the Public Debt. They are the debt financing instruments of the U.S. Federal government, and they are often referred to simply as Treasuries or Treasurys. There are four types of marketable _____: Treasury bills, Treasury notes, Treasury bonds, and Treasury Inflation Protected Securities (TIPS.)

a. 4-4-5 Calendar
c. Treasury Inflation-Protected Securities
b. Treasury Inflation Protected Securities
d. Treasury Securities

30. In economics and finance, _____ is the practice of taking advantage of a price differential between two or more markets: striking a combination of matching deals that capitalize upon the imbalance, the profit being the difference between the market prices. When used by academics, an _____ is a transaction that involves no negative cash flow at any probabilistic or temporal state and a positive cash flow in at least one state; in simple terms, a risk-free profit.

Chapter 16. Foreign Direct Investment and Cross-Border Acquisitions, 153

a. Issuer
b. Efficient-market hypothesis
c. Initial margin
d. Arbitrage

31. _____ refers to the methods of practicing and using another person's business philosophy. The franchisor grants the independent operator the right to distribute its products, techniques, and trademarks for a percentage of gross monthly sales and a royalty fee. Various tangibles and intangibles such as national or international advertising, training, and other support services are commonly made available by the franchisor.
   a. 529 plan
   b. Franchising
   c. 4-4-5 Calendar
   d. 7-Eleven

32. The American Oil Company founded in Baltimore in 1910 and incorporated in 1922 by Louis Blaustein and his son Jacob, but is now part of BP. The firm's early innovations include the gasoline tanker truck and the drive-through filling station.

In 1923 the Blausteins sold a half interest in _____ to the Pan American Petroleum ' Transport company in exchange for a guaranteed supply of oil.

   a. AAB
   b. ABN Amro
   c. A Random Walk Down Wall Street
   d. Amoco

33. _____ or amalgamation is the act of merging many things into one. In business, it often refers to the mergers or acquisitions of many smaller companies into much larger ones. The financial accounting term of _____ refers to the aggregated financial statements of a group company as consolidated account.
   a. Cost of goods sold
   b. Retained earnings
   c. Consolidation
   d. Write-off

34. _____ is a fee paid on borrowed assets. It is the price paid for the use of borrowed money, or, money earned by deposited funds. Assets that are sometimes lent with _____ include money, shares, consumer goods through hire purchase, major assets such as aircraft, and even entire factories in finance lease arrangements.
   a. AAB
   b. Interest
   c. Insolvency
   d. A Random Walk Down Wall Street

35. A _____ is a private or public market for the trading of company stock and derivatives of company stock at an agreed price; these are securities listed on a stock exchange as well as those only traded privately.

The size of the world _____ is estimated at about $36.6 trillion US at the beginning of October 2008. The world derivatives market has been estimated at about $480 trillion face or nominal value, 12 times the size of the entire world economy.

   a. Adolph Coors
   b. Andrew Tobias
   c. Anton Gelonkin
   d. Stock market

36. In business, _____ is the total assets minus total outside liabilities of an individual or a company. For a company, this is called shareholders' equity and may be referred to as book value. _____ is stated as at a particular point in time.
   a. Moneylender
   b. Net worth
   c. Restructuring
   d. Certified International Investment Analyst

37. _____ refers to confiscation of private property with the stated purpose of establishing social equality.

Unlike eminent domain, _____ takes place beyond the common law legal systems and refers to socially-motivated confiscations of any property rather than to taking away the real estate. Just compensation to owners is given.

_____ is one of the political risks involved with Foreign Direct Investment. It is characterized by confiscation of the foreign asset, and a pittance payment.

a. A Random Walk Down Wall Street
b. AAB
c. ABN Amro
d. Expropriation

38. _____ is a type of risk faced by investors, corporations, and governments. It is a risk that can be understood and managed with proper aforethought and investment.

Broadly, _____ refers to the complications businesses and governments may face as a result of what are commonly referred to as political decisions--or 'any political change that alters the expected outcome and value of a given economic action by changing the probability of achieving business objectives.' .

a. Political risk
b. Capital asset
c. Mid price
d. Single-index model

39. _____, in auditing, is the risk that a company's internal controls are insufficient to mitigate or detect errors or fraud.

- Risk Assessment
- Inherent risk
- Detection Risk

a. 4-4-5 Calendar
b. 529 plan
c. Detection Risk
d. Control risk

40. An _____ is a risk arising from execution of a company's business functions. As such, it is a very broad concept including e.g. fraud risks, legal risks, physical or environmental risks, etc. The term _____ is most commonly found in risk management programs of financial institutions that must organize their risk management program according to Basel II.

a. A Random Walk Down Wall Street
b. AAB
c. ABN Amro
d. Operational risk

41. _____ is the incidence or process of transferring ownership of a business, enterprise, agency or public service from the public sector (government) to the private sector (business.) In a broader sense, _____ refers to transfer of any government function to the private sector including governmental functions like revenue collection and law enforcement.

The term '_____' also has been used to describe two unrelated transactions. The first is a buyout, by the majority owner, of all shares of a public corporation or holding company's stock, privatizing a publicly traded stock. The second is a demutualization of a mutual organization or cooperative to form a joint stock company.

Chapter 16. Foreign Direct Investment and Cross-Border Acquisitions, 155

a. 4-4-5 Calendar
c. 7-Eleven
b. 529 plan
d. Privatization

42. _____ is the quality of paper money substitutes which entitles the holder to redeem them on demand into money proper.

Historically, the banknote has followed a common or very similar pattern in the western nations. Originally decentralized and issued from various independent banks, it was gradually brought under state control and became a monopoly privilege of the central banks.

a. Convertibility
c. Devaluation
b. Functional currency
d. Petrodollar recycling

43. _____ refers to the likelihood that changes in the business environment adversely affect operating profits or the value of assets in a specific country. For example, financial factors such as currency controls, devaluation or regulatory changes, or stability factors such as mass riots, civil war and other potential events contribute to companies' operational risks. This term is also sometimes referred to as political risk, however _____ is a more general term, which generally only refers to risks affecting all companies operating within a particular country.

a. Country risk
c. Solvency
b. Single-index model
d. Capital asset

44. _____ is a term used for a number of concepts involving either the performance of an investigation of a business or person, or the performance of an act with a certain standard of care. It can be a legal obligation, but the term will more commonly apply to voluntary investigations. A common example of _____ in various industries is the process through which a potential acquirer evaluates a target company or its assets for acquisition.

a. Down payment
c. Quiet period
b. Bond indenture
d. Due diligence

45. The _____ is an important selective, mainly private, international organization designed by its founders to supervise and liberalize international trade. The organization officially commenced on 1 January 1995, under the Marrakesh Agreement, succeeding the 1947 General Agreement on Tariffs and Trade (GATT.)

The _____ deals with regulation of trade between participating countries; it provides a framework for negotiating and formalising trade agreements, and a dispute resolution process aimed at enforcing participants' adherence to _____ agreements which are signed by representatives of member governments and ratified by their parliaments.

a. Financial Crimes Enforcement Network
c. Public Company Accounting Oversight Board
b. Gamelan Council
d. World Trade Organization

Chapter 17. International Capital Structure and the Cost of Capital,

1. In finance, _____ refers to the way a corporation finances its assets through some combination of equity, debt, or hybrid securities. A firm's _____ is then the composition or 'structure' of its liabilities. For example, a firm that sells $20 billion in equity and $80 billion in debt is said to be 20% equity-financed and 80% debt-financed.
   a. Market for corporate control
   b. Capital structure
   c. Book building
   d. Rights issue

2. The institution most often referenced by the word '_____' is a public or publicly traded _____, the shares of which are traded on a public stock exchange (e.g., the New York Stock Exchange or Nasdaq in the United States) where shares of stock of _____s are bought and sold by and to the general public. Most of the largest businesses in the world are publicly traded _____s. However, the majority of _____s are said to be closely held, privately held or close _____s, meaning that no ready market exists for the trading of shares.
   a. Corporation
   b. Federal Home Loan Mortgage Corporation
   c. Depository Trust Company
   d. Protect

3. In economics, business, and accounting, a _____ is the value of money that has been used up to produce something, and hence is not available for use anymore. In business, the _____ may be one of acquisition, in which case the amount of money expended to acquire it is counted as _____. In this case, money is the input that is gone in order to acquire the thing.
   a. Fixed costs
   b. Sliding scale fees
   c. Marginal cost
   d. Cost

4. The _____ is an expected return that the provider of capital plans to earn on their investment.

Capital (money) used for funding a business should earn returns for the capital providers who risk their capital. For an investment to be worthwhile, the expected return on capital must be greater than the _____.

   a. 4-4-5 Calendar
   b. Capital intensity
   c. Weighted average cost of capital
   d. Cost of capital

5. A _____, securities exchange or (in Europe) bourse is a corporation or mutual organization which provides 'trading' facilities for stock brokers and traders, to trade stocks and other securities. _____s also provide facilities for the issue and redemption of securities as well as other financial instruments and capital events including the payment of income and dividends. The securities traded on a _____ include: shares issued by companies, unit trusts and other pooled investment products and bonds.
   a. Stock Exchange
   b. 529 plan
   c. 4-4-5 Calendar
   d. 7-Eleven

6. The phrase _____ refers to the aspect of corporate strategy, corporate finance and management dealing with the buying, selling and combining of different companies that can aid, finance, or help a growing company in a given industry grow rapidly without having to create another business entity.

An acquisition, also known as a takeover, is the buying of one company (the 'target') by another. An acquisition may be friendly or hostile.

   a. 529 plan
   b. 4-4-5 Calendar
   c. 7-Eleven
   d. Mergers and acquisitions

Chapter 17. International Capital Structure and the Cost of Capital, 157

7. In business and finance, a _____ (also referred to as equity _____) of stock means a _____ of ownership in a corporation (company.) In the plural, stocks is often used as a synonym for _____s especially in the United States, but it is less commonly used that way outside of North America.

In the United Kingdom, South Africa, and Australia, stock can also refer to completely different financial instruments such as government bonds or, less commonly, to all kinds of marketable securities.

a. Bucket shop
b. Margin
c. Procter ' Gamble
d. Share

8. _____ is the planning process used to determine whether a firm's long term investments such as new machinery, replacement machinery, new plants, new products, and research development projects are worth pursuing. It is budget for major capital, or investment, expenditures.

Many formal methods are used in _____, including the techniques such as

- Net present value
- Profitability index
- Internal rate of return
- Modified Internal Rate of Return
- Equivalent annuity

These methods use the incremental cash flows from each potential investment, or project. Techniques based on accounting earnings and accounting rules are sometimes used - though economists consider this to be improper - such as the accounting rate of return, and 'return on investment.' Simplified and hybrid methods are used as well, such as payback period and discounted payback period.

a. Shareholder value
b. Capital budgeting
c. Preferred stock
d. Financial distress

9. _____ is a fee paid on borrowed assets. It is the price paid for the use of borrowed money , or, money earned by deposited funds . Assets that are sometimes lent with _____ include money, shares, consumer goods through hire purchase, major assets such as aircraft, and even entire factories in finance lease arrangements.
a. Insolvency
b. A Random Walk Down Wall Street
c. AAB
d. Interest

10. An _____ is the price a borrower pays for the use of money they do not own, and the return a lender receives for deferring the use of funds, by lending it to the borrower. _____s are normally expressed as a percentage rate over the period of one year.

_____s targets are also a vital tool of monetary policy and are used to control variables like investment, inflation, and unemployment.

a. Interest rate
c. ABN Amro
b. A Random Walk Down Wall Street
d. AAB

11. The _____ is a capital budgeting metric used by firms to decide whether they should make investments. It is an indicator of the efficiency or quality of an investment, as opposed to net present value (NPV), which indicates value or magnitude.

The IRR is the annualized effective compounded return rate which can be earned on the invested capital, i.e., the yield on the investment.

a. Internal rate of return
c. ABN Amro
b. A Random Walk Down Wall Street
d. AAB

12. The _____ is the rate that a company is expected to pay to finance its assets. WACC is the minimum return that a company must earn on existing asset base to satisfy its creditors, owners, and other providers of capital.

Companies raise money from a number of sources: common equity, preferred equity, straight debt, convertible debt, exchangeable debt, warrants, options, pension liabilities, executive stock options, governmental subsidies, and so on.

a. Cost of capital
c. Weighted average cost of capital
b. 4-4-5 Calendar
d. Capital intensity

13. In finance, _____, also known as return on investment is the ratio of money gained or lost on an investment relative to the amount of money invested. The amount of money gained or lost may be referred to as interest, profit/loss, gain/loss, or net income/loss. The money invested may be referred to as the asset, capital, principal, or the cost basis of the investment.

a. Doctrine of the Proper Law
c. Rate of return
b. Stock or scrip dividends
d. Composiition of Creditors

14. In business and accounting, _____s are everything of value that is owned by a person or company. The balance sheet of a firm records the monetary value of the _____s owned by the firm. The two major _____ classes are tangible _____s and intangible _____s.

a. Accounts payable
c. Asset
b. EBITDA
d. Income

15. In finance, _____ is the process of estimating the potential market value of a financial asset or liability. they can be done on assets (for example, investments in marketable securities such as stocks, options, business enterprises, or intangible assets such as patents and trademarks) or on liabilities (e.g., Bonds issued by a company.) _____s are required in many contexts including investment analysis, capital budgeting, merger and acquisition transactions, financial reporting, taxable events to determine the proper tax liability, and in litigation.

a. Procter ' Gamble
c. Share
b. Margin
d. Valuation

Chapter 17. International Capital Structure and the Cost of Capital,

16. The term _____ has three unrelated technical definitions, and is also used in a variety of non-technical ways.

- In financial economics, it refers to any asset used to make money, as opposed to assets used for personal enjoyment or consumption. This is an important distinction because two people can disagree sharply about the value of personal assets, one person might think a sports car is more valuable than a pickup truck, another person might have the opposite taste. But if an asset is held for the purpose of making money, taste has nothing to do with it, only differences of opinion about how much money the asset will produce. With the further assumption that people agree on the probability distribution of future cash flows, it is possible to have an objective _____ pricing model. Even without the assumption of agreement, it is possible to set rational limits on _____ value.
- In governmental accounting, it is defined as any asset used in operations with an initial useful life extending beyond one reporting period. Generally, government managers have a 'stewardship' duty to maintain _____s under their control. See International Public Sector Accounting Standards for details.
- In US tax accounting, it is defined as any property other than a list of exceptions. The main exceptions are anything held for sale, and any real estate or depreciable property used in business. Almost everything you own and use for personal purposes, pleasure or investment is a _____. If something is a _____ for tax purposes, gains or losses on sale or disposition are capital gains or capital losses. For individuals, however, capital losses on property held for personal use are generally not deductible. See the IRS publication Tax Facts about Capital Gains and Losses for details.

A well-known financial accounting textbook advises that the term be avoided except in tax accounting because it is used in so many different senses, not all of them well-defined. For example it is often used as a synonym for fixed assets or for investments in securities.

A common non-technical usage occurs when people ask that employees or the environment or something else be treated as a _____.

a. Solvency
c. Settlement date
b. Political risk
d. Capital Asset

17. In finance, the _____ is used to determine a theoretically appropriate required rate of return of an asset, if that asset is to be added to an already well-diversified portfolio, given that asset's non-diversifiable risk. The model takes into account the asset's sensitivity to non-diversifiable risk (also known as systemic risk or market risk), often represented by the quantity beta (β) in the financial industry, as well as the expected return of the market and the expected return of a theoretical risk-free asset.

The model was introduced by Jack Treynor (1961, 1962), William Sharpe (1964), John Lintner (1965a,b) and Jan Mossin (1966) independently, building on the earlier work of Harry Markowitz on diversification and modern portfolio theory.

a. Cox-Ingersoll-Ross model
c. Hull-White model
b. Random walk hypothesis
d. Capital Asset Pricing Model

18. _____ is the branch of economics that studies the dynamics of exchange rates, foreign investment, and how these affect international trade. It also studies international projects, international investments and capital flows, and trade deficits. It includes the study of futures, options and currency swaps.

Chapter 17. International Capital Structure and the Cost of Capital,

a. AAB
c. ABN Amro
b. A Random Walk Down Wall Street
d. International finance

19. A _____ is a portfolio consisting of a weighted sum of every asset in the market, with weights in the proportions that they exist in the market (with the necessary assumption that these assets are infinitely divisible.)

Neha Tyagi's critique (1977) states that this is only a theoretical concept, as to create a _____ for investment purposes in practice would necessarily include every single possible available asset, including real estate, precious metals, stamp collections, jewelry, and anything with any worth, as the theoretical market being referred to would be the world market. As a result, proxies for the market are used in practice by investors.

a. Market price
c. Central Securities Depository
b. Delta neutral
d. Market portfolio

20. In finance, _____ is that risk which is common to an entire market and not to any individual entity or component thereof. It should be distinguished from systemic risk which is the risk that the entire financial system will collapse as a result of some catastrophic event.

Risks can be reduced in four main ways: Avoidance, Reduction, Retention and Transfer.

a. Capital surplus
c. Primary market
b. Systematic risk
d. Conglomerate merger

21. _____ is the removal or simplification of government rules and regulations that constrain the operation of market forces. _____ does not mean elimination of laws against fraud, but eliminating or reducing government control of how business is done, thereby moving toward a more free market.

The stated rationale for '_____' is often that fewer and simpler regulations will lead to a raised level of competitiveness, therefore higher productivity, more efficiency and lower prices overall.

a. Value added
c. Supply shock
b. Deregulation
d. Demand shock

22. An _____ represents the ownership in the shares of a foreign company trading on US financial markets. The stock of many non-US companies trades on US exchanges through the use of _____s. _____s enable US investors to buy shares in foreign companies without undertaking cross-border transactions.

a. A Random Walk Down Wall Street
c. AAB
b. ABN Amro
d. American depository receipt

23. A _____ is a certificate issued by a depository bank, which purchases shares of foreign companies and deposits it on the account. _____s represent ownership of an underlying number of shares.

They facilitate trade of shares, and are commonly used to invest in companies from developing or emerging markets.

Chapter 17. International Capital Structure and the Cost of Capital,

a. Short positions
c. Special journals
b. The Security Industry Association
d. Global depository receipt

24. The _____ is an American stock exchange. It is the largest electronic screen-based equity securities trading market in the United States. With approximately 3,200 companies, it has more trading volume per day than any other stock exchange in the world.
a. 529 plan
c. 7-Eleven
b. 4-4-5 Calendar
d. NASDAQ

25. The _____ is a stock exchange based in New York City, New York. It is the largest stock exchange in the world by dollar value of its listed companies securities. As of October 2008, the combined capitalization of all domestic _____ listed companies was $10.1 trillion.
a. 529 plan
c. 7-Eleven
b. New York Stock Exchange
d. 4-4-5 Calendar

26. The U.S. _____ is an independent agency of the United States government which holds primary responsibility for enforcing the federal securities laws and regulating the securities industry, the nation's stock and options exchanges, and other electronic securities markets. The SEC was created by section 4 of the SEC of 1934 (now codified as 15 U.S.C. Â§ 78d and commonly referred to as the 1934 Act.)
a. 4-4-5 Calendar
c. 7-Eleven
b. 529 plan
d. Securities and Exchange Commission

27. A _____ is a fungible, negotiable instrument representing financial value. They are broadly categorized into debt securities (such as banknotes, bonds and debentures), and equity securities; e.g., common stocks. The company or other entity issuing the _____ is called the issuer.
a. Securities lending
c. Tracking stock
b. Book entry
d. Security

28. In economics, the _____, measures the payments that flow between any individual country and all other countries. It is used to summarize all international economic transactions for that country during a specific time period, usually a year. The _____ is determined by the country's exports and imports of goods, services, and financial capital, as well as financial transfers.
a. Purchasing power parity
c. Balance of payments
b. Gross national product
d. 4-4-5 Calendar

29. The _____ is the financial market where previously issued securities and financial instruments such as stock, bonds, options, and futures are bought and sold. The term '_____' is also used refer to the market for any used goods or assets, or an alternative use for an existing product or asset where the customer base is the second market

With primary issuances of securities or financial instruments, or the primary market, investors purchase these securities directly from issuers such as corporations issuing shares in an IPO or private placement, or directly from the federal government in the case of treasuries.

a. Secondary market
c. Delta neutral
b. Financial market
d. Performance attribution

Chapter 17. International Capital Structure and the Cost of Capital,

30. _____, adopted pursuant to the U.S. Securities Act of 1933, as amended (the 'Securities Act') provides a safe harbor from the registration requirements of the Securities Act of 1933 for certain private resales of restricted securities to QIBs (qualified institutional buyers), which generally are large institutional investors with over $100 million in investable assets. When a broker or dealer is selling securities in reliance on _____, it is subject to the condition that it may not make offers to persons other than those it reasonably believes to be QIBs.

Since its adoption, _____ has greatly increased the liquidity of the securities affected.

a. Rule 144A
c. SIPC

b. Prudent man rule
d. Securities Investor Protection Corporation

31. In finance, a _____ is a debt security, in which the authorized issuer owes the holders a debt and, depending on the terms of the _____, is obliged to pay interest (the coupon) and/or to repay the principal at a later date, termed maturity.

Thus a _____ is a loan: the issuer is the borrower, the _____ holder is the lender, and the coupon is the interest. _____s provide the borrower with external funds to finance long-term investments, or, in the case of government _____s, to finance current expenditure.

a. Bond
c. Convertible bond

b. Puttable bond
d. Catastrophe bonds

32. The _____ is a financial market where participants buy and sell debt securities, usually in the form of bonds. As of 2006, the size of the international _____ is an estimated $45 trillion, of which the size of the outstanding U.S. _____ debt was $25.2 trillion.

Nearly all of the $923 billion average daily trading volume in the U.S. _____ takes place between broker-dealers and large institutions in a decentralized, over-the-counter market.

a. Fixed income
c. 529 plan

b. Bond market
d. 4-4-5 Calendar

33. _____ is that which is owed; usually referencing assets owed, but the term can cover other obligations. In the case of assets, _____ is a means of using future purchasing power in the present before a summation has been earned. Some companies and corporations use _____ as a part of their overall corporate finance strategy.

a. Debt
c. Partial Payment

b. Credit cycle
d. Cross-collateralization

34. _____ is a financial ratio that indicates the percentage of a company's assets are provided via debt. It is the ratio of total debt (the sum of current liabilities and long-term liabilities) and total assets (the sum of current assets, fixed assets, and other assets such as 'goodwill'.)

or alternatively:

For example, a company with $2 million in total assets and $500,000 in total liabilities would have a _____ of 25%

Like all financial ratios, a company's _____ should be compared with their industry average or other competing firms.

a. Capitalization rate
b. Cash management
c. Cash concentration
d. Debt ratio

35. A _____, in law and finance, is a purchaser of securities that is deemed financially sophisticated and is legally recognized by security market regulators to need less protection from issuers than most public investors.

A _____ is an investing entity owning and investing large amounts of securities on a discretionary basis. The threshold is defined as ownership of at least $100 million of securities not affiliated with the entity and dependent on the type of entity. Additionally, they must be entities that fall under one of several categories including an insurance company, investment company, employee benefit plan, trust fund, Business Development Company, 501(c)(3) not-for-profit organization, corporation, partnership, business trust or investment adviser. An individual cannot be designated as a _____ without first establishing an entity falling under one of the previous categories.

a. 4-4-5 Calendar
b. Qualified institutional buyer
c. 7-Eleven
d. 529 plan

36. In political science and economics, the _____ or agency dilemma treats the difficulties that arise under conditions of incomplete and asymmetric information when a principal hires an agent. Various mechanisms may be used to try to align the interests of the agent with those of the principal, such as piece rates/commissions, profit sharing, efficiency wages, performance measurement (including financial statements), the agent posting a bond, or fear of firing. The _____ is found in most employer/employee relationships, for example, when stockholders hire top executives of corporations.

a. 4-4-5 Calendar
b. 7-Eleven
c. Principal-agent problem
d. 529 plan

37. In United States banking, _____ is a marketing term for certain services offered primarily to larger business customers. It may be used to describe all bank accounts (such as checking accounts) provided to businesses of a certain size, but it is more often used to describe specific services such as cash concentration, zero balance accounting, and automated clearing house facilities. Sometimes, private banking customers are given _____ services.

a. Global tactical asset allocation
b. Capitalization rate
c. Profitability index
d. Cash management

Chapter 17. International Capital Structure and the Cost of Capital,

38. In finance, _____ occurs when a debtor has not met its legal obligations according to the debt contract, e.g. it has not made a scheduled payment, or has violated a loan covenant (condition) of the debt contract. _____ may occur if the debtor is either unwilling or unable to pay their debt. This can occur with all debt obligations including bonds, mortgages, loans, and promissory notes.

   a. Credit crunch
   b. Default
   c. Debt validation
   d. Vendor finance

39. _____ is the risk of loss due to a debtor's non-payment of a loan or other line of credit (either the principal or interest (coupon) or both)

Most lenders employ their own models (credit scorecards) to rank potential and existing customers according to risk, and then apply appropriate strategies. With products such as unsecured personal loans or mortgages, lenders charge a higher price for higher risk customers and vice versa. With revolving products such as credit cards and overdrafts, risk is controlled through careful setting of credit limits.

   a. Liquidity risk
   b. Market risk
   c. Credit risk
   d. Transaction risk

40. A _____ is a set of companies with interlocking business relationships and shareholdings. It is a type of business group.

The prototypical _____ are those which appeared in Japan during the 'economic miracle' following World War II.

   a. Relative strength Index
   b. Keiretsu
   c. Stock split
   d. Zero-coupon bond

41. A mutual shareholder or _____ is an individual or company (including a corporation) that legally owns one or more shares of stock in a joint stock company. A company's shareholders collectively own that company. Thus, the typical goal of such companies is to enhance shareholder value.

   a. Stockholder
   b. Stock market bubble
   c. Trading curb
   d. Limit order

42. A _____ is an international bond that is denominated in a currency not native to the country where it is issued. It can be categorised according to the currency in which it is issued. London is one of the centers of the _____ market, but _____s may be traded throughout the world - for example in Singapore or Tokyo.

   a. Interest rate option
   b. Economic entity
   c. Eurobond
   d. Education production function

43. _____ or financing is to provide capital (funds), which means money for a project, a person, a business or any other private or public institutions.

Those funds can be allocated for either short term or long term purposes. The health fund is a new way of _____ private healthcare centers.

Chapter 17. International Capital Structure and the Cost of Capital, 165

    a. Synthetic CDO
    b. Product life cycle
    c. Proxy fight
    d. Funding

44. _____ is the set of processes, customs, policies, laws and institutions affecting the way a corporation is directed, administered or controlled. _____ also includes the relationships among the many stakeholders involved and the goals for which the corporation is governed. The principal stakeholders are the shareholders, management and the board of directors.
    a. Corporate governance
    b. Foreign Corrupt Practices Act
    c. Due diligence
    d. Patent

45. _____ is a measure of the ability of a debtor to pay their debts as and when they fall due. It is usually expressed as a ratio or a percentage of current liabilities.

For a corporation with a published balance sheet there are various ratios used to calculate a measure of liquidity.

    a. Operating leverage
    b. Operating profit margin
    c. Invested capital
    d. Accounting liquidity

46. _____ most frequently refers to the standard deviation of the continuously compounded returns of a financial instrument with a specific time horizon. It is often used to quantify the risk of the instrument over that time period. _____ is typically expressed in annualized terms, and it may either be an absolute number ($5) or a fraction of the mean (5%).
    a. Currency swap
    b. Portfolio insurance
    c. Volatility
    d. Seasoned equity offering

47. In economics and finance, _____ represents passive holdings of securities such as foreign stocks, bonds, or other financial assets, none of which entails active management or control of the securities' issuer by the investor; where such control exists, it is known as foreign direct investment. Generally, this means the investor holds less than 10% of the total shares or less than the amount needed to hold the majority vote.

Some examples of _____ are:

- purchase of shares in a foreign company.
- purchase of bonds issued by a foreign government.
- acquisition of assets in a foreign country.

Factors affecting international _____:

- tax rates on interest or dividends (investors will normally prefer countries where the tax rates are relatively low)
- interest rates (money tends to flow to countries with high interest rates)
- exchange rates (foreign investors may be attracted if the local currency is expected to strengthen)

_____ is part of the capital account on the balance of payments statistics.

a. Portable alpha
c. Divestment

b. Portfolio investment
d. Tactical asset allocation

48. _____ is the value on a given date of a future payment or series of future payments, discounted to reflect the time value of money and other factors such as investment risk. _____ calculations are widely used in business and economics to provide a means to compare cash flows at different times on a meaningful 'like to like' basis.

The most commonly applied model of the time value of money is compound interest.

a. Negative gearing
c. Net present value

b. Present value of benefits
d. Present value

49. _____ is a concept in economics, finance, and psychology related to the behaviour of consumers and investors under uncertainty. _____ Is the reluctance of a person to accept a bargain with an uncertain payoff rather than another bargain with a more certain, but possibly lower, expected payoff.

The inverse of a person's _____ is sometimes called their risk tolerance

a. Risk adjusted return on capital
c. Risk premium

b. Discount factor
d. Risk aversion

50. _____ are costs incurred on the purchase of land, buildings, construction and equipment to be used in the production of goods or the rendering of services. In other words, the total cost needed to bring a project to a commercially operable status. However, _____ are not limited to the initial construction of a factory or other business.

a. Capital outflow
c. Defined contribution plan

b. Trade-off
d. Capital costs

51. _____ is the risk that the value of an investment will decrease due to moves in market factors. The five standard _____ factors are:

- Equity risk, the risk that stock prices will change.
- Interest rate risk, the risk that interest rates will change.
- Currency risk, the risk that foreign exchange rates will change.
- Commodity risk, the risk that commodity prices (e.g. grains, metals) will change.

As with other forms of risk, _____ may be measured in a number of ways. Traditionally, this is done using a Value at Risk methodology. Value at risk is well established as a risk management technique, but it contains a number of limiting assumptions that constrain its accuracy.

a. Currency risk
c. Transaction risk

b. Tracking error
d. Market Risk

52. The _____ is the market for securities, where companies and governments can raise longterm funds. The _____ includes the stock market and the bond market. Financial regulators, such as the U.S. Securities and Exchange Commission, oversee the _____ s in their designated countries to ensure that investors are protected against fraud.

Chapter 17. International Capital Structure and the Cost of Capital,

a. Forward market
b. Spot rate
c. Capital market
d. Delta neutral

53. In economics, a _____ is a mechanism that allows people to easily buy and sell (trade) financial securities (such as stocks and bonds), commodities (such as precious metals or agricultural goods), and other fungible items of value at low transaction costs and at prices that reflect the efficient-market hypothesis.

_____s have evolved significantly over several hundred years and are undergoing constant innovation to improve liquidity.

Both general markets (where many commodities are traded) and specialized markets (where only one commodity is traded) exist.

a. Cost of carry
b. Delta hedging
c. Secondary market
d. Financial market

54. A _____ is a document that indicates that the bearer of the document has title to property, such as shares or bonds. They differ from normal registered instruments, in that no records are kept of who owns the underlying property, or of the transactions involving transfer of ownership. Whoever physically holds the bearer bond papers owns the property.

a. Book entry
b. Bearer instrument
c. Marketable
d. Securities lending

55. _____ in its classic form is defined as a company from one country making a physical investment into building a factory in another country. It is the establishment of an enterprise by a foreigner. Its definition can be extended to include investments made to acquire lasting interest in enterprises operating outside of the economy of the investor.

a. Dow Jones ' Company
b. Public company
c. Foreign direct investment
d. MicroPlace

56. A _____ is heuristic and has the following assumptions :

- Rationality of all market actors (Rationality in meaning of the actor's utility maximization)
- No transaction costs (particularly no information costs and no taxes)
- Price taking behavior - there is a sufficiently large number of participants such that no individual can affect the market
- given rare resources
- freedom of decision to do something or to let it be (no external effects)

Share and foreign exchange markets are commonly seen to be the most similar to the _____. The real estate market is an example of a very imperfect market. a free market economy is also related to this _____ system as the public have free will

Other characteristics of a _____ include:-

- No barriers to entry to (or exit from) the market
- Perfect knowledge
- Normal profits

Normal profits are defined as that level of profit which just induces the participants to stay in the market. In other words companies in a _____ pay no dividends, as super-normal profits would induce other participants into the market and drive profits back to the 'normal' level.

This attribute of _____s has profound political and economic implications, as many people assume that the purpose of the market is to enable participants to make profits.

a. 4-4-5 Calendar
b. 7-Eleven
c. 529 plan
d. Perfect market

57. _____ is an economic concept with commonplace familiarity. It is the price that a good or service is offered at, or will fetch, in the marketplace. It is of interest mainly in the study of microeconomics.

a. Central Securities Depository
b. Delta hedging
c. Convertible arbitrage
d. Market price

58. A _____, in business matters, is an entity that is controlled by a bigger and more powerful entity. The controlled entity is called a company, corporation, or limited liability company, and the controlling entity is called its parent (or the parent company.) The reason for this distinction is that a lone company cannot be a _____ of any organization; only an entity representing a legal fiction as a separate entity can be a _____.

a. 529 plan
b. Subsidiary
c. Joint stock company
d. 4-4-5 Calendar

59. _____ is an area of finance dealing with the financial decisions corporations make and the tools and analysis used to make these decisions. The primary goal of _____ is to maximize corporate value while managing the firm's financial risks. Although it is in principle different from managerial finance which studies the financial decisions of all firms, rather than corporations alone, the main concepts in the study of _____ are applicable to the financial problems of all kinds of firms.

a. Gross profit
b. Special purpose entity
c. Cash flow
d. Corporate finance

60. _____ is a type of risk faced by investors, corporations, and governments. It is a risk that can be understood and managed with proper aforethought and investment.

Broadly, _____ refers to the complications businesses and governments may face as a result of what are commonly referred to as political decisions--or 'any political change that alters the expected outcome and value of a given economic action by changing the probability of achieving business objectives.' .

a. Mid price
b. Political risk
c. Single-index model
d. Capital asset

Chapter 18. International Capital Budgeting, 169

1. _____ is the planning process used to determine whether a firm's long term investments such as new machinery, replacement machinery, new plants, new products, and research development projects are worth pursuing. It is budget for major capital, or investment, expenditures.

Many formal methods are used in _____, including the techniques such as

- Net present value
- Profitability index
- Internal rate of return
- Modified Internal Rate of Return
- Equivalent annuity

These methods use the incremental cash flows from each potential investment, or project. Techniques based on accounting earnings and accounting rules are sometimes used - though economists consider this to be improper - such as the accounting rate of return, and 'return on investment.' Simplified and hybrid methods are used as well, such as payback period and discounted payback period.

a. Financial distress	b. Shareholder value
c. Preferred stock	d. Capital budgeting

2. _____ is the balance of the amounts of cash being received and paid by a business during a defined period of time, sometimes tied to a specific project. Measurement of _____ can be used

- to evaluate the state or performance of a business or project.
- to determine problems with liquidity. Being profitable does not necessarily mean being liquid. A company can fail because of a shortage of cash, even while profitable.
- to generate project rate of returns. The time of _____s into and out of projects are used as inputs to financial models such as internal rate of return, and net present value.
- to examine income or growth of a business when it is believed that accrual accounting concepts do not represent economic realities. Alternately, _____ can be used to 'validate' the net income generated by accrual accounting.

_____ as a generic term may be used differently depending on context, and certain _____ definitions may be adapted by analysts and users for their own uses. Common terms include operating _____ and free _____.

_____s can be classified into:

1. Operational _____s: Cash received or expended as a result of the company's core business activities.
2. Investment _____s: Cash received or expended through capital expenditure, investments or acquisitions.
3. Financing _____s: Cash received or expended as a result of financial activities, such as interests and dividends.

All three together - the net _____ - are necessary to reconcile the beginning cash balance to the ending cash balance. Loan draw downs or equity injections, that is just shifting of capital but no expenditure as such, are not considered in the net _____.

a. Shareholder value
c. Real option
b. Corporate finance
d. Cash flow

3. _____ or net present worth (NPW) is defined as the total present value (PV) of a time series of cash flows. It is a standard method for using the time value of money to appraise long-term projects. Used for capital budgeting, and widely throughout economics, it measures the excess or shortfall of cash flows, in present value terms, once financing charges are met.
   a. Present value of costs
   c. Negative gearing
   b. Tax shield
   d. Net present value

4. _____ is a business valuation method. _____ is the net present value of a project if financed solely by ownership equity plus the present value of all the benefits of financing. Usually, the main benefit is a tax shield resulted from tax deductibility of interest payments. Another one can be a subsidized borrowing.
   a. ABN Amro
   c. A Random Walk Down Wall Street
   b. AAB
   d. Adjusted present value

5. _____ is the value on a given date of a future payment or series of future payments, discounted to reflect the time value of money and other factors such as investment risk. _____ calculations are widely used in business and economics to provide a means to compare cash flows at different times on a meaningful 'like to like' basis.

The most commonly applied model of the time value of money is compound interest.

   a. Negative gearing
   c. Present value
   b. Present value of benefits
   d. Net present value

6. In United States banking, _____ is a marketing term for certain services offered primarily to larger business customers. It may be used to describe all bank accounts (such as checking accounts) provided to businesses of a certain size, but it is more often used to describe specific services such as cash concentration, zero balance accounting, and automated clearing house facilities. Sometimes, private banking customers are given _____ services.
   a. Cash management
   c. Global tactical asset allocation
   b. Capitalization rate
   d. Profitability index

7. The _____ is a capital budgeting metric used by firms to decide whether they should make investments. It is an indicator of the efficiency or quality of an investment, as opposed to net present value (NPV), which indicates value or magnitude.

The IRR is the annualized effective compounded return rate which can be earned on the invested capital, i.e., the yield on the investment.

   a. AAB
   c. ABN Amro
   b. Internal rate of return
   d. A Random Walk Down Wall Street

8. _____ identifies the relationship of investment to payoff of a proposed project. The ratio is calculated as follows:

-

_____ is also known as Profit Investment Ratio, abbreviated to P.I. and Value Investment Ratio (V.I.R.). _____ is a good tool for ranking projects because it allows you to clearly identify the amount of value created per unit of investment, thus if you are capital constrained you wish to invest in those projects which create value most efficiently first.

a. Conditional prepayment rate
c. Total return
b. Capitalization rate
d. Profitability index

9. The institution most often referenced by the word '_____' is a public or publicly traded _____, the shares of which are traded on a public stock exchange (e.g., the New York Stock Exchange or Nasdaq in the United States) where shares of stock of _____s are bought and sold by and to the general public. Most of the largest businesses in the world are publicly traded _____s. However, the majority of _____s are said to be closely held, privately held or close _____s, meaning that no ready market exists for the trading of shares.

a. Protect
c. Depository Trust Company
b. Federal Home Loan Mortgage Corporation
d. Corporation

10. In finance, _____, also known as return on investment is the ratio of money gained or lost on an investment relative to the amount of money invested. The amount of money gained or lost may be referred to as interest, profit/loss, gain/loss, or net income/loss. The money invested may be referred to as the asset, capital, principal, or the cost basis of the investment.

a. Doctrine of the Proper Law
c. Rate of return
b. Stock or scrip dividends
d. Composiition of Creditors

11. _____ is a term used in accounting, economics and finance to spread the cost of an asset over the span of several years.

In simple words we can say that _____ is the reduction in the value of an asset due to usage, passage of time, wear and tear, technological outdating or obsolescence, depletion or other such factors.

In accounting, _____ is a term used to describe any method of attributing the historical or purchase cost of an asset across its useful life, roughly corresponding to normal wear and tear.

a. Matching principle
c. Bottom line
b. Depreciation
d. Deferred financing costs

12. _____ is a fee paid on borrowed assets. It is the price paid for the use of borrowed money , or, money earned by deposited funds . Assets that are sometimes lent with _____ include money, shares, consumer goods through hire purchase, major assets such as aircraft, and even entire factories in finance lease arrangements.

a. Insolvency
c. Interest
b. A Random Walk Down Wall Street
d. AAB

13. An _____ represents the ownership in the shares of a foreign company trading on US financial markets. The stock of many non-US companies trades on US exchanges through the use of _____s. _____s enable US investors to buy shares in foreign companies without undertaking cross-border transactions.

    a. A Random Walk Down Wall Street
    b. ABN Amro
    c. AAB
    d. American depository receipt

14. In economics, business, and accounting, a _____ is the value of money that has been used up to produce something, and hence is not available for use anymore. In business, the _____ may be one of acquisition, in which case the amount of money expended to acquire it is counted as _____. In this case, money is the input that is gone in order to acquire the thing.

    a. Sliding scale fees
    b. Cost
    c. Fixed costs
    d. Marginal cost

15. The _____ is an expected return that the provider of capital plans to earn on their investment.

    Capital (money) used for funding a business should earn returns for the capital providers who risk their capital. For an investment to be worthwhile, the expected return on capital must be greater than the _____.

    a. 4-4-5 Calendar
    b. Capital intensity
    c. Weighted average cost of capital
    d. Cost of capital

16. A _____ is a certificate issued by a depository bank, which purchases shares of foreign companies and deposits it on the account. _____s represent ownership of an underlying number of shares.

    They facilitate trade of shares, and are commonly used to invest in companies from developing or emerging markets.

    a. The Security Industry Association
    b. Special journals
    c. Short positions
    d. Global depository receipt

17. _____ is that which is owed; usually referencing assets owed, but the term can cover other obligations. In the case of assets, _____ is a means of using future purchasing power in the present before a summation has been earned. Some companies and corporations use _____ as a part of their overall corporate finance strategy.

    a. Cross-collateralization
    b. Debt
    c. Credit cycle
    d. Partial Payment

18. _____ is a financial ratio that indicates the percentage of a company's assets are provided via debt. It is the ratio of total debt (the sum of current liabilities and long-term liabilities) and total assets (the sum of current assets, fixed assets, and other assets such as 'goodwill'.)

$\boxed{}$ >

or alternatively:

Chapter 18. International Capital Budgeting,

For example, a company with $2 million in total assets and $500,000 in total liabilities would have a _____ of 25%

Like all financial ratios, a company's _____ should be compared with their industry average or other competing firms.

a. Cash management
b. Capitalization rate
c. Cash concentration
d. Debt ratio

19. _____ refers to a tax levied by various jurisdictions on the profits made by companies or associations. It is a tax on the value of the corporation's profits.

The measure of taxable profits varies from country to country.

a. Corporate tax
b. Trade finance
c. Proxy fight
d. First-mover advantage

20. In finance, a _____ is a debt security, in which the authorized issuer owes the holders a debt and, depending on the terms of the _____, is obliged to pay interest (the coupon) and/or to repay the principal at a later date, termed maturity.

Thus a _____ is a loan: the issuer is the borrower, the _____ holder is the lender, and the coupon is the interest. _____s provide the borrower with external funds to finance long-term investments, or, in the case of government _____s, to finance current expenditure.

a. Convertible bond
b. Puttable bond
c. Catastrophe bonds
d. Bond

21. The _____ is a financial market where participants buy and sell debt securities, usually in the form of bonds. As of 2006, the size of the international _____ is an estimated $45 trillion, of which the size of the outstanding U.S. _____ debt was $25.2 trillion.

Nearly all of the $923 billion average daily trading volume in the U.S. _____ takes place between broker-dealers and large institutions in a decentralized, over-the-counter market.

a. Bond market
b. 4-4-5 Calendar
c. 529 plan
d. Fixed income

22. _____ are various forms of controls imposed by a government on the purchase/sale of foreign currencies by residents or on the purchase/sale of local currency by nonresidents.

Common _____ include:

- Banning the use of foreign currency within the country
- Banning locals from possessing foreign currency
- Restricting currency exchange to government-approved exchangers
- Fixed exchange rates
- Restrictions on the amount of currency that may be imported or exported

Countries with _____ are also known as 'Article 14 countries,' after the provision in the International Monetary Fund agreement allowing exchange controls for transitional economies. Such controls used to be common in most countries, particularly poorer ones, until the 1990s when free trade and globalization started a trend towards economic liberalization. Today, countries which still impose exchange controls are the exception rather than the rule.

a. Forex scam
b. Foreign exchange option
c. Spot market
d. Foreign exchange controls

23. In economics, the _____, measures the payments that flow between any individual country and all other countries. It is used to summarize all international economic transactions for that country during a specific time period, usually a year. The _____ is determined by the country's exports and imports of goods, services, and financial capital, as well as financial transfers.

a. Gross national product
b. 4-4-5 Calendar
c. Purchasing power parity
d. Balance of payments

24. The _____ is a daily reference rate based on the interest rates at which banks borrow unsecured funds from banks in the London wholesale money market (or interbank market.) It is roughly comparable to the U.S. Federal funds rate.

During 1984 it became apparent that an increasing number of banks were trading actively in a variety of relatively new market instruments, notably interest rate swaps, foreign currency options and forward rate agreements.

a. Fixed interest
b. Shanghai Interbank Offered Rate
c. London Interbank Offered Rate
d. Risk-free interest rate

25. _____ right are usage-based payments made by one party to another (the 'licensor') for ongoing use of an asset, sometimes an intellectual property (IP) right..

_____ can be determined as a percentage of gross or net sales derived from use of the asset or a fixed price per unit sold. but there are also other modes and metrics of compensation.

a. Royalties
b. Celler-Kefauver Act
c. Financial Institutions Reform Recovery and Enforcement Act
d. Due diligence

26. _____ refers to the pricing of contributions (assets, tangible and intangible, services, and funds) transferred within an organization. For example, goods from the production division may be sold to the marketing division, or goods from a parent company may be sold to a foreign subsidiary. Since the prices are set within an organization (i.e. controlled), the typical market mechanisms that establish prices for such transactions between third parties may not apply.
   a. Transfer pricing
   b. Price discrimination
   c. Discounts and allowances
   d. Price index

27. The _____ is the rate that a company is expected to pay to finance its assets. WACC is the minimum return that a company must earn on existing asset base to satisfy its creditors, owners, and other providers of capital.

Companies raise money from a number of sources: common equity, preferred equity, straight debt, convertible debt, exchangeable debt, warrants, options, pension liabilities, executive stock options, governmental subsidies, and so on.

   a. Cost of capital
   b. 4-4-5 Calendar
   c. Capital intensity
   d. Weighted average cost of capital

28. The _____ is published by The Economist as an informal way of measuring the purchasing power parity (PPP) between two currencies and provides a test of the extent to which market exchange rates result in goods costing the same in different countries. It 'seeks to make exchange-rate theory a bit more digestible'.
   a. 529 plan
   b. Big Mac index
   c. 4-4-5 Calendar
   d. Divisia index

29. In finance, the _____ between two currencies specifies how much one currency is worth in terms of the other. For example an _____ of 102 Japanese yen to the United States dollar means that JPY 102 is worth the same as USD 1. The foreign exchange market is one of the largest markets in the world.
   a. A Random Walk Down Wall Street
   b. ABN Amro
   c. AAB
   d. Exchange rate

30. The _____ is where currency trading takes place. It is where banks and other official institutions facilitate the buying and selling of foreign currencies. FX transactions typically involve one party purchasing a quantity of one currency in exchange for paying a quantity of another.
   a. Foreign exchange option
   b. Spot market
   c. Floating exchange rate
   d. Foreign exchange market

31. The _____ was a December 1971 agreement that ended the fixed exchange rates established at the Bretton Woods Conference of 1944.

The Bretton Woods Conference of 1944 established an international fixed exchange rate regime in which currencies were pegged to the United States dollar, which was based on the gold standard.

By 1970, however, it was clear that the exchange rate regime was under threat, as the United States dollar was greatly overvalued because of heavy American spending on Lyndon B. Johnson's Great Society and the Vietnam War.

a. Smithsonian Agreement
c. 7-Eleven
b. 4-4-5 Calendar
d. 529 plan

32. In financial accounting, _____ , cash flow provided by operations or cash flow from operating activities, refers to the amount of cash a company generates from the revenues it brings in, excluding costs associated with long-term investment on capital items or investment in securities.

_____ = Cash generated from operations less taxation and interest paid, investment income received and less dividends paid gives rise to _____s per International Financial Reporting Standards.

To calculate cash generated from operations, one must calculate cash generated from customers and cash paid to suppliers.

a. Operating Cash flow
c. Other Comprehensive Basis of Accounting
b. Appreciation
d. A Random Walk Down Wall Street

33. The _____ is the guaranteed payoff at which a person is 'indifferent' between accepting the guaranteed payoff and a higher but uncertain payoff. (It is the amount of the higher payout minus the risk premium).
a. 7-Eleven
c. Certainty equivalent
b. 4-4-5 Calendar
d. 529 plan

34. _____ means regulating, adapting or settling in a variety of contexts:

In commercial law, _____ means the settlement of a loss incurred on insured goods. The calculation of the amounts of compensation to be paid by or to the several interests is a complicated matter. It involves much detail and arithmetic, and requires a full and accurate knowledge of the principles of the subject.

a. Asset recovery
c. Adjustment
b. Equity method
d. Intelligent investor

35. A '_____' is a 'Charge' that is paid to obtain the right to delay a payment. Essentially, the payer purchases the right to make a given payment in the future instead of in the Present. The '_____', or 'Charge' that must be paid to delay the payment, is simply the difference between what the payment amount would be if it were paid in the present and what the payment amount would be paid if it were paid in the future.
a. Value at risk
c. Risk aversion
b. Risk modeling
d. Discount

36. The _____ is a private, not-for-profit organization whose primary purpose is to develop generally accepted accounting principles (GAAP) within the United States in the public's interest. The Securities and Exchange Commission (SEC) designated the _____ as the organization responsible for setting accounting standards for public companies in the U.S. It was created in 1973, replacing the Accounting Principles Board and the Committee on Accounting Procedure of the American Institute of Certified Public Accountants. The _____'s mission is 'to establish and improve standards of financial accounting and reporting for the guidance and education of the public, including issuers, auditors, and users of financial information.'

The _____ is not a governmental body.

Chapter 18. International Capital Budgeting, 177

a. MRU Holdings
b. FASB
c. PlaNet Finance
d. Credit karma

37. In economics, _____ is a rise in the general level of prices of goods and services in an economy over a period of time. The term '_____' once referred to increases in the money supply (monetary _____); however, economic debates about the relationship between money supply and price levels have led to its primary use today in describing price _____. _____ can also be described as a decline in the real value of money--a loss of purchasing power in the medium of exchange which is also the monetary unit of account.

a. ABN Amro
b. Inflation
c. A Random Walk Down Wall Street
d. AAB

38. In corporate finance, _____ analysis applies put option and call option valuation techniques to capital budgeting decisions. A _____ itself, is the right--but not the obligation--to undertake some business decision; typically the option to make, or abandon, a capital investment. For example, the opportunity to invest in the expansion of a firm's factory, or alternatively to sell the factory, is a _____.

a. Cash flow
b. Capital budgeting
c. Book building
d. Real option

39. _____ is the study of how the variation (uncertainty) in the output of a mathematical model can be apportioned, qualitatively or quantitatively, to different sources of variation in the input of a model .

In more general terms uncertainty and sensitivity analyses investigate the robustness of a study when the study includes some form of mathematical modelling. While uncertainty analysis studies the overall uncertainty in the conclusions of the study, _____ tries to identify what source of uncertainty weights more on the study's conclusions.

a. Synthetic CDO
b. Sensitivity analysis
c. Proxy fight
d. Golden parachute

40. An _____ is a contract written by a seller that conveys to the buyer the right -- but not the obligation -- to buy (in the case of a call _____) or to sell (in the case of a put _____) a particular asset, such as a piece of property such as, among others, a futures contract. In return for granting the _____, the seller collects a payment (the premium) from the buyer.

For example, buying a call _____ provides the right to buy a specified quantity of a security at a set strike price at some time on or before expiration, while buying a put _____ provides the right to sell.

a. Option
b. AT'T Mobility LLC
c. Annuity
d. Amortization

41. _____ refers to a business or organization attempting to acquire goods or services to accomplish the goals of the enterprise. Though there are several organizations that attempt to set standards in the _____ process, processes can vary greatly between organizations. Typically the word '_____' is not used interchangeably with the word 'procurement', since procurement typically includes Expediting, Supplier Quality, and Traffic and Logistics (T'L) in addition to _____.

Chapter 18. International Capital Budgeting,

a. 529 plan
b. 4-4-5 Calendar
c. 7-Eleven
d. Purchasing

42. _____ is the value of goods/services compared to the amount paid with a currency. Currency can be either a commodity money, like gold or silver, or fiat currency like US dollars which are the world reserve currency. As Adam Smith noted, having money gives one the ability to 'command' others' labor, so _____ to some extent is power over other people, to the extent that they are willing to trade their labor or goods for money or currency.

a. 4-4-5 Calendar
b. 529 plan
c. 7-Eleven
d. Purchasing power

43. The _____ theory uses the long-term equilibrium exchange rate of two currencies to equalize their purchasing power. Developed by Gustav Cassel in 1920, it is based on the law of one price: the theory states that, in ideally efficient markets, identical goods should have only one price.

This purchasing power SEM rate equalizes the purchasing power of different currencies in their home countries for a given basket of goods.

a. 4-4-5 Calendar
b. Gross national product
c. TED spread
d. Purchasing power parity

44. _____ is a type of risk faced by investors, corporations, and governments. It is a risk that can be understood and managed with proper aforethought and investment.

Broadly, _____ refers to the complications businesses and governments may face as a result of what are commonly referred to as political decisions--or 'any political change that alters the expected outcome and value of a given economic action by changing the probability of achieving business objectives.'.

a. Capital asset
b. Single-index model
c. Mid price
d. Political risk

45. _____s are deposits denominated in United States dollars at banks outside the United States, and thus are not under the jurisdiction of the Federal Reserve. Consequently, such deposits are subject to much less regulation than similar deposits within the United States, allowing for higher margins. There is nothing 'European' about _____ deposits; a US dollar-denominated deposit in Tokyo or Caracas would likewise be deemed _____ deposits.

a. AAB
b. ABN Amro
c. A Random Walk Down Wall Street
d. Eurodollar

46. _____ was an arrangement established in 1979 under the Jenkins European Commission where most nations of the European Economic Community (EEC) linked their currencies to prevent large fluctuations relative to one another.

After the collapse of the Bretton Woods system in 1971, most of the EEC countries agreed in 1972 to maintain stable exchange rates by preventing exchange fluctuations of more than 2.25% (the European 'currency snake'.) In March 1979, this system was replaced by the _____, and the European Currency Unit (ECU) was defined.

Chapter 18. International Capital Budgeting,

a. A Random Walk Down Wall Street
b. Euro Interbank Offered Rate
c. European Monetary System
d. Exchange Rate Mechanism

47. A _____ secures the proper functioning of money by regulating economic agents, transaction types, and money supply.

They are traditionally formed by the policy decisions of individual governments and administrated as a domestic economic issue.

The current trend, however, is to use international trade and investment to alter the policy and legislation of individual governments.

a. Payback period
b. Monetary System
c. Bond credit rating
d. Pattern day trader

48. In business, _____ is income that a company receives from its normal business activities, usually from the sale of goods and services to customers. Some companies also receive _____ from interest, dividends or royalties paid to them by other companies. _____ may refer to business income in general, or it may refer to the amount, in a monetary unit, received during a period of time, as in 'Last year, Company X had _____ of $32 million.'

In many countries, including the UK, _____ is referred to as turnover.

a. Furniture, Fixtures and Equipment
b. Bottom line
c. Matching principle
d. Revenue

Chapter 19. Multinational Cash Management,

1. In United States banking, _____ is a marketing term for certain services offered primarily to larger business customers. It may be used to describe all bank accounts (such as checking accounts) provided to businesses of a certain size, but it is more often used to describe specific services such as cash concentration, zero balance accounting, and automated clearing house facilities. Sometimes, private banking customers are given _____ services.

   a. Cash management
   b. Capitalization rate
   c. Profitability index
   d. Global tactical asset allocation

2. The _____ is a private, not-for-profit organization whose primary purpose is to develop generally accepted accounting principles (GAAP) within the United States in the public's interest. The Securities and Exchange Commission (SEC) designated the _____ as the organization responsible for setting accounting standards for public companies in the U.S. It was created in 1973, replacing the Accounting Principles Board and the Committee on Accounting Procedure of the American Institute of Certified Public Accountants. The _____'s mission is 'to establish and improve standards of financial accounting and reporting for the guidance and education of the public, including issuers, auditors, and users of financial information.'

   The _____ is not a governmental body.

   a. FASB
   b. PlaNet Finance
   c. MRU Holdings
   d. Credit karma

3. _____ refers to the various forms of financial support and financial transactions used in international trade. _____ uses a range of instruments to provide finance to exporters and importers, including documentary credits such as letters of credit.

   While a seller (the exporter) can require the purchaser (an importer) to prepay for goods shipped, the purchaser (importer) may wish to reduce risk by requiring the seller to document that the goods have been shipped.

   a. Debtor-in-possession financing
   b. Trade finance
   c. Free cash flow
   d. Forfaiting

4. In economics and finance, _____ is the practice of taking advantage of a price differential between two or more markets: striking a combination of matching deals that capitalize upon the imbalance, the profit being the difference between the market prices. When used by academics, an _____ is a transaction that involves no negative cash flow at any probabilistic or temporal state and a positive cash flow in at least one state; in simple terms, a risk-free profit.

   a. Issuer
   b. Efficient-market hypothesis
   c. Initial margin
   d. Arbitrage

5. In general, _____ means to allow a positive value and a negative value to set-off and partially or entirely cancel each other out.

Chapter 19. Multinational Cash Management, 181

In the context of credit risk, there are at least three specific types of _____:

- Close-out _____

- _____ by novation

- Settlement or payment _____

_____ decreases credit exposure, increases business with existing counterparties, and reduces both operational and settlement risk and operational costs.

a. Forward price
c. Reinvestment risk
b. Moneylender
d. Netting

6. _____ refers to the pricing of contributions (assets, tangible and intangible, services, and funds) transferred within an organization. For example, goods from the production division may be sold to the marketing division, or goods from a parent company may be sold to a foreign subsidiary. Since the prices are set within an organization (i.e. controlled), the typical market mechanisms that establish prices for such transactions between third parties may not apply.

a. Price index
c. Price discrimination
b. Discounts and allowances
d. Transfer pricing

7. Working capital requirements of a business should be monitored at all times to ensure that there are sufficient funds available to meet short-term expenses.

The _____ is basically a detailed plan that shows all expected sources and uses of cash

a. Loans and interest, in Judaism
c. Mitigating Control
b. Cash budget
d. Rate of return

8. _____ is the balance of the amounts of cash being received and paid by a business during a defined period of time, sometimes tied to a specific project. Measurement of _____ can be used

- to evaluate the state or performance of a business or project.
- to determine problems with liquidity. Being profitable does not necessarily mean being liquid. A company can fail because of a shortage of cash, even while profitable.
- to generate project rate of returns. The time of _____s into and out of projects are used as inputs to financial models such as internal rate of return, and net present value.
- to examine income or growth of a business when it is believed that accrual accounting concepts do not represent economic realities. Alternately, _____ can be used to 'validate' the net income generated by accrual accounting.

_____ as a generic term may be used differently depending on context, and certain _____ definitions may be adapted by analysts and users for their own uses. Common terms include operating _____ and free _____.

_____s can be classified into:

1. Operational _____s: Cash received or expended as a result of the company's core business activities.
2. Investment _____s: Cash received or expended through capital expenditure, investments or acquisitions.
3. Financing _____s: Cash received or expended as a result of financial activities, such as interests and dividends.

All three together - the net _____ - are necessary to reconcile the beginning cash balance to the ending cash balance. Loan draw downs or equity injections, that is just shifting of capital but no expenditure as such, are not considered in the net _____.

a. Corporate finance
c. Shareholder value
b. Real option
d. Cash flow

9. _____ is a business valuation method. _____ is the net present value of a project if financed solely by ownership equity plus the present value of all the benefits of financing. Usually, the main benefit is a tax shield resulted from tax deductibility of interest payments. Another one can be a subsidized borrowing.
a. ABN Amro
c. A Random Walk Down Wall Street
b. AAB
d. Adjusted present value

10. _____ is the value on a given date of a future payment or series of future payments, discounted to reflect the time value of money and other factors such as investment risk. _____ calculations are widely used in business and economics to provide a means to compare cash flows at different times on a meaningful 'like to like' basis.

The most commonly applied model of the time value of money is compound interest.

a. Negative gearing
c. Present value of benefits
b. Net present value
d. Present value

11. _____ is a legally enforceable arrangement between a bank and a counterparty that creates a single legal obligation covering all included individual contracts. This means that a bank'e;s obligation, in the event of the default or insolvency of one of the parties, would be the net sum of all positive and negative fair values of contracts included in the _____ arrangement.
a. Deposit account
c. Contractum trinius
b. 4-4-5 Calendar
d. Bilateral netting

12. _____ is the process of dispersing decision-making governance closer to the people or citizen. It includes the dispersal of administration or governance in sectors or areas like engineering, management science, political science, political economy, sociology and economics. _____ is also possible in the dispersal of population and employment.
a. Decentralization
c. Management by exception
b. Corporate Transparency
d. Cash cow

Chapter 19. Multinational Cash Management, 183

13. In finance, the _____ between two currencies specifies how much one currency is worth in terms of the other. For example an _____ of 102 Japanese yen to the United States dollar means that JPY 102 is worth the same as USD 1. The foreign exchange market is one of the largest markets in the world.

a. AAB
c. ABN Amro
b. A Random Walk Down Wall Street
d. Exchange rate

14. The free _____ of a public company is an estimate of the proportion of shares that are not held by large owners and that are not stock with sales restrictions (restricted stock that cannot be sold until they become unrestricted stock.)

The free _____ or a public _____ is usually defined as being all shares held by investors other than:

- shares held by owners owning more than 5% of all shares (those could be institutional investors, 'strategic shareholders,' founders, executives, and other insiders' holdings)
- restricted stocks (granted to executives that can be, but don't have to be, registered insiders)
- insider holdings (it is assumed that insiders hold stock for the very long term)

The free _____ is an important criterion in quoting a share on the stock market.

To _____ a company means to list its shares on a public stock exchange through an initial public offering (or 'flotation'.)

- Open market
- Outstanding shares
- Market capitalization
- Public _____ loat
- Reverse takeover

a. Synthetic CDO
c. Trade finance
b. Golden parachute
d. Float

15. _____ proposes how rational investors will use diversification to optimize their portfolios, and how a risky asset should be priced. The basic concepts of the theory are Markowitz diversification, the efficient frontier, capital asset pricing model, the alpha and beta coefficients, the Capital Market Line and the Securities Market Line.

_____ models an asset's return as a random variable, and models a portfolio as a weighted combination of assets so that the return of a portfolio is the weighted combination of the assets' returns.

a. Market value
c. Consumer basket
b. Payback period
d. Modern portfolio theory

16. In probability and statistics, the _____ of a collection of numbers is a measure of the dispersion of the numbers from their expected (mean) value. It can apply to a probability distribution, a random variable, a population or a data set. The _____ is usually denoted with the letter σ (lowercase sigma.)

a. Kurtosis
b. Mean
c. Sample size
d. Standard deviation

17. _____ refers to a tax levied by various jurisdictions on the profits made by companies or associations. It is a tax on the value of the corporation's profits.

The measure of taxable profits varies from country to country.

a. First-mover advantage
b. Proxy fight
c. Trade finance
d. Corporate tax

18. _____, refers to consumption opportunity gained by an entity within a specified time frame, which is generally expressed in monetary terms. However, for households and individuals, '_____ is the sum of all the wages, salaries, profits, interests payments, rents and other forms of earnings received... in a given period of time.' For firms, _____ generally refers to net-profit: what remains of revenue after expenses have been subtracted.

a. Accrual
b. OIBDA
c. Annual report
d. Income

19. An _____ is a tax levied on the financial income of people, corporations, or other legal entities. Various _____ systems exist, with varying degrees of tax incidence. Income taxation can be progressive, proportional, or regressive.

a. Income tax
b. ABN Amro
c. A Random Walk Down Wall Street
d. AAB

20. The _____ was a December 1971 agreement that ended the fixed exchange rates established at the Bretton Woods Conference of 1944.

The Bretton Woods Conference of 1944 established an international fixed exchange rate regime in which currencies were pegged to the United States dollar, which was based on the gold standard.

By 1970, however, it was clear that the exchange rate regime was under threat, as the United States dollar was greatly overvalued because of heavy American spending on Lyndon B. Johnson's Great Society and the Vietnam War.

a. 4-4-5 Calendar
b. 7-Eleven
c. Smithsonian Agreement
d. 529 plan

21. _____s is a real estate appraisal term referring to properties with characteristics that are similar to a subject property whose value is being sought. This can be accomplished either by a real estate agent who attempts to establish the value of a potential client's home or property through market analysis or, by a licensed or certified appraiser or surveyor using more defined methods, when performing a real estate appraisal.

Chapter 19. Multinational Cash Management, 185

Five factors are usually considered when determining _____s:

- Conditions of Sale -- Did the _____ recently transact under conditions (e.g. -- arms length, distress sale, estate settlement) which are consistent with the standard of value under which the appraisal is being performed?
- Financing Conditions -- Was the _____ transaction influenced by non-market or other favorable (or even unfavorable) financing terms? For example, if the _____ sold with a below-market interest rate provided by the seller, and if the standard of value (e.g. -- market value) assumes no such abnormal financing, then the appraiser may need to adjust the _____ price by an amount equal to the estimated impact of the favorable financing.
- Market Conditions -- This is often referred to as the time adjustment and accounts for changing prices over time.
- Locational Comparability -- Are the _____ and the subject property influenced by the same locational characteristics? For example, even two houses in the same neighborhood may have different views which cause one to be more valuable than the other.
- Physical Comparability -- This includes such factors as size, condition, quality, and age.

A real estate appraisal is like any other statistical sampling process. The _____s are the samples drawn and measured, and the outcome is an estimate of value -- called an 'opinion of value' in the terminology of real estate appraisal.

a. Bucket shop
c. Margin

b. Procter ' Gamble
d. Comparable

22. _____ is a pricing method used by companies. It is used primarily because it is easy to calculate and requires little information. There are several varieties, but the common thread in all of them is that one first calculates the cost of the product, then includes an additional amount to represent profit.

a. Discounts and allowances
c. Price discrimination

b. Cost-plus pricing
d. Transfer pricing

23. A _____ is a private or public market for the trading of company stock and derivatives of company stock at an agreed price; these are securities listed on a stock exchange as well as those only traded privately.

The size of the world _____ is estimated at about $36.6 trillion US at the beginning of October 2008. The world derivatives market has been estimated at about $480 trillion face or nominal value, 12 times the size of the entire world economy.

a. Anton Gelonkin
c. Adolph Coors

b. Andrew Tobias
d. Stock market

24. In business, _____ is income that a company receives from its normal business activities, usually from the sale of goods and services to customers. Some companies also receive _____ from interest, dividends or royalties paid to them by other companies. _____ may refer to business income in general, or it may refer to the amount, in a monetary unit, received during a period of time, as in 'Last year, Company X had _____ of $32 million.'

Chapter 19. Multinational Cash Management,

In many countries, including the UK, _____ is referred to as turnover.

a. Furniture, Fixtures and Equipment
c. Bottom line
b. Matching principle
d. Revenue

25. In finance, a _____ is a debt security, in which the authorized issuer owes the holders a debt and, depending on the terms of the _____, is obliged to pay interest (the coupon) and/or to repay the principal at a later date, termed maturity.

Thus a _____ is a loan: the issuer is the borrower, the _____ holder is the lender, and the coupon is the interest. _____s provide the borrower with external funds to finance long-term investments, or, in the case of government _____s, to finance current expenditure.

a. Puttable bond
c. Convertible bond
b. Bond
d. Catastrophe bonds

26. The _____ is a financial market where participants buy and sell debt securities, usually in the form of bonds. As of 2006, the size of the international _____ is an estimated $45 trillion, of which the size of the outstanding U.S. _____ debt was $25.2 trillion.

Nearly all of the $923 billion average daily trading volume in the U.S. _____ takes place between broker-dealers and large institutions in a decentralized, over-the-counter market.

a. Bond market
c. Fixed income
b. 4-4-5 Calendar
d. 529 plan

27. _____ is the long dimension of any object. The _____ of a thing is the distance between its ends, its linear extent as measured from end to end. This may be distinguished from height, which is vertical extent, and width or breadth, which are the distance from side to side, measuring across the object at right angles to the _____.
a. 7-Eleven
c. 4-4-5 Calendar
b. 529 plan
d. Length

28. An _____ represents the ownership in the shares of a foreign company trading on US financial markets. The stock of many non-US companies trades on US exchanges through the use of _____s. _____s enable US investors to buy shares in foreign companies without undertaking cross-border transactions.
a. AAB
c. A Random Walk Down Wall Street
b. ABN Amro
d. American depository receipt

29. The European _____, was a system introduced by the European Community in March 1979, as part of the European Monetary System (EMS), to reduce exchange rate variability and achieve monetary stability in Europe, in preparation for Economic and Monetary Union and the introduction of a single currency, the euro, which took place on 1 January 1999. Subsequent exchange rate agreements made with countries wishing to join the Eurozone are known as _____ II.

Chapter 19. Multinational Cash Management,

The _____ is based on the concept of fixed currency exchange rate margins, but with exchange rates variable within those margins.

a. Exchange Rate Mechanism
b. European Monetary System
c. A Random Walk Down Wall Street
d. Euro Interbank Offered Rate

30. _____ are defined as identifiable non-monetary assets that cannot be seen, touched or physically measured, which are created through time and/or effort and that are identifiable as a separate asset. There are two primary forms of intangibles - legal intangibles (such as trade secrets (e.g., customer lists), copyrights, patents, trademarks, and goodwill) and competitive intangibles (such as knowledge activities (know-how, knowledge), collaboration activities, leverage activities, and structural activities.) Legal intangibles generate legal property rights defensible in a court of law.

a. A Random Walk Down Wall Street
b. AAB
c. ABN Amro
d. Intangible assets

31. _____ describes something which a person or corporation can have ownership of and can transfer ownership of to another person or corporation, but has no physical substance. It generally refers to statutory creations such as copyright, trademarks, or patents. It excludes tangible property like real property and personal property.

a. AAB
b. A Random Walk Down Wall Street
c. ABN Amro
d. Intangible property

32. A _____ is an expenditure creating future benefits. A _____ is incurred when a business spends money either to buy fixed assets or to add to the value of an existing fixed asset with a useful life that extends beyond the taxable year. Capex are used by a company to acquire or upgrade physical assets such as equipment, property, or industrial buildings.

a. Cost of capital
b. 4-4-5 Calendar
c. Weighted average cost of capital
d. Capital expenditure

33. _____ in its classic form is defined as a company from one country making a physical investment into building a factory in another country. It is the establishment of an enterprise by a foreigner. Its definition can be extended to include investments made to acquire lasting interest in enterprises operating outside of the economy of the investor.

a. Public company
b. Dow Jones ' Company
c. Foreign direct investment
d. MicroPlace

34. A standard, commercial _____ is a document issued mostly by a financial institution, used primarily in trade finance, which usually provides an irrevocable payment undertaking.

The _____ can also be the source of payment for a transaction, meaning that redeeming the _____ will pay an exporter. Letters of credit are used primarily in international trade transactions of significant value, for deals between a supplier in one country and a customer in another.

a. Letter of credit
b. McFadden Act
c. Bond indenture
d. Duty of loyalty

35. A _____ occurs when a financial sponsor acquires a controlling interest in a company's equity and where a significant percentage of the purchase price is financed through leverage (borrowing.) The assets of the acquired company are used as collateral for the borrowed capital, sometimes with assets of the acquiring company. The bonds or other paper issued for _____s are commonly considered not to be investment grade because of the significant risks involved.
   a. Leverage
   b. Leveraged buyout
   c. Limited partnership
   d. Pension fund

36. A _____, in business matters, is an entity that is controlled by a bigger and more powerful entity. The controlled entity is called a company, corporation, or limited liability company, and the controlling entity is called its parent (or the parent company.) The reason for this distinction is that a lone company cannot be a _____ of any organization; only an entity representing a legal fiction as a separate entity can be a _____.
   a. 4-4-5 Calendar
   b. Subsidiary
   c. 529 plan
   d. Joint stock company

37. _____ is the provision of resources (such as granting a loan) by one party to another party where that second party does not reimburse the first party immediately, thereby generating a debt, and instead arranges either to repay or return those resources (or material(s) of equal value) at a later date. The first party is called a creditor, also known as a lender, while the second party is called a debtor, also known as a borrower.

   Movements of financial capital are normally dependent on either _____ or equity transfers.

   a. Comparable
   b. Credit
   c. Warrant
   d. Clearing house

38. _____ is the process of comparing the cost, time or quality of what one organization does against what another organization does. The result is often a business case for making changes in order to make improvements.

   Also referred to as 'best practice _____' or 'process _____', it is a process used in management and particularly strategic management, in which organizations evaluate various aspects of their processes in relation to best practice, usually within their own sector.

   a. 7-Eleven
   b. 4-4-5 Calendar
   c. 529 plan
   d. Benchmarking

39. The institution most often referenced by the word '_____' is a public or publicly traded _____, the shares of which are traded on a public stock exchange (e.g., the New York Stock Exchange or Nasdaq in the United States) where shares of stock of _____s are bought and sold by and to the general public. Most of the largest businesses in the world are publicly traded _____s. However, the majority of _____s are said to be closely held, privately held or close _____s, meaning that no ready market exists for the trading of shares.
   a. Depository Trust Company
   b. Protect
   c. Federal Home Loan Mortgage Corporation
   d. Corporation

Chapter 20. International Trade Finance,

1. _____ is exchanging goods or services that are paid for, in whole or part, with other goods or services.

There are five main variants of _____:

- Barter: Exchange of goods or services directly for other goods or services without the use of money as means of purchase or payment.
- Switch trading: Practice in which one company sells to another its obligation to make a purchase in a given country.
- Counter purchase: Sale of goods and services to a country by a company that promises to make a future purchase of a specific product from the country.
- Buyback: occurs when a firm builds a plant in a country - or supplies technology, equipment, training, or other services to the country and agrees to take a certain percentage of the plant's output as partial payment for the contract.
- Offset: Agreement that a company will offset a hard - currency purchase of an unspecified product from that nation in the future. Agreement by one nation to buy a product from another, subject to the purchase of some or all of the components and raw materials from the buyer of the finished product, or the assembly of such product in the buyer nation.

_____ also occurs when countries lack sufficient hard currency, or when other types of market trade are impossible85 a barrel while Iraq oil sales into Asia were valued at about $22 a barrel. In 2001, India agreed to swap 1.5 million tonnes of Iraqi crude under the oil-for-food program.

   a. 4-4-5 Calendar   b. Countertrade
   c. Going concern   d. 529 plan

2. The _____ is the official export credit agency of the United States federal government. It was established in 1934 by an executive order, and made an independent agency in the Executive branch by Congress in 1945, for the purposes of financing and insuring foreign purchases of United States goods for customers unable or unwilling to accept credit risk. The mission of the Bank is to create and sustain U.S. jobs by financing sales of U.S. exports to international buyers.
   a. AAB   b. ABN Amro
   c. A Random Walk Down Wall Street   d. Export-Import Bank of the United States

3. _____ refers to the various forms of financial support and financial transactions used in international trade.
_____ uses a range of instruments to provide finance to exporters and importers, including documentary credits such as letters of credit.

While a seller (the exporter) can require the purchaser (an importer) to prepay for goods shipped, the purchaser (importer) may wish to reduce risk by requiring the seller to document that the goods have been shipped.

   a. Free cash flow   b. Debtor-in-possession financing
   c. Trade finance   d. Forfaiting

4. _____ is the act of consigning, which is placing a person or thing in the hand of another, but retaining ownership until the goods are sold or person is transferred. This may be done for shipping, transfer of prisoners, or for sale in a store (i.e. a _____ shop.)

Features of _____ are as follows: 1)The Relation between the two parties is that of consignor and consignee and not that of buyer and seller 2)The consignor is entitled to receive all the expenses in connection with _____ 3)The consignee is not responsible for damage of goods during transport or any other procedure.

 a. 529 plan   b. 7-Eleven
 c. 4-4-5 Calendar   d. Consignment

5. A standard, commercial _____ is a document issued mostly by a financial institution, used primarily in trade finance, which usually provides an irrevocable payment undertaking.

The _____ can also be the source of payment for a transaction, meaning that redeeming the _____ will pay an exporter. Letters of credit are used primarily in international trade transactions of significant value, for deals between a supplier in one country and a customer in another.

 a. Duty of loyalty   b. Bond indenture
 c. Letter of credit   d. McFadden Act

6. In finance, the _____ is the global financial market for short-term borrowing and lending. It provides short-term liquidity funding for the global financial system. The _____ is where short-term obligations such as Treasury bills, commercial paper and bankers' acceptances are bought and sold.

 a. Cramdown   b. Money market
 c. Debt-for-equity swap   d. Consumer debt

7. A _____ can require immediate payment by the second party to the third upon presentation of the _____. This is called a sight _____. A Cheques is a sight _____. An importer might write a _____ promising payment to an exporter for delivery of goods with payment to occur 60 days after the goods are delivered. Such a _____ is called a time _____.

 a. Cashflow matching   b. Second lien loan
 c. Gross profit margin   d. Draft

8. _____ is the provision of resources (such as granting a loan) by one party to another party where that second party does not reimburse the first party immediately, thereby generating a debt, and instead arranges either to repay or return those resources (or material(s) of equal value) at a later date. The first party is called a creditor, also known as a lender, while the second party is called a debtor, also known as a borrower.

Movements of financial capital are normally dependent on either _____ or equity transfers.

 a. Credit   b. Warrant
 c. Clearing house   d. Comparable

9. A _____, referred to as a note payable in accounting, is a contract where one party (the maker or issuer) makes an unconditional promise in writing to pay a sum of money to the other (the payee), either at a fixed or determinable future time or on demand of the payee, under specific terms. They differ from IOUs in that they contain a specific promise to pay, rather than simply acknowledging that a debt exists.

Chapter 20. International Trade Finance, 191

The terms of a note typically include the principal amount, the interest rate if any, and the maturity date.

- a. Title loan
- b. Financial plan
- c. Credit repair software
- d. Promissory note

10. In trade finance, _____ involves the purchasing of receivables from exporters. The forfaiter will take on all the risks involved with the receivables. It is different from the factoring operation in the sense that _____ is a transaction based operation while factoring is a firm based operation - meaning, in factoring, a firm sells all its receivables while in _____, the firm sells one of its transactions.
- a. Funding
- b. Forfaiting
- c. Sensitivity analysis
- d. Pac-Man defense

11. The _____ was a period of financial crisis that gripped much of Asia beginning in July 1997, and raised fears of a worldwide economic meltdown (financial contagion).

The crisis started in Thailand with the financial collapse of the Thai baht caused by the decision of the Thai government to float the baht, cutting its peg to the USD, after exhaustive efforts to support it in the face of a severe financial overextension that was in part real estate driven. At the time, Thailand had acquired a burden of foreign debt that made the country effectively bankrupt even before the collapse of its currency.

- a. OTC Bulletin Board
- b. Asian Financial Crisis
- c. International trade
- d. Internal control

12. The _____ of monetary management established the rules for commercial and financial relations among the world's major industrial states in the mid 20th Century. The _____ was the first example of a fully negotiated monetary order intended to govern monetary relations among independent nation-states.

Preparing to rebuild the international economic system as World War II was still raging, 730 delegates from all 44 Allied nations gathered at the Mount Washington Hotel in Bretton Woods, New Hampshire, United States, for the United Nations Monetary and Financial Conference.

- a. The Hong Kong Securities Institute
- b. Fixed Asset Register
- c. Bretton Woods system
- d. Cash budget

13. A _____ product means that when an investor buys this specific derivative security, he is guaranteed to get back at maturity a part or the totality of the money he invested on day one. Examples of _____s include bond plus option, usually bond plus call, and constant proportion portfolio insurance.
- a. Capital Guarantee
- b. No-arbitrage bounds
- c. Cash on delivery
- d. Market neutral

14. The institution most often referenced by the word '_____' is a public or publicly traded _____, the shares of which are traded on a public stock exchange (e.g., the New York Stock Exchange or Nasdaq in the United States) where shares of stock of _____s are bought and sold by and to the general public. Most of the largest businesses in the world are publicly traded _____s. However, the majority of _____s are said to be closely held, privately held or close _____s, meaning that no ready market exists for the trading of shares.

192   *Chapter 20. International Trade Finance,*

    a. Corporation
    c. Depository Trust Company
    b. Federal Home Loan Mortgage Corporation
    d. Protect

15. _____ or financing is to provide capital (funds), which means money for a project, a person, a business or any other private or public institutions.

Those funds can be allocated for either short term or long term purposes. The health fund is a new way of _____ private healthcare centers.

    a. Synthetic CDO
    c. Product life cycle
    b. Proxy fight
    d. Funding

16. In economic models, the _____ time frame assumes no fixed factors of production. Firms can enter or leave the marketplace, and the cost (and availability) of land, labor, raw materials, and capital goods can be assumed to vary. In contrast, in the short-run time frame, certain factors are assumed to be fixed, because there is not sufficient time for them to change.
    a. 529 plan
    c. 4-4-5 Calendar
    b. Short-run
    d. Long-run

17. _____ is a financial metric which represents operating liquidity available to a business. Along with fixed assets such as plant and equipment, _____ is considered a part of operating capital. It is calculated as current assets minus current liabilities.
    a. Working capital management
    c. 529 plan
    b. 4-4-5 Calendar
    d. Working Capital

18. The _____ is a bank that provides financial and technical assistance to developing countries for development programs (e.g. bridges, roads, schools, etc.) with the stated goal of reducing poverty.

The _____ differs from the _____ Group, in that the _____ comprises only two institutions:

- International Bank for Reconstruction and Development (IBRD)
- International Development Association (IDA)

Whereas the latter incorporates these two in addition to three more:

- International Finance Corporation (IFC)
- Multilateral Investment Guarantee Agency (MIGA)
- International Centre for Settlement of Investment Disputes (ICSID)

John Maynard Keynes (right) represented the UK at the conference, and Harry Dexter White represented the US.

The _____ was created following the ratification of the United Nations Monetary and Financial Conference | Bretton Woods agreement. The concept was originally conceived in July 1944 at the United Nations Monetary and Financial Conference.

Chapter 20. International Trade Finance,

a. 7-Eleven
c. 529 plan
b. 4-4-5 Calendar
d. World Bank

19. _____ is a business valuation method. _____ is the net present value of a project if financed solely by ownership equity plus the present value of all the benefits of financing. Usually, the main benefit is a tax shield resulted from tax deductibility of interest payments. Another one can be a subsidized borrowing.
   a. Adjusted present value
   b. AAB
   c. ABN Amro
   d. A Random Walk Down Wall Street

20. In banking and finance, _____ denotes all activities from the time a commitment is made for a transaction until it is settled. _____ is necessary because the speed of trades is much faster than the cycle time for completing the underlying transaction.

In its widest sense _____ involves the management of post-trading, pre-settlement credit exposures, to ensure that trades are settled in accordance with market rules, even if a buyer or seller should become insolvent prior to settlement.

   a. Clearing house
   b. Share
   c. Clearing
   d. Procter ' Gamble

21. _____ in its classic form is defined as a company from one country making a physical investment into building a factory in another country. It is the establishment of an enterprise by a foreigner. Its definition can be extended to include investments made to acquire lasting interest in enterprises operating outside of the economy of the investor.
   a. Foreign direct investment
   b. Public company
   c. MicroPlace
   d. Dow Jones ' Company

22. In finance, the _____ between two currencies specifies how much one currency is worth in terms of the other. For example an _____ of 102 Japanese yen to the United States dollar means that JPY 102 is worth the same as USD 1. The foreign exchange market is one of the largest markets in the world.
   a. ABN Amro
   b. Exchange rate
   c. A Random Walk Down Wall Street
   d. AAB

23. The _____ is where currency trading takes place. It is where banks and other official institutions facilitate the buying and selling of foreign currencies. FX transactions typically involve one party purchasing a quantity of one currency in exchange for paying a quantity of another.
   a. Floating exchange rate
   b. Foreign exchange option
   c. Spot market
   d. Foreign exchange market

24. _____ is a type of trade policy that allows traders to act and transact without interference from government. Thus, the policy permits trading partners mutual gains from trade, with goods and services produced according to the theory of comparative advantage.

Under a _____ policy, prices are a reflection of true supply and demand, and are the sole determinant of resource allocation.

a. Monte Carlo methods
b. Seasoned equity offering
c. Yield spread
d. Free trade

25. In economics and finance, _____ is the practice of taking advantage of a price differential between two or more markets: striking a combination of matching deals that capitalize upon the imbalance, the profit being the difference between the market prices. When used by academics, an _____ is a transaction that involves no negative cash flow at any probabilistic or temporal state and a positive cash flow in at least one state; in simple terms, a risk-free profit.
   a. Initial margin
   b. Efficient-market hypothesis
   c. Issuer
   d. Arbitrage

26. A _____ secures the proper functioning of money by regulating economic agents, transaction types, and money supply.

They are traditionally formed by the policy decisions of individual governments and administrated as a domestic economic issue.

The current trend, however, is to use international trade and investment to alter the policy and legislation of individual governments.

   a. Pattern day trader
   b. Monetary system
   c. Bond credit rating
   d. Payback period

27. _____ is exchange of capital, goods, and services across international borders or territories. In most countries, it represents a significant share of gross domestic product (GDP.) While _____ has been present throughout much of history, its economic, social, and political importance has been on the rise in recent centuries.
   a. Index number
   b. United States Treasury security
   c. OTC Bulletin Board
   d. International trade

28. A _____ or directed economy is an economic system in which the government or workers' councils manages the economy. It is an economic system in which the central government makes all decisions on the production and consumption of goods and services. Its most extensive form is referred to as a command economy, centrally _____, or command and control economy.
   a. Planned economy
   b. 529 plan
   c. 7-Eleven
   d. 4-4-5 Calendar

Chapter 21. International Tax Environment, 195

1. A _____ is a pool of assets forming an independent legal entity that are bought with the contributions to a pension plan for the exclusive purpose of financing pension plan benefits.

   _____s are important shareholders of listed and private companies. They are especially important to the stock market where large institutional investors like the Ontario Teachers' Pension Plan dominate.

   a. Limited liability company
   b. Leverage
   c. Leveraged buyout
   d. Pension fund

2. _____ is the planning process used to determine whether a firm's long term investments such as new machinery, replacement machinery, new plants, new products, and research development projects are worth pursuing. It is budget for major capital, or investment, expenditures.

   Many formal methods are used in _____, including the techniques such as

   - Net present value
   - Profitability index
   - Internal rate of return
   - Modified Internal Rate of Return
   - Equivalent annuity

   These methods use the incremental cash flows from each potential investment, or project. Techniques based on accounting earnings and accounting rules are sometimes used - though economists consider this to be improper - such as the accounting rate of return, and 'return on investment.' Simplified and hybrid methods are used as well, such as payback period and discounted payback period.

   a. Preferred stock
   b. Shareholder value
   c. Financial distress
   d. Capital budgeting

3. _____ refers to a tax levied by various jurisdictions on the profits made by companies or associations. It is a tax on the value of the corporation's profits.

   The measure of taxable profits varies from country to country.

   a. Proxy fight
   b. Trade finance
   c. Corporate Tax
   d. First-mover advantage

4. _____ in its classic form is defined as a company from one country making a physical investment into building a factory in another country. It is the establishment of an enterprise by a foreigner. Its definition can be extended to include investments made to acquire lasting interest in enterprises operating outside of the economy of the investor.
   a. Public company
   b. MicroPlace
   c. Dow Jones ' Company
   d. Foreign direct investment

Chapter 21. International Tax Environment,

5. _____, refers to consumption opportunity gained by an entity within a specified time frame, which is generally expressed in monetary terms. However, for households and individuals, '_____ is the sum of all the wages, salaries, profits, interests payments, rents and other forms of earnings received... in a given period of time.' For firms, _____ generally refers to net-profit: what remains of revenue after expenses have been subtracted.

   a. OIBDA
   b. Income
   c. Annual report
   d. Accrual

6. _____ (or PwC) is one of the world's largest professional services firms. It was formed in 1998 from a merger between Price Waterhouse and Coopers ' Lybrand, both formed in London.

   _____ earned aggregated worldwide revenues of $28 billion for fiscal 2008, and employed over 146,000 people in 150 countries.

   a. PriceWaterhouseCoopers
   b. Texas ratio
   c. Lending Club
   d. Credit karma

7. The phrase _____ refers to the aspect of corporate strategy, corporate finance and management dealing with the buying, selling and combining of different companies that can aid, finance, or help a growing company in a given industry grow rapidly without having to create another business entity.

   An acquisition, also known as a takeover, is the buying of one company (the 'target') by another. An acquisition may be friendly or hostile.

   a. 4-4-5 Calendar
   b. 7-Eleven
   c. Mergers and acquisitions
   d. 529 plan

8. _____ is the provision of resources (such as granting a loan) by one party to another party where that second party does not reimburse the first party immediately, thereby generating a debt, and instead arranges either to repay or return those resources (or material(s) of equal value) at a later date. The first party is called a creditor, also known as a lender, while the second party is called a debtor, also known as a borrower.

   Movements of financial capital are normally dependent on either _____ or equity transfers.

   a. Comparable
   b. Clearing house
   c. Warrant
   d. Credit

9. The term _____ describes two different concepts:

   - The first is a recognition of partial payment already made towards taxes due.
   - The second is a state benefit paid to workers through the tax system, which has the effect of increasing (rather than reducing) net income.

   Within the Australian, Canadian, United Kingdom, and United States tax systems, a _____ is a recognition of partial payment already made towards taxes due. A similar concept exists (fr:Avoir fiscal) in the French tax system. This situation arises, for example, when standard rate tax has been deducted at source, but the tax-payer is subject to further taxation at a higher rate. It also applies in dividend imputation systems.

a. 529 plan	b. 7-Eleven
c. Tax credit	d. 4-4-5 Calendar

10. The term _____ is used to describe a nation's social, or business activity in the process of rapid industrialization. _____ are generally less-wealthy than the developed world, and are wealthier (or the wealthiest of) the developing world. According to The Economist many people find the term dated, but a new term has yet to gain much traction.

a. AAB	b. ABN Amro
c. A Random Walk Down Wall Street	d. Emerging Markets

11. A _____ is a payment made by a corporation to its shareholder members. When a corporation earns a profit or surplus, that money can be put to two uses: it can either be re-invested in the business (called retained earnings), or it can be paid to the shareholders as a _____. Many corporations retain a portion of their earnings and pay the remainder as a _____.

a. Dividend	b. Special dividend
c. Dividend puzzle	d. Dividend yield

12. _____ is a rent received on a regular basis, with little effort required to maintain it. It is advocated by some authors, especially by Robert Kiyosaki.

Some examples of _____ are:

- Repeated regular income, earned by a sales person, generated from the payment of a product or service that must be renewed on a regular basis, in order to continue receiving its benefits - also called residual income.
- Rental from property;
- Royalties from publishing a book or from licensing a patent or other form of intellectual property;
- Earnings from internet advertisement on your websites;
- Earnings from a business that does not require direct involvement from the owner or merchant;
- Dividend and interest income from owning securities, such as stocks and bonds, are usually referred to as portfolio income, which can be considered a form of _____;
- Pensions.

_____ is usually taxable. The American Internal Revenue Service defines _____ as 'any activity...

a. 4-4-5 Calendar	b. Horizontal merger
c. Fixed exchange rate system	d. Passive income

13. _____ refers to the additional value of a commodity over the cost of commodities used to produce it from the previous stage of production. An example is the price of gasoline at the pump over the price of the oil in it. In national accounts used in macroeconomics, it refers to the contribution of the factors of production, i.e., land, labor, and capital goods, to raising the value of a product and corresponds to the incomes received by the owners of these factors.

a. Value added	b. Supply shock
c. Deregulation	d. Demand shock

14. _____ generally refers to two kinds of taxes: Taxes which employers are required to withhold from employees' pay Pay-As-You-Earn or Pay-As-You-Go tax; and taxes which are paid from the employer's own funds and which are directly related to employing a worker, which may be either fixed charges or proportionally linked to an employee's pay.

In China, the _____ is a specific tax which is paid to states and territories by employers, not by employees. The tax is not deducted from the worker's pay.

- a. Tax brackets
- b. Withholding tax
- c. Payroll tax
- d. Capital gain

15. _____ is an amount withheld by the party making a payment to another (payee) and paid to the taxation authorities. The amount the payer deducts may vary, depending on the nature of the product or service being paid for. The payee is assessed on the gross amount, and the tax to be withheld (the _____) is computed in that assessment.
- a. Tax holiday
- b. Capital gains tax
- c. Capital gain
- d. Withholding tax

16. _____ is the imposition of two or more taxes on the same income (in the case of income taxes), asset (in the case of capital taxes), or financial transaction (in the case of sales taxes.) It refers to two distinct situations:

- taxation of dividend income without relief or credit for taxes paid by the company paying the dividend on the income from which the dividend is paid. This arises in the so-called 'classical' system of corporate taxation, used in the United States.
- taxation by two or more countries of the same income, asset or transaction, for example income paid by an entity of one country to a resident of a different country. The double liability is often mitigated by tax treaties between countries.

It is not unusual for a business or individual who is resident in one country to make a taxable gain (earnings, profits) in another. This person may find that he is obliged by domestic laws to pay tax on that gain locally and pay again in the country in which the gain was made. Since this is inequitable, many nations make bilateral _____ agreements with each other.

- a. 7-Eleven
- b. 4-4-5 Calendar
- c. Double taxation
- d. 529 plan

17. _____ is a fee paid on borrowed assets. It is the price paid for the use of borrowed money, or, money earned by deposited funds. Assets that are sometimes lent with _____ include money, shares, consumer goods through hire purchase, major assets such as aircraft, and even entire factories in finance lease arrangements.
- a. Interest
- b. Insolvency
- c. AAB
- d. A Random Walk Down Wall Street

18. An _____ is the price a borrower pays for the use of money they do not own, and the return a lender receives for deferring the use of funds, by lending it to the borrower. _____s are normally expressed as a percentage rate over the period of one year.

_____s targets are also a vital tool of monetary policy and are used to control variables like investment, inflation, and unemployment.

Chapter 21. International Tax Environment, 199

    a. ABN Amro
    b. Interest rate
    c. AAB
    d. A Random Walk Down Wall Street

19. _____, are a legal construction of the tax authorities around the world. A _____ is a legal entity that exists in one jurisdiction but is owned or controlled primarily by taxpayers of a different jurisdiction. _____ laws were introduced to stop tax evasion through the use of offshore companies in low-tax or no-tax jurisdictions such as tax havens.
    a. Controlled foreign corporations
    b. Naked call
    c. Casino credit
    d. BootStrap Method

20. The institution most often referenced by the word '_____' is a public or publicly traded _____, the shares of which are traded on a public stock exchange (e.g., the New York Stock Exchange or Nasdaq in the United States) where shares of stock of _____s are bought and sold by and to the general public. Most of the largest businesses in the world are publicly traded _____s. However, the majority of _____s are said to be closely held, privately held or close _____s, meaning that no ready market exists for the trading of shares.
    a. Protect
    b. Corporation
    c. Depository Trust Company
    d. Federal Home Loan Mortgage Corporation

21. The _____ is a private, not-for-profit organization whose primary purpose is to develop generally accepted accounting principles (GAAP) within the United States in the public's interest. The Securities and Exchange Commission (SEC) designated the _____ as the organization responsible for setting accounting standards for public companies in the U.S. It was created in 1973, replacing the Accounting Principles Board and the Committee on Accounting Procedure of the American Institute of Certified Public Accountants. The _____'s mission is 'to establish and improve standards of financial accounting and reporting for the guidance and education of the public, including issuers, auditors, and users of financial information.'

The _____ is not a governmental body.

    a. PlaNet Finance
    b. MRU Holdings
    c. Credit karma
    d. FASB

22. An _____ is a tax levied on the financial income of people, corporations, or other legal entities. Various _____ systems exist, with varying degrees of tax incidence. Income taxation can be progressive, proportional, or regressive.
    a. ABN Amro
    b. AAB
    c. A Random Walk Down Wall Street
    d. Income tax

23. A _____, in business matters, is an entity that is controlled by a bigger and more powerful entity. The controlled entity is called a company, corporation, or limited liability company, and the controlling entity is called its parent (or the parent company.) The reason for this distinction is that a lone company cannot be a _____ of any organization; only an entity representing a legal fiction as a separate entity can be a _____.
    a. Subsidiary
    b. 4-4-5 Calendar
    c. Joint stock company
    d. 529 plan

24. _____ refers to the pricing of contributions (assets, tangible and intangible, services, and funds) transferred within an organization. For example, goods from the production division may be sold to the marketing division, or goods from a parent company may be sold to a foreign subsidiary. Since the prices are set within an organization (i.e. controlled), the typical market mechanisms that establish prices for such transactions between third parties may not apply.
   a. Price discrimination
   b. Price index
   c. Discounts and allowances
   d. Transfer pricing

25. In United States banking, _____ is a marketing term for certain services offered primarily to larger business customers. It may be used to describe all bank accounts (such as checking accounts) provided to businesses of a certain size, but it is more often used to describe specific services such as cash concentration, zero balance accounting, and automated clearing house facilities. Sometimes, private banking customers are given _____ services.
   a. Cash management
   b. Profitability index
   c. Capitalization rate
   d. Global tactical asset allocation

26. _____ is the value on a given date of a future payment or series of future payments, discounted to reflect the time value of money and other factors such as investment risk. _____ calculations are widely used in business and economics to provide a means to compare cash flows at different times on a meaningful 'like to like' basis.

The most commonly applied model of the time value of money is compound interest.

   a. Net present value
   b. Negative gearing
   c. Present value
   d. Present value of benefits

27. A _____ is a temporary reduction or elimination of a tax. Governments usually create a _____ as an incentive for business investment. The taxes that are most commonly reduced by national and local governments are sales taxes.
   a. Tax brackets
   b. Capital gains tax
   c. Withholding tax
   d. Tax holiday

28. _____ is the long dimension of any object. The _____ of a thing is the distance between its ends, its linear extent as measured from end to end. This may be distinguished from height, which is vertical extent, and width or breadth, which are the distance from side to side, measuring across the object at right angles to the _____.
   a. 7-Eleven
   b. 4-4-5 Calendar
   c. 529 plan
   d. Length

29. An _____ is an investment vehicle traded on stock exchanges, much like stocks. An ETF holds assets such as stocks or bonds and trades at approximately the same price as the net asset value of its underlying assets over the course of the trading day. Most ETFs track an index, such as the Dow Jones Industrial Average or the S'P 500.
   a. AAB
   b. A Random Walk Down Wall Street
   c. ABN Amro
   d. Exchange-traded fund

30. _____ is that which is owed; usually referencing assets owed, but the term can cover other obligations. In the case of assets, _____ is a means of using future purchasing power in the present before a summation has been earned. Some companies and corporations use _____ as a part of their overall corporate finance strategy.

Chapter 21. International Tax Environment,

a. Credit cycle
c. Partial Payment

b. Cross-collateralization
d. Debt

31. A _____ can require immediate payment by the second party to the third upon presentation of the _____. This is called a sight _____. A Cheques is a sight _____. An importer might write a _____ promising payment to an exporter for delivery of goods with payment to occur 60 days after the goods are delivered. Such a _____ is called a time _____.

a. Cashflow matching
c. Draft

b. Second lien loan
d. Gross profit margin

32. Procter is a surname, and may also refer to:

- Bryan Waller Procter (pseud. Barry Cornwall), English poet
- Goodwin Procter, American law firm
- _____, consumer products multinational

a. Clearing house
c. Valuation

b. Bucket shop
d. Procter ' Gamble

33. _____ is a Fortune 500, American multinational corporation headquartered in Cincinnati, Ohio, that manufactures a wide range of consumer goods. As of 2008, P'G is the 8th largest corporation in the world by market capitalization and 14th largest US company by profit.

a. 4-4-5 Calendar
c. 7-Eleven

b. 529 plan
d. Procter ' Gamble Co.

34. The _____ is a capital budgeting metric used by firms to decide whether they should make investments. It is an indicator of the efficiency or quality of an investment, as opposed to net present value (NPV), which indicates value or magnitude.

The IRR is the annualized effective compounded return rate which can be earned on the invested capital, i.e., the yield on the investment.

a. A Random Walk Down Wall Street
c. ABN Amro

b. AAB
d. Internal rate of return

35. In business, _____ is income that a company receives from its normal business activities, usually from the sale of goods and services to customers. Some companies also receive _____ from interest, dividends or royalties paid to them by other companies. _____ may refer to business income in general, or it may refer to the amount, in a monetary unit, received during a period of time, as in 'Last year, Company X had _____ of $32 million.'

In many countries, including the UK, _____ is referred to as turnover.

a. Furniture, Fixtures and Equipment
c. Matching principle

b. Bottom line
d. Revenue

36. _____ in finance is a risk management technique, related to hedging, that mixes a wide variety of investments within a portfolio. Because the fluctuations of a single security have less impact on a diverse portfolio, _____ minimizes the risk from any one investment.

A simple example of _____ is the following: On a particular island the entire economy consists of two companies: one that sells umbrellas and another that sells sunscreen.

    a. 7-Eleven   b. Diversification
    c. 529 plan   d. 4-4-5 Calendar

37. In finance, _____, also known as return on investment is the ratio of money gained or lost on an investment relative to the amount of money invested. The amount of money gained or lost may be referred to as interest, profit/loss, gain/loss, or net income/loss. The money invested may be referred to as the asset, capital, principal, or the cost basis of the investment.

    a. Composition of Creditors   b. Stock or scrip dividends
    c. Rate of return   d. Doctrine of the Proper Law

ANSWER KEY

Chapter 1
1. d	2. d	3. d	4. c	5. d	6. d	7. d	8. c	9. b	10. a
11. b	12. d	13. c	14. b	15. d	16. a	17. d	18. b	19. d	20. d
21. b	22. b	23. a	24. d	25. d	26. a	27. b	28. d	29. d	30. d
31. d	32. b	33. c	34. c	35. b	36. d	37. d	38. d	39. b	40. b
41. d	42. a	43. d	44. b	45. a	46. b	47. d	48. a	49. d	50. c
51. d	52. d	53. c	54. b	55. d	56. a	57. b	58. b	59. d	

Chapter 2
1. d	2. d	3. d	4. d	5. d	6. d	7. b	8. d	9. a	10. a
11. a	12. c	13. a	14. d	15. a	16. c	17. a	18. a	19. c	20. d
21. b	22. a	23. a	24. d	25. d	26. d	27. d	28. d	29. d	30. d
31. c	32. d	33. d	34. b	35. b	36. a	37. d	38. a	39. c	40. a
41. b	42. d	43. d	44. b	45. d	46. b	47. d	48. d		

Chapter 3
1. b	2. c	3. d	4. d	5. d	6. d	7. d	8. d	9. c	10. d
11. a	12. d	13. a	14. d	15. d	16. c	17. a	18. d	19. d	20. d
21. d	22. a	23. d	24. b	25. d	26. b	27. d	28. d	29. b	30. d
31. d	32. b	33. b	34. d	35. b	36. b	37. d	38. d	39. a	40. c
41. d	42. c	43. d	44. d	45. d	46. d				

Chapter 4
1. a	2. d	3. c	4. d	5. c	6. d	7. d	8. c	9. d	10. d
11. c	12. c	13. b	14. c	15. d	16. a	17. b	18. d	19. d	20. b
21. b	22. d	23. d	24. d	25. d	26. b	27. b	28. a	29. d	30. c
31. c	32. d	33. d	34. a	35. a	36. b	37. d	38. a	39. d	40. b

Chapter 5
1. d	2. d	3. c	4. a	5. d	6. d	7. b	8. a	9. a	10. c
11. c	12. b	13. c	14. a	15. b	16. d	17. d	18. b	19. c	20. d
21. d	22. d	23. c	24. d	25. d	26. a	27. d	28. a	29. b	30. a
31. c	32. b	33. d	34. d	35. d	36. a	37. a	38. d	39. d	40. d
41. b	42. d	43. d	44. c	45. d	46. d	47. d			

Chapter 6
1. d	2. d	3. c	4. c	5. d	6. c	7. c	8. d	9. b	10. c
11. c	12. c	13. d	14. a	15. b	16. d	17. b	18. d	19. d	20. a
21. a	22. c	23. a	24. d	25. d	26. d	27. d	28. b	29. d	30. d
31. b	32. d	33. d	34. d	35. d	36. c	37. b	38. d	39. d	40. b
41. d	42. a	43. d	44. a	45. d					

Chapter 7

1. d	2. a	3. d	4. a	5. a	6. a	7. d	8. c	9. a	10. d
11. c	12. d	13. a	14. a	15. a	16. b	17. d	18. a	19. a	20. d
21. d	22. d	23. a	24. c	25. a	26. d	27. a	28. c	29. d	30. d
31. d	32. b	33. a	34. d	35. b	36. b	37. d	38. d	39. b	40. b
41. d	42. b	43. d	44. d						

Chapter 8

1. b	2. a	3. a	4. b	5. c	6. b	7. d	8. d	9. b	10. d
11. d	12. c	13. d	14. b	15. d	16. c	17. d	18. a	19. b	20. c
21. d	22. d	23. a	24. c	25. d	26. c	27. d	28. d	29. d	30. d
31. d	32. a	33. a	34. d	35. c	36. b	37. d	38. d	39. c	40. d
41. d	42. b	43. d	44. c	45. d	46. d	47. a	48. c	49. d	50. d
51. d	52. d								

Chapter 9

1. d	2. d	3. d	4. d	5. a	6. d	7. d	8. d	9. b	10. d
11. a	12. d	13. d	14. d	15. d	16. b	17. a	18. b	19. d	20. d
21. d	22. a	23. d	24. d	25. d	26. c	27. c	28. a	29. a	30. a
31. a	32. d	33. a	34. d	35. b	36. d	37. d	38. d	39. b	

Chapter 10

1. c	2. d	3. d	4. a	5. c	6. b	7. b	8. d	9. c	10. b
11. d	12. d	13. d	14. d	15. d	16. a	17. d	18. b	19. a	20. d
21. d	22. b	23. d	24. a	25. d	26. d	27. b	28. a	29. d	30. d
31. c	32. d	33. a	34. a	35. a					

Chapter 11

1. d	2. d	3. d	4. d	5. d	6. d	7. b	8. b	9. d	10. b
11. d	12. d	13. d	14. d	15. d	16. d	17. b	18. b	19. b	20. a
21. c	22. d	23. d	24. c	25. b	26. d	27. c	28. c	29. d	30. d
31. c	32. d	33. d	34. d	35. d	36. d	37. d	38. a	39. d	40. d
41. b	42. b	43. d	44. d	45. d	46. d	47. d	48. a	49. d	50. c
51. d	52. d	53. d	54. b	55. a					

Chapter 12

1. d	2. d	3. d	4. d	5. a	6. d	7. d	8. a	9. a	10. a
11. b	12. d	13. d	14. a	15. a	16. a	17. d	18. d	19. d	20. d
21. d	22. b	23. d	24. d	25. c	26. d	27. d	28. d	29. b	30. a
31. d	32. d	33. b	34. c	35. c	36. c	37. a	38. b	39. d	40. a
41. d	42. d	43. c	44. d	45. d					

ANSWER KEY

Chapter 13
1. c   2. b   3. d   4. d   5. d   6. b   7. b   8. a   9. d   10. d
11. c   12. b   13. d   14. a   15. d   16. a   17. d   18. c   19. a   20. c
21. d   22. d   23. a   24. a   25. d   26. c   27. d   28. b   29. d   30. a
31. a   32. c   33. d   34. c   35. a   36. d   37. d   38. a   39. b   40. d
41. b   42. c   43. c   44. d   45. d

Chapter 14
1. d   2. c   3. c   4. d   5. a   6. b   7. b   8. d   9. d   10. b
11. a   12. d   13. a   14. d   15. a   16. d   17. c   18. b   19. d   20. d
21. c   22. c   23. d   24. d   25. c   26. b   27. a   28. d   29. b   30. d
31. a   32. b   33. d

Chapter 15
1. d   2. d   3. c   4. a   5. d   6. d   7. b   8. d   9. a   10. d
11. a   12. d   13. d   14. d   15. d   16. d   17. c   18. d   19. d   20. b
21. c   22. d   23. a   24. c   25. d   26. d   27. b   28. a   29. d   30. a
31. d   32. c   33. c   34. c   35. b   36. c   37. d   38. d   39. b   40. d
41. d   42. d   43. c   44. a   45. d   46. b   47. d   48. d   49. d   50. d
51. a   52. d   53. d   54. d   55. d   56. d   57. a   58. d   59. c   60. d
61. d   62. d   63. d   64. d

Chapter 16
1. a   2. d   3. a   4. d   5. d   6. b   7. d   8. d   9. d   10. d
11. a   12. a   13. d   14. d   15. d   16. a   17. d   18. d   19. d   20. d
21. a   22. d   23. d   24. b   25. b   26. d   27. d   28. d   29. d   30. d
31. b   32. d   33. c   34. b   35. d   36. b   37. d   38. a   39. d   40. d
41. d   42. a   43. a   44. d   45. d

Chapter 17
1. b   2. a   3. d   4. d   5. a   6. d   7. d   8. b   9. d   10. a
11. a   12. c   13. c   14. c   15. d   16. d   17. d   18. d   19. d   20. b
21. b   22. d   23. d   24. d   25. b   26. d   27. d   28. c   29. a   30. a
31. a   32. b   33. a   34. d   35. b   36. c   37. d   38. b   39. c   40. b
41. a   42. c   43. d   44. a   45. d   46. c   47. b   48. d   49. d   50. d
51. d   52. c   53. d   54. b   55. c   56. d   57. d   58. b   59. d   60. b

Chapter 18
1. d   2. d   3. d   4. d   5. c   6. a   7. b   8. d   9. d   10. c
11. b   12. c   13. d   14. b   15. d   16. d   17. b   18. d   19. a   20. d
21. a   22. d   23. d   24. c   25. a   26. a   27. d   28. b   29. d   30. d
31. a   32. a   33. c   34. c   35. d   36. b   37. b   38. d   39. b   40. a
41. d   42. d   43. d   44. d   45. d   46. c   47. b   48. d

Chapter 19

1. a	2. a	3. b	4. d	5. d	6. d	7. b	8. d	9. d	10. d
11. d	12. a	13. d	14. d	15. d	16. d	17. d	18. d	19. a	20. c
21. d	22. b	23. d	24. d	25. b	26. a	27. d	28. d	29. a	30. d
31. d	32. d	33. c	34. a	35. b	36. b	37. b	38. d	39. d	

Chapter 20

1. b	2. d	3. c	4. d	5. c	6. b	7. d	8. a	9. d	10. b
11. b	12. c	13. a	14. a	15. d	16. d	17. d	18. d	19. a	20. c
21. a	22. b	23. d	24. d	25. d	26. b	27. d	28. a		

Chapter 21

1. d	2. d	3. c	4. d	5. b	6. a	7. c	8. d	9. c	10. d
11. a	12. d	13. a	14. c	15. d	16. c	17. a	18. b	19. a	20. b
21. d	22. d	23. a	24. d	25. a	26. c	27. d	28. d	29. d	30. d
31. c	32. d	33. d	34. d	35. d	36. b	37. c